Camping
Washington

Steve Giordano

FALCON®

HELENA, MONTANA

A FALCON GUIDE®

Falcon® Publishing is continually expanding its list of recreation guidebooks. All books include detailed descriptions, accurate maps, and all the information necessary for enjoyable trips. You can order extra copies of this book and get information and prices for other Falcon® guidebooks by writing Falcon, P.O. Box 1718, Helena, MT 59624 or calling toll free 1-800-582-2665. Also, please ask for a free copy of our current catalog. Visit our website at www.FalconOutdoors.com or contact us by e-mail at falcon@falcon.com.

Project Editor: Gayle Shirley
Production Editor: Jessica Solberg
Copyeditor: Ross Johnson
Maps by Tony Moore
Page Compositor: Marita Martiniak
Book design by Falcon® Publishing, Inc.

All photos by the author unless otherwise noted.
Cover photo of Mount Rainier by Larry Carver.

Cataloging-in-Publication Data is on record at the Library of Congress.

CAUTION

Outdoor recreational activities are by their very nature potentially hazardous. All participants in such activities must assume the responsibility for their own actions and safety. The information contained in this guidebook cannot replace sound judgment and good decision-making skills, which help reduce risk exposure, nor does the scope of this book allow for disclosure of all the potential hazards and risks involved in such activities.

Learn as much as possible about the outdoor recreational activities in which you participate, prepare for the unexpected, and be cautious. The reward will be a safer and more enjoyable experience.

♻ Text pages printed on recycled paper.

Contents

Acknowledgments 4

Introduction 5

Camping in Washington 7

How to Use This Guide 8

Washington Map 9

Coastal Region 12

    Rain Forest 14

    Beaches 34

    Hood Canal/Kitsap Peninsula 41

    Strait of Juan de Fuca 53

Western Region 58

    North Puget Sound 60

    San Juan Islands and Island County 86

    South Puget Sound 93

Eastern Region 127

    North Cascades 129

    South Cascades 161

    Columbia Plateau 182

    Spokane and Northeastern Washington 202

    Southeastern Washington 227

Contact Information 235

    Managing Agencies 235

    Reservation Services 236

Index 237

About the Author 240

Acknowledgments

I could not have written this book without the extreme cooperation of the many public agencies that operate campground facilities in Washington State. These include the Washington State Parks and Recreation Commission, the Forest Service, the U.S. Army Corps of Engineers, the Washington Department of Natural Resources, the National Park Service, and many municipalities and public utility districts. The help of their staffs was invaluable.

I also owe great appreciation to my parents Roy and Jeanne Giordano for getting me started properly on a lifetime of camping. In the early days, our equipment consisted of three war-surplus mummy bags, period. We slept on the beach or among the sand dunes, with me in the middle. Equipment added through the years, including a tent and stove, seemed like luxuries, and they still do today. I must confess, though, that the western Washington climate fairly calls out for an RV—they have theirs and I have mine.

I must also credit my Falcon editor, Gayle Shirley, for seeing me through to the completion of *Camping Washington*. She never even got grumpy over the state of my submissions and did not cajole as the deadlines slipped by. Any mistakes in the book are mine, and she gets the credit for the way it works with you the reader in mind. Happy camping!

Introduction

The popular image of Washington State, outside of the Pacific Northwest, is of a rain-soaked wilderness somewhere near Alaska. People know of Seattle and its high-tech coffee and its industries like Boeing and Microsoft, but they tend to think the state is chock-full of mountains and forests with a few roads cut through the trees. In some parts of the state, that is true. For example, the famed North Cross State Highway, now known as the North Cascades Highway, opened as recently as 1972. However, it closes every winter, usually from November to March or April, because the mountain snows get too deep to plow. Washington has about 81,300 miles of federal, state, and local roads, including 757 miles of interstate highway. Federal lands comprise nearly 30 percent of the state's 71,300 square miles.

Nearly 60 years ago, when the immense Bonneville and Grand Coulee Dams on the Columbia River were completed, the Bonneville Power Administration produced a movie for Pacific Northwest residents in rural areas. The film encouraged them to electrify their homes and farms with the dam's newly generated power. Folk singer Woody Guthrie wrote 26 songs for the movie, for about $10 per song. The most famous of them is "Roll On, Columbia, Roll On."

Washington mountains lack the height of the Rockies, but they excel by any standard of grandeur. Swift-moving streams fall away on all sides, rock walls jut straight up from the roadside, forest canopy hangs entirely over the road in some places, and in the fall the changing of the leaves in the mountain passes creates a near-neon glow.

The scale of the mountains is enormous, their contrasting terrain is striking, their gorges and river valleys seem sculpted by giants, and their perpetually snow- and ice-covered peaks appear as beacons to everyone within 100 miles.

Western Washington's rain, in spite of its distressing reputation, is not really all that bad. Seattle gets about 38 inches per year—less than New York City. In the "rain shadow" of the Olympic Peninsula, the town of Sequim (pronounced "Squim") gets about 17 inches of rain per year, and some of the San Juan Islands get around 22 inches. Cactus grows on at least one of the islands. Of course, the mountains that cause this dryness, the Olympics, absorb the southwesterly brunt of Pacific storms and receive up to 160 inches of rain per year. A two-story rain gauge behind the Quinault Lodge in Olympic National Forest measures the rainfall in feet.

A popular activity for some hardy people is winter storm-watching on the coast of the Olympic Peninsula. The experience is an actual tourism draw, as travelers pull their rigs into coastal campgrounds and Seattle weekenders rent cottages and lodge rooms all for the sake of experiencing the brute beauty of a winter storm.

Two states border Washington: Idaho on the east and Oregon on the south. The Canadian province of British Columbia is to the north, while the straits, Puget Sound, and the Pacific Ocean are to the west. A series of interlaced channels, the Straits of Juan de Fuca and Georgia, along with Haro Strait, separate the state from Canada's Vancouver Island.

The geographic center of Washington is the town of George. The Columbia River Gorge Amphitheater is nearby, a national-caliber concert venue during the summer.

Forest covers about half of Washington's land area. The temperate rain forest extends down the western side of the Olympic Peninsula south to the Columbia River. It has a high biomass of spruce, cedar, and hemlock. The forest floor is dense with ferns and mosses.

The more heavily logged area from Puget Sound into the western Cascade Range contains cedar, hemlock, and Douglas-fir. Higher in the Cascades, the forest tends toward silver fir and Douglas-fir. The eastern slope of the Cascades is ponderosa pine habitat. Douglas-fir is the most common tree in northeastern Washington. The central Columbia Plateau is actually a steppe covered by short grasses. Much of southeastern Washington is a prairie of taller grasses.

Washington's major attractions are outdoors. They include three national parks (Mount Rainier, Olympic, and North Cascades), three national recreation areas (Lake Chelan, Lake Roosevelt, and Ross Lake), plus the Mount St. Helens National Scenic Monument and the Columbia River Gorge National Scenic Area. On the Olympic Peninsula alone, there are nearly a million acres of forest.

Camping in Washington

Campgrounds in Washington are as diverse as the landscape. They include sites in the rain forest of the Olympic Peninsula; on the beaches of the Pacific Ocean, Hood Canal, and Puget Sound; in the alpine forests and meadows; and, in some eastern sections of the state, in desertlike conditions. The vast majority of campgrounds are at the edge of a body of water; Washington is riddled with lakes and laced with rivers.

A high percentage of campgrounds are open all year, offering access to both summer and winter recreation. Some parks close their campsites but remain open for day use through the winter.

Annual moorage permits, boat-launch permits, disability passes, and senior citizen passes are available by calling the Washington State Parks and Recreation Commission (see contact information on page 235). An application will be mailed to you.

The Washington State Parks system is one of the 10 largest in the nation in terms of acreage managed (250,000 acres) and visitation (51 million visits annually). Nearly all public parks in Washington have some degree of wheelchair accessibility, and almost all allow leashed pets. Pets must be on a leash no longer than 8 feet and under your control.

Through Reservations Northwest, you can make campsite reservations for many state parks as much as 11 months in advance. The phone center is open from Mondays through Fridays, 8 A.M. to 5 P.M., with extended hours in the summer. The best times to call are Wednesdays through Fridays after 1 P.M. For the phone number, see the contact information on page 236. Only about half of the state parks take reservations; the rest offer campsites on a first-come, first-served basis. Reservations can also be made through e-mail. Instructions are posted on the parks commission website: www.parks.wa.gov.

The National Recreation Reservation Service takes reservations for most Forest Service and U. S. Army Corps of Engineers campgrounds. There is a fee to make reservations at Forest Service campgrounds, but not at Corps of Engineers campgrounds.

How to Use This Guide

Camping Washington is designed for quick and easy reference. You should be able to find what you are looking for at a glance, whether by location on one of the many campground locator maps or in the quick-reference tables for each region.

I have divided Washington into three broad regions, corresponding to the state's designated tourism regions, and each of these is further divided into several subregions:

The Coastal Region includes all of the Olympic Peninsula south to the border with Oregon. The Coastal Region contains the rain forest, coastal beaches, Hood Canal, the Kitsap Peninsula, and the Strait of Juan de Fuca.

The Western Region includes everything else in western Washington eastward to the crest of the Cascade Mountains. This region is divided into three subsections: the islands of the San Juans and Island County, from Everett north to the Canadian border, and from Seattle south to the Oregon border. The volcanoes, Mounts Baker, Rainier, St. Helens, and Adams, are all in the Western Region.

The Eastern Region stretches from the crest of the Cascades eastward to the Idaho border. It includes the North and South Cascades, the Columbia Plateau, the northeastern highlands, and the rolling Palouse and the Blue Mountains in the state's southeastern corner.

Nearly 400 campgrounds are described in this guide. All of them are publicly owned and all are accessible by car. Four-wheel-drive is not necessary to reach any of them. However, you may not be able to tow trailers to a few of the campgrounds, notably those in the Harts Pass area near Winthrop. When that is the case, the text will say so. Everything you need to know about any particular campground before setting out is discussed in the text. Complete driving directions are given from a nearby city, as are the number of campsites, RV length restrictions, elevation of the campground, things to do in the vicinity, the managing agency, cost, a comprehensive list of amenities, and a narrative description of the campground.

Each campground description will tell you at a glance whether a campground offers tent sites, RV sites, or both. Most offer both, but many require RVs to be self-contained. The "Sites" listing will say so when that's the case.

For easy comparison with other campgrounds in a subregion, the quick-reference guide gives the information in chart form. For example, if your camping style requires a restroom with showers, just scan the "showers" column to find the campgrounds for you. From that point, turn to the page of one you are interested in and read the complete description.

Since camping fees change frequently by a dollar or two and we do not want to mislead you, we have indicated overnight costs with dollar signs for comparative purposes. The key is:

$ = less than $10
$$ = $10 to $15
$$$ = $16 to $20
$$$$ = more than $20

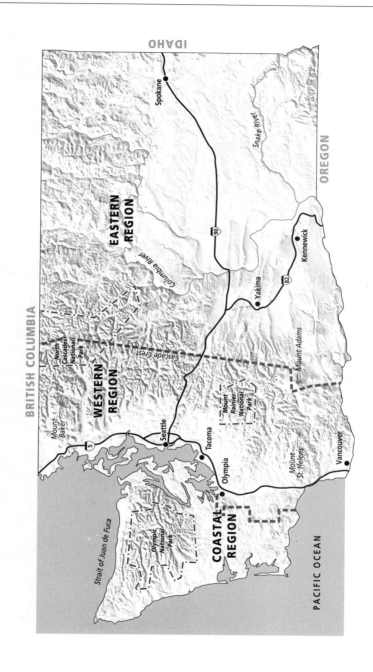

The Campgrounds

COASTAL REGION

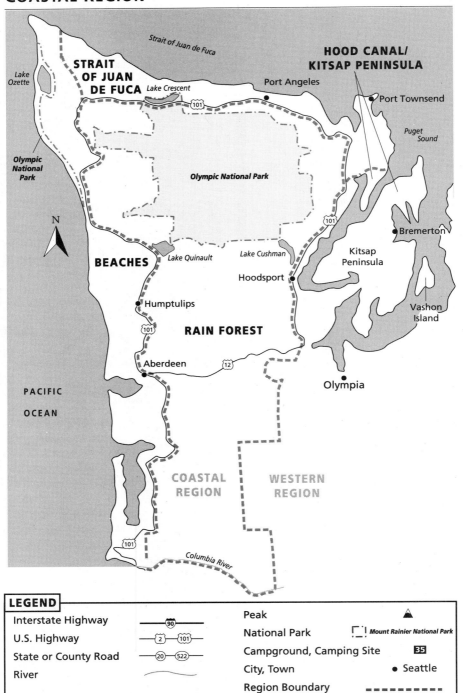

Strait of Juan de Fuca

STRAIT OF JUAN DE FUCA

Lake Ozette

Lake Crescent

Port Angeles

HOOD CANAL/ KITSAP PENINSULA

Port Townsend

Puget Sound

Olympic National Park

Olympic National Park

N

BEACHES

Lake Quinault

Lake Cushman

Kitsap Peninsula

Bremerton

Hoodsport

Vashon Island

Humptulips

RAIN FOREST

Aberdeen

Olympia

PACIFIC OCEAN

COASTAL REGION

WESTERN REGION

Columbia River

LEGEND

Interstate Highway	90	
U.S. Highway	2 101	
State or County Road	20 522	
River		

Peak	▲
National Park	Mount Rainier National Park
Campground, Camping Site	35
City, Town	● Seattle
Region Boundary	- - - - - -

Coastal Region

There is a lot of watching to be done on the Olympic Peninsula: storm watching, whale watching, storm watching, bird watching, storm watching. From July through September, the region is relatively dry and temperatures get into the 70s. But the Olympic Peninsula is basically a temperate rain forest (nearly a million acres of it) and much of what there is to do there concerns water: fishing, boating, river rafting, beach walking, oyster harvesting. Even just going for a walk can mean wet feet. Good water-resistant boots and rain gear will keep you a happy camper.

U.S. Highway 101 is the only way around the peninsula. The road makes a loop, starting just west of Olympia, but there are also enough side trips to keep you busy for days.

Westport is well known for its charter fishing and whale watching, and Ocean Shores is a bit of beach-resort paradise. On the north end of the peninsula, the community of Neah Bay attracts those interested in charter fishing, but the Makah Tribal Museum is another attraction worth experiencing. It exhibits the best of the Ozette archaeological digs.

On the peninsula, it is sometimes hard to see the forest for the trees, and there are only 38 miles of road in Olympic National Park, so the best view of the park is from Hurricane Ridge. It is a 17-mile drive from Port Angeles on the north shore.

RV parks and campgrounds abound on the peninsula. There are as many campsites in Grays Harbor County (2,146) as motel rooms. So take a long week-end, or even a week or so, and explore the possibilities. The beaches and forests seem endless.

In the Olympic National Forest, many campsites go begging because campers assume they will all be full. Over Labor Day Weekend 1999, three-quarters of them were vacant, while all state park campgrounds were full. Even though no reservations are taken for Olympic National Forest campgrounds, be sure to call ahead and ask about campsite availability—do not assume they will all be full.

Hood Canal is a long, narrow saltwater inlet that begins where the Juan de Fuca and Georgia Straits meet near Port Townsend. Hood Canal runs south along the eastern side of the Olympic Peninsula and bends northeast to the town of Belfair. US 101 runs most of the length of the western shore of the canal.

The Strait of Juan de Fuca separates the Olympic Peninsula from Vancouver Island. It is about 17 miles wide, and its shores collect an abundance of flotsam and jetsam during incoming tides from the Pacific Ocean.

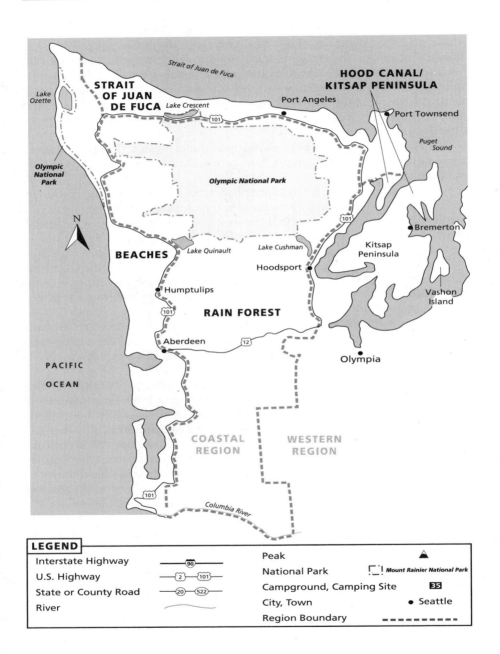

RAIN FOREST

	Group sites	RV sites	Total # of sites	Max. RV length	Hookups	Toilets	Showers	Drinking water	Dump station	Pets	Wheelchair	Recreation	Fee	Season	Can reserve	Stay limit
1 Big Creek		•	23	21		V	•			•		HFBS	$	May–mid Nov		14
2 Bogachiel State Park		•	42	30	WES	F	•	•	•	•	•	HFB	$$			10
3 Brown Creek		•	19	21		V	•		•			HF	$			14
4 Campbell Tree Grove		•	11	16		V	•		•			HF				14
5 Coho		•	58	36		F	•		•	•		HFB	$	May–mid Nov		14
6 Collins		•	16	21		V	•		•			HFS		mid May–Sep		14
7 Coppermine Bottom		•	9			V			•			FB				14
8 Cottonwood		•	9			V	•		•			HFB				14
9 Dungeness Forks			10			V	•		•			HF	$	May–Sep		14
10 East Crossing			9			V	•		•			HF	$	mid May–Sep		14
11 Elkhorn		•	20	21		V	•		•			HF	$	mid May–Sep		14
12 Falls Creek		•	31	16		F	•		•			FHBS	$$	Mem Day–Lab Day		14
13 Falls View		•	30	21		F	•		•			HF	$$	mid May–mid Sep		14
14 Gatton Creek			5			V	•		•			HFBS	$$	mid May 'til Nov		14
15 Hamma Hamma		•	15	21		V	•		•	•		HFSC	$	May–mid Nov		14
16 Hoh Oxbow		•	7			V				•		FB				14
17 Klahowya		•	45	20		F	•		•			HBFC	$$	mid May–mid Oct		14
18 Lake Cushman State Park		•	82	60	WES	F	•	•	•	•	•	HFB	$$	Apr until Nov	•	10
19 Lena Creek		•	14	21		V	•		•	•		HF	$	mid May thru Sep		14
20 Lilliwaup		•	6			V	•		•			HF				14
21 Lake Sylvia State Park		•	37	30		F	•	•	•	•	•	HFSB	$$–$$$	May–Labor Day		10
22 Melbourne		•	5			V			•			HFB				14
23 Minnie Peterson		•	8			V			•			HFB				14
24 Olympic Natl Park: Altaire		•	30	21		F	•		•	•		HF	$$	June–Sep		14
25 Olympic Natl Park: Deer Park			18			V	•		•			H		mid June–Oct		14
26 Olympic Natl Park: Dosewallips			30			F	•		•			FH	$$	May–Sep		14
27 Olympic Natl Park: Elwha		•	41	21		F	•		•	•		HF	$$			14
28 Olympic Natl Park: Fairholm		•	87	21		F		•	•	•		HFB	$$			14
29 Olympic Natl Park: Graves Creek		•	30	21		F	•		•	•		HF				14
30 Olympic Natl Park: Heart o'the Hills		•	105	21		F	•		•	•		H	$			14
31 Olympic Natl Park: Hoh		•	89	21		F		•	•	•	•	HF	$			14
32 Olympic Natl Park: Queets			20			V			•			HF		May 30–Sep 30		14
33 Olympic Natl Park: Sol Duc		•	80	21		F		•	•	•	•	HF	$	May–late Oct		14
34 Olympic Natl Park: Staircase		•	59	21		F	•		•	•		HF	$			14
35 Schafer State Park		•	55		WE	F	•	•	•	•	•	HFB	$–$$			10
36 South Fork Hoh		•	3			V			•			HFB				14

continued on following page

	Group sites	RV sites	Total # of sites	Max. RV length	Hookups	Toilets	Showers	Drinking water	Dump station	Pets	Wheelchair	Recreation	Fee	Season	Can reserve	Stay limit
37 Upper Clearwater		•	9			V				•		HFB				14
38 Western Lakes			3			V				•		H				14
39 Willaby		•	22	16		F	•			•		HFBCS	$$	mid April–mid Sep		14
40 Willoughby Creek		•	3			V				•		HF				14

Hookups: W = Water E = Electric S = Sewer
Toilets: F = Flush V = Vault P = Pit
Recreation: C = Bicycling/Mountain Biking H = Hiking S = Swimming F = Fishing B = Boating O = Off-highway driving R = Horseback Riding
Maximum Trailer/RV Length given in feet. **Stay Limit** given in days.
Fee $ = less than $10; $$ = $10-$15; $$$ = $16–20; $$$$ = more than $20.
If no entry under **Season,** campground is open all year. If no entry under **Fee,** camping is free.

1 Big Creek

Location: 9 miles west of Hoodsport, near Lake Cushman.
Sites: 23 sites for tents or self-contained RVs no longer than 21 feet.
Facilities: Drinking water, sheltered picnic tables, firewood, vault toilets, groceries, boat rentals, nature trails.
Fee per night: $.
Elevation: 731 feet.
Management: Olympic National Forest, Hood Canal Ranger District.
Activities: Hiking, fishing, boating, swimming, waterskiing.
Finding the campground: From U.S. Highway 101 in the town of Hoodsport on Hood Canal, take Washington Highway 119 (Lake Cushman Road) west and then north for 9 miles to the campground.

About the campground: The price is right at this 30-acre campground near Lake Cushman in Olympic National Forest. The big sites offer more privacy than you find at most public campgrounds. The lake, which is about 8 miles long, is 1.5 miles south of camp. The campground is open from May through mid-November.

2 Bogachiel State Park

Location: 6 miles south of Forks on the Bogachiel River.
Sites: 34 tent sites, 6 sites with hookups for RVs no longer than 30 feet, 2 primitive sites.
Facilities: Drinking water, picnic tables, fire grills, dump station, restrooms, coin-operated showers, boat ramp.
Fee per night: $$.
Elevation: 310 feet.

Management: Washington State Parks and Recreation Commission.
Activities: Hiking, fishing, boating, hunting, rafting.
Finding the campground: Bogachiel State Park is 6 miles south of the town of Forks on U.S. Highway 101.

About the campground: This sizable campground covers 123 acres and features 2,800 feet of shoreline frontage along the Bogachiel River. It is a good location for steelhead fishing along the river or hiking on a half-mile of marked trails nearby. The campground is located on both sides of US 101 and is open year-round.

3 Brown Creek

Location: About 40 miles northwest of Olympia on Brown Creek.
Sites: 7 tent sites, 12 sites for trailers and RVs no longer than 21 feet.
Facilities: Drinking water, picnic tables, vault toilets.
Fee per night: $.
Elevation: 650 feet.
Management: Olympic National Forest, Hood Canal Ranger District.
Activities: Hiking, fishing.
Finding the campground: Use a Forest Service map to find this remote campground. Drive west on U.S. Highway 101 from Interstate 5 exit 104 at Olympia. Continue for 29 miles, turn left onto Skokomish Valley Road, and drive 5 miles. Take Forest Road 23 for 9 miles, then FR 2353 for 0.75 mile. Turn onto FR 2340 and drive into the campground.

About the campground: Brown Creek Campground encompasses 6 acres within Olympic National Forest. It is rarely crowded because it is difficult to find and not many people know about it. Camping conditions are primitive. So is the access road, but four-wheel drive is not necessary, except perhaps in muddy weather. The campground is open year-round.

4 Campbell Tree Grove

Location: 27 miles northeast of Humptulips on the East Fork Humptulips River.
Sites: 8 tent sites, 3 sites for tents or self-contained RVs no longer than 16 feet.
Facilities: Drinking water, picnic tables, vault toilets.
Fee per night: None.
Elevation: 1,100 feet.
Management: Olympic National Forest, Quinault Ranger District.
Activities: Hiking, fishing.
Finding the campground: From Humptulips on U.S. Highway 101, drive 5 miles north and turn right (northeast) onto Donkey Creek Road (Forest Road 22). Continue for 8 miles and turn left onto FR 2204. Stay on FR 2204 for 14 miles to the campground.

About the campground: This 3-acre riverside campground in Olympic National Forest next to the Colonel Bob Wilderness. This is way out in the boonies, but small, nice, and peaceful. Good hiking trails are in the area. The campground is open year-round.

5 Coho

Location: About 33 miles north of Montesano on Wynoochee Lake.
Sites: 58 sites for tents or RVs no longer than 36 feet.
Facilities: Drinking water, picnic tables, flush toilets, wheelchair-accessible restroom, boat docks, boat ramp.
Fee per night: $.
Elevation: 900 feet.
Management: Olympic National Forest, Hood Canal Ranger District.
Activities: Hiking, fishing, canoeing, boating, swimming.
Finding the campground: From Montesano, 37 miles west of Interstate 5 on Washington Highway 8/U.S. Highway 12, turn north onto Wynoochee Valley Road/Forest Road 22. After 32 miles, bear west on FR 22 for a quarter-mile, then north on FR 2294 for just over a mile to the campground.

About the campground: Wynoochee Lake is about 4 miles long and more than a half-mile wide. A hiking trail goes all the way around it. The campground is at the southern end of the lake on the west shore, near Wynoochee Dam. When the weather is nice, Coho is a wonderful campground for relaxing and exploring this part of Olympic National Forest. It is open from May to mid-November.

6 Collins

Location: 26 miles north of Hoodsport on the Duckabush River.
Sites: 6 sites for tents, 10 sites for RVs no longer than 21 feet.
Facilities: Drinking water, picnic tables, vault toilets.
Fee per night: None.
Elevation: 200 feet.
Management: Olympic National Forest, Hood Canal Ranger District.
Activities: Fishing, hiking, swimming.
Finding the campground: From Hoodsport on Hood Canal, drive 21 miles north on U.S. Highway 101. Half a mile south of Duckabush, turn left (west) onto Duckabush Road (Forest Road 2510) and drive 5 miles to the campground.

About the campground: Collins Campground is small, shady, and nicely situated on the shore of the Duckabush River in the Olympic National Forest. It is open from mid-May through September.

7 Coppermine Bottom

Location: About 64 miles north of Hoquiam on the Clearwater River.
Sites: 9 sites for tents or self-contained RVs.
Facilities: Picnic tables, fire grills, tent pads, vault toilets, group shelter, boat ramp; no drinking water.

Fee per night: None.
Elevation: 620 feet.
Management: Washington Department of Natural Resources, Olympic Region.
Activities: Fishing, boating.
Finding the campground: From Hoquiam, drive north on U.S. Highway 101 for about 50 miles. At milepost 147, midway between the towns of Amanda Park and Queets, turn north onto Hoh-Clearwater Mainline and drive for 12.6 miles. Turn right onto C-1010 Road and continue for 1.5 miles to the campground on the left. The last 1.5 miles are on a one-lane gravel road.

About the campground: Well away from US 101, this secluded campground offers nice sites next to the Clearwater River. This is in the Olympic Experimental State Forest, also known as the Bert Cole State Forest. The campground is open year-round.

8 Cottonwood

Location: About 18 miles south of Forks on the Hoh River.
Sites: 9 sites for tents or self-contained RVs.
Facilities: Drinking water, picnic tables, fire grills, tent pads, vault toilets, boat ramp.
Fee per night: None.
Elevation: 160 feet.
Management: Washington Department of Natural Resources, Olympic Region.
Activities: Hiking, fishing, boating, river rafting.
Finding the campground: About 15 miles south of the town of Forks, between mileposts 177 and 178 on U.S. Highway 101, turn west onto Lower Hoh Road (also called Oil City Road). Drive for 2.3 miles and turn left onto H-4060, a gravel road. Continue 0.9 mile to the campground.

About the campground: The Hoh is a swift, wide, and wondrous river, and this campground sits just above its bank. The camp is primitive but pleasantly isolated and peaceful. It is in the Olympic Experimental State Forest, also known as the Bert Cole State Forest. The campground is open year-round.

9 Dungeness Forks

Location: About 12 miles south of Sequim at the confluence of the Dungeness and Gray Wolf Rivers.
Sites: 10 tent sites.
Facilities: Drinking water, picnic tables, vault toilets.
Fee per night: $.
Elevation: 1,180 feet.
Management: Olympic National Forest, Quilcene Ranger District.
Activities: Hiking, fishing.
Finding the campground: From Sequim, drive 3 miles southeast on U.S. Highway 101 and turn right (south) onto Palo Alto Road. Follow it for 7 miles, then

turn right (west) onto Forest Road 2880. Continue 1.5 miles to the campground.

About the campground: Situated in Olympic National Forest, Dungeness Forks Campground is comfortable, shady, and quiet. It is located at the confluence of the Dungeness and Gray Wolf Rivers, in the rain shadow of the Olympic Mountains. That means it is drier than campgrounds on the west side of the Olympic Peninsula. It is open from May through September.

10 East Crossing

Location: About 13 miles southeast of Sequim on the Dungeness River.
Sites: 9 tent sites.
Facilities: Drinking water, picnic tables, vault toilets.
Fee per night: $.
Elevation: 1,200 feet.
Management: Olympic National Forest, Quilcene Ranger District.
Activities: Hiking, fishing.
Finding the campground: From Sequim, drive 3 miles southeast on U.S. Highway 101, turn right (south) onto Palo Alto Road, and drive about 8 miles. Turn left (south) onto Forest Road 28. In 1 mile, turn right (south) onto FR2860 and drive 1 mile to the campground. A Forest Service map would be helpful.

About the campground: Like Dungeness Forks Campground (above), East Crossing is small. It sits on 7 acres on the shady east side of the Dungeness River in a very undisturbed pocket of Olympic National Forest. The campground is open from mid-May through September.

11 Elkhorn

Location: About 36 miles northwest of Hoodsport on the Dosewallips River.
Sites: 20 sites for tents or RVs no longer than 21 feet.
Facilities: Drinking water, picnic tables, vault toilets.
Fee per night: $.
Elevation: 600 feet.
Management: Olympic National Forest, Quilcene Ranger District.
Activities: Fishing, hiking.
Finding the campground: From Hoodsport, drive north on U.S. Highway 101 along Hood Canal for nearly 25 miles. Just south of Brinnon, turn left (west) onto Dosewallips Road (Forest Road 2610) and drive along the Dosewallips River for 11 miles to the campground.

About the campground: Elkhorn's 4 wooded acres sit on the north bank of the Dosewallips River in Olympic National Forest. The setting is peaceful and the fishing is supposed to be good. The campground is open from mid-May through September.

12 Falls Creek

Location: About 45 miles north of Aberdeen on Lake Quinault.
Sites: 15 tent sites, 16 sites for RVs no longer than 16 feet.
Facilities: Drinking water, picnic tables, flush toilets; nearby boat rentals, docks, and ramps.
Fee per night: $$.
Elevation: 200 feet.
Management: Olympic National Forest, Quinault Ranger District.
Activities: Fishing, hiking, boating, swimming.
Finding the campground: From Aberdeen, drive 42 miles north on U.S. Highway 101 to the Quinault turnoff (South Shore Road). Turn right (northeast) and drive 2.5 miles to the campground on the east shore of Lake Quinault.

About the campground: Falls Creek Campground is located in Olympic National Forest, where Falls Creek flows into Lake Quinault. It is near the Quinault Ranger Station and Lake Quinault Lodge. There is a boat ramp and a rocky beach. The swimming is good in the warmer months of July and August. Signed nature trails go near and through the campground, which is open from Memorial Day through Labor Day.

13 Falls View

Location: About 29 miles south of Port Townsend on the Big Quilcene River.
Sites: 30 sites for tents or RVs no longer than 21 feet.
Facilities: Drinking water, picnic tables, flush toilets.
Fee per night: $$.
Elevation: 635 feet.
Management: Olympic National Forest, Quilcene Ranger District.
Activities: Hiking, fishing.
Finding the campground: The entrance to Falls View Campground is on U.S. Highway 101, 3.5 miles south of Quilcene, which is 25 miles south of Port Townsend.

About the campground: Within hiking distance of nearby Mount Walker, Falls View is a popular campground on the eastern side of the Big Quilcene River. It is located in Olympic National Forest and is open from mid-May to mid-September.

14 Gatton Creek

Location: 45 miles north of Aberdeen on Lake Quinault.
Sites: 5 tent sites.
Facilities: Drinking water, picnic tables, firewood, vault toilets, nature trail.
Fee per night: $$.
Elevation: 200 feet.
Management: Olympic National Forest, Quinault Ranger District.

Activities: Hiking, fishing, boating, swimming.
Finding the campground: From Aberdeen, drive 42 miles north on U.S. Highway 101 to the Quinault turnoff (South Shore Road). Turn right (northeast) and drive 3 miles to the campground on the eastern shore of Lake Quinault.

About the campground: Gatton Creek Campground was named for the creek that runs into Lake Quinault at this site. Situated in Olympic National Forest, the camp is small but lovely and peaceful. Signed nature trails pass through the rain forest nearby. The campground is open from mid-May through October.

15 Hamma Hamma

Location: About 19 miles north of Hoodsport on the Hamma Hamma River.
Sites: 3 sites for tents, 12 sites for tents or self-contained RVs no longer than 21 feet.
Facilities: Drinking water, picnic tables, vault toilets.
Fee per night: $.
Elevation: 600 feet.
Management: Olympic National Forest, Hood Canal Ranger District.
Activities: Hiking, fishing, swimming, mountain biking.
Finding the campground: From Hoodsport on Hood Canal, drive 13 miles north on U.S. Highway 101. Two miles past Eldon, turn left (northwest) onto Hamma Hamma River Road (Forest Road 25) and drive 6 miles to the campground.

About the campground: This 5-acre, primitive camp is located in Olympic National Forest, just below the spot where Cabin Creek enters the Hamma Hamma River. The fishing is fine here on the "dry" side of the Olympic Mountains. The campground is open from May to mid-November.

16 Hoh Oxbow

Location: About 16 miles south of Forks on the Hoh River.
Sites: 7 sites for tents or self-contained RVs, including 1 wheelchair-accessible site.
Facilities: Picnic tables, fire grills, tent pads, vault toilets, boat ramp; no drinking water.
Fee per night: None.
Elevation: 317 feet.
Management: Washington Department of Natural Resources, Olympic Region.
Activities: Fishing, boating, river rafting.
Finding the campground: The campground is about 16 miles south of the town of Forks between mileposts 176 and 177 on U.S. Highway 101. It is on the east side of the highway between the road and the Hoh River.

About the campground: Hoh Oxbow, named for the oxbow made by the river here, is popular with anglers. The campground is very primitive and there is no water, but it is an easy trip north to Forks for supplies. This camp is in the Olympic Experimental State Forest, also known as the Bert Cole State Forest. It is open year-round.

17 Klahowya

Location: About 20 miles northeast of Forks on the Soleduck River.
Sites: 25 sites for tents, 20 sites for RVs no longer than 20 feet.
Facilities: Drinking water, picnic tables, vault and flush toilets, boat ramp.
Fee per night: $$.
Elevation: 850 feet.
Management: Olympic National Forest, Soleduck Ranger District.
Activities: Hiking, boating, fishing, mountain biking.
Finding the campground: From the town of Forks, drive 20 miles northeast on U.S. Highway 101.

About the campground: This 32-acre campground in Olympic National Forest is quite popular because of its easy access from US 101 and its thickly forested surroundings. It is nicely situated on the comparative flats of the Soleduck River Valley next to the river. The campground is open from mid-May to mid-October with all services. It stays open the rest of the year, but with limited services.

18 Lake Cushman State Park

Location: 6 miles west of Hoodsport on Lake Cushman.
Sites: 30 sites for tents or self-contained RVs no longer than 60 feet, 50 sites for tents only, 2 primitive sites.
Facilities: Drinking water, fire grills, picnic tables, restrooms, showers, playground, dump station, 3 boat ramps.
Fee per night: $$.
Elevation: 731 feet.
Management: Washington State Parks and Recreation Commission.
Activities: Hiking, fishing, boating, waterskiing.
Finding the campground: From Hoodsport on Hood Canal, take Washington Highway 119 (Lake Cushman Road) west for 6 miles to the campground.

About the campground: This park encompasses 600 acres and nearly 8 miles of shoreline on Lake Cushman. Four miles of marked hiking trails wind through the park, and good hiking can be found right outside the park as well. The campground is very popular with families and is often full. Late summer is the most dependable time to find dry weather. The campground is open from April through October. For a fee, you can make reservations by calling Reservations Northwest (see contact information on page 236).

19 Lena Creek

Location: 21 miles northwest of Hoodsport on the Hamma Hamma River.
Sites: 14 sites for tents or self-contained RVs no longer than 21 feet.
Facilities: Drinking water, picnic tables, vault toilets.
Fee per night: $.
Elevation: 900 feet.
Management: Olympic National Forest, Hood Canal Ranger District.
Activities: Hiking, fishing.
Finding the campground: From the town of Hoodsport on Hood Canal, drive 11 miles north on U.S. Highway 101 to Eldon. Continue 2 miles north on US 101 and then turn left (northwest) onto Hamma Hamma River Road (Forest Road 25). Drive 8 miles to the campground.

About the campground: This 7-acre campground is very basic, good for roughing it if you are so inclined. Save some energy for the 1.5-mile hike up Lena Creek past the Mason/Jefferson county line to Lena Lake. The lake is about a half-mile long, and, 1 mile beyond the lake, the trail crosses from Olympic National Forest into Olympic National Park. From there, it is another 3 miles to Upper Lena Lake. The campground is open from mid-May through September.

20 Lilliwaup

Location: About 20 miles north of Hoodsport on Lilliwaup Creek.
Sites: 6 sites for tents or self-contained RVs.
Facilities: Drinking water, picnic tables, fire grills, tent pads, vault toilets.
Fee per night: None.
Elevation: 900 feet.
Management: Washington Department of Natural Resources, South Puget Sound Region.
Activities: Hiking, fishing.
Finding the campground: From Hoodsport, drive 8 miles north along Hood Canal via U.S. Highway 101. Turn left (west) onto Jorsted Creek Road (Forest Road 24). Continue for 5.5 miles and then turn left onto a gravel one-lane road and drive 6.6 miles to the campground.

About the campground: Lilliwaup Campground is small, quiet, and primitive. It is nicely situated on Lilliwaup Creek and is open year-round.

21 Lake Sylvia State Park

Location: About 2 miles north of Montesano on Lake Sylvia.
Sites: 35 sites for tents or self-contained RVs no longer than 30 feet, 2 primitive tent sites.
Facilities: Drinking water, picnic tables, fire grills, dump station, toilets, coin-operated showers, store, boat ramp, boat rentals, playground.
Fee per night: $$ to $$$.
Elevation: 125 feet.

Management: Washington State Parks and Recreation Commission.
Activities: Hiking, fishing, swimming, boating.
Finding the campground: From U.S. Highway 12 in Montesano, head north at the sign for Lake Sylvia State Park. Drive 1.5 miles through town to reach the park.

About the campground: Lake Sylvia State Park encompasses 234 acres and features 15,000 feet of shoreline, 270 feet of which comprise a developed swimming beach. Other attractions are a swimming float and 5 miles of hiking trail. The lake was formed when Sylvia Creek was dammed for log impoundment and power production. The power operated a downstream lumber mill for 60 years beginning in 1871. The campground is open from May through Labor Day weekend.

22 Melbourne

Location: About 16 miles north of Hoodsport on Melbourne Lake.
Sites: 5 sites for tents or self-contained RVs.
Facilities: Picnic tables, fire grills, tent pads, vault toilets; no drinking water.
Fee per night: None.
Elevation: 820 feet.
Management: Washington Department of Natural Resources, South Puget Sound Region.
Activities: Hiking, fishing, boating.
Finding the campground: From Hoodsport, drive 8 miles north along Hood Canal via U.S. Highway 101. Turn left (west) onto Jorsted Creek Road (Forest Road 24). Continue for 5.5 miles and then turn left onto a gravel one-lane road. Drive 1.7 miles, bear left, and drive 0.75 mile to the camp.

About the campground: Located in Olympic National Forest, Melbourne Campground is, like many DNR sites, rustic, private, and not well known. The price is right, too. Melbourne Lake is less than a half-mile long. The campground is open year-round.

23 Minnie Peterson

Location: About 18 miles southeast of Forks on the Hoh River.
Sites: 8 sites for tents or self-contained RVs.
Facilities: Undrinkable water, picnic tables, fire grills, tent pads, vault toilets.
Fee per night: None.
Elevation: 120 feet.
Management: Washington Department of Natural Resources, South Puget Sound Region.
Activities: Hiking, fishing, boating, river rafting.
Finding the campground: From Forks, drive about 13 miles south on U.S. Highway 101. Turn left (east) between mileposts 178 and 179 onto Upper Hoh Road. Drive 4.5 miles to reach the campground on the left.

About the campground: This campground sits at the edge of the Hoh Rain Forest in the Olympic Experimental State Forest (or Bert Cole State Forest). It is just outside the boundary of Olympic National Park. It is primitive and free, and the sites are nicely placed along the riverbank. The campground is open year-round.

24 Olympic National Park: Altaire

Location: About 13 miles southwest of Port Angeles on the Elwha River in Olympic National Park.
Sites: 30 sites for tents or RVs no longer than 21 feet.
Facilities: Drinking water, picnic tables, fire grills, restrooms, some wheelchair-accessible facilities.
Fee per night: $$.
Elevation: 450 feet.
Management: Olympic National Park, Elwha Ranger Station.
Activities: Hiking, fishing.
Finding the campground: From Port Angeles on the Strait of Juan de Fuca, take U.S. Highway 101 west for 9 miles to the turnoff onto Olympic Hot Springs Road, just past Lake Aldwell. The campground is about 4 miles south on Olympic Hot Springs Road.

About the campground: Altaire feels more remote than it actually is. It is secluded and private, with good access to hiking trails in both Olympic National Forest and Olympic National Park. It is open from June to September.

25 Olympic National Park: Deer Park

Location: About 22 miles southeast of Port Angeles in Olympic National Park.
Sites: 18 tent sites.
Facilities: Drinking water, picnic tables, fire grills, vault toilets.
Fee per night: None.
Elevation: 5,400 feet.
Management: Olympic National Park.
Activities: Hiking.
Finding the campground: From U.S. Highway 101, 4 miles east of downtown Port Angeles, head south into the park on Deer Park Road. Continue for 18 miles to the campground.

About the campground: Access to alpine hiking trails is the main appeal of Deer Park, a primitive campground for tents only. Its elevation of more than a mile allows you to get acclimated before tackling the trails. The campground is open from mid-June to late September and has limited winter facilities. Unseasonable snows can close the winding dirt access road.

Fifty species of animals thrive in Olympic National Park, site of the largest evergreen forest in the contiguous United States.

26 Olympic National Park: Dosewallips

Location: 39 miles northwest of Hoodsport on the Dosewallips River in Olympic National Park.
Sites: 30 tent sites; trailers not recommended.
Facilities: Drinking water, picnic tables, fire grills, restrooms.
Fee per night: $$.
Elevation: 1,540 feet.
Management: Olympic National Park, Hood Canal Ranger District.
Activities: Fishing, nature trails.
Finding the campground: From Hoodsport on Hood Canal, drive north on U.S. Highway 101 for nearly 25 miles to just south of the town of Brinnon. Turn west onto Dosewallips Road (Forest Road 2610) and drive along the Dosewallips River for 14 miles to the campground.

About the campground: Dosewallips Campground is about the end of the road for cars, but you could hike along rivers to the Pacific Coast from here. The riverside campsites are nice, which attracts a lot of people who want to hike the trail network in Olympic National Park. The campground is open from mid-May to late September.

27 Olympic National Park: Elwha

Location: About 12 miles southwest of Port Angeles on the Elwha River in Olympic National Park.
Sites: 41 sites for tents or RVs no longer than 21 feet.
Facilities: Drinking water, picnic tables, fire grills, restrooms, some wheelchair-accessible facilities.
Fee per night: $$.
Elevation: 390 feet.
Management: Olympic National Park.
Activities: Hiking, fishing.
Finding the campground: From Port Angeles on the Strait of Juan de Fuca, take U.S. Highway 101 west for 9 miles to the turnoff onto Olympic Hot Springs Road, just past Lake Aldwell. The campground is about 2.5 miles south on Olympic Hot Springs Road.

About the campground: The Elwha River is a lovely, north-draining river on the Olympic Peninsula, and this campground is right on the riverbank. It affords good access to hiking trails in both Olympic National Forest and Olympic National Park. The campground is open year-round.

28 Olympic National Park: Fairholm

Location: About 22 miles west of Port Angeles on Lake Crescent in Olympic National Park.
Sites: 87 sites for tents or RVs no longer than 21 feet.
Facilities: Drinking water, picnic tables, fire grills, dump station, restrooms.
Fee per night: $$.
Elevation: 580 feet.
Management: Olympic National Park.
Activities: Hiking, fishing, boating.
Finding the campground: From Port Angeles, drive 22 miles west on U.S. Highway 101 to the western end of Lake Crescent. Turn right (north) onto North Shore Road. The campground is on the right within a half-mile.

About the campground: Lake Crescent is a study in just how lovely a remote subalpine lake can be—except that it sits right next to the highway at a low elevation. Plenty of boaters use the lake; there is even a paddle wheeler for tourists. But if the lake were not in Olympic National Park, there would be subdivisions all around it. Fairholm's amenities make it one of the more comfortable campgrounds in the park. It is open year-round.

29 Olympic National Park: Graves Creek

Location: 60 miles north of Aberdeen on the Quinault River in Olympic National Park.
Sites: 30 sites for tents or RVs no longer than 21 feet.

Facilities: Drinking water, picnic tables, fire grills, wheelchair-accessible restrooms.
Fee per night: None.
Elevation: 600 feet.
Management: Olympic National Park.
Activities: Hiking, fishing.
Finding the campground: From Aberdeen, drive 42 miles north on U.S. Highway 101 to the Quinault turnoff (South Shore Road). Turn right (northeast) and drive 18 miles to the campground. Graves Creek Ranger Station is here, too.

About the campground: Graves Creek Campground, located near the spot at which Graves Creek empties into the Quinault River, is a good base site from which to launch hikes into the Olympic backcountry. It is open year-round, but in the winter amenities are limited.

30 Olympic National Park: Heart o' the Hills

Location: 6 miles south of Port Angeles in Olympic National Park.
Sites: 105 sites for tents or RVs no longer than 21 feet.
Facilities: Drinking water, picnic tables, restrooms, wheelchair-accessible facilities.
Fee per night: $.
Elevation: 1,800 feet.
Management: Olympic National Park.
Activities: Nature program, hiking.
Finding the campground: From U.S. Highway 101 in Port Angeles, head south toward Hurricane Ridge on Mount Angeles Road. Continue 6 miles to the campground.

About the campground: Heart o' the Hills covers just 35 acres, but it offers good access to the "rain shadow" side of Olympic National Park. The paved road continues to Hurricane Ridge, an alpine and cross-country ski area with excellent winter programs. The campground is open year-round, but heavy snow can close Hurricane Ridge Road.

31 Olympic National Park: Hoh

Location: 33 miles southeast of Forks in Olympic National Park.
Sites: 89 sites for tents or RVs no longer than 21 feet.
Facilities: Drinking water, picnic tables, fire grills, restrooms, wheelchair-accessible facilities, dump station.
Fee per night: $.
Elevation: 500 feet.
Management: Olympic National Park, Hoh Ranger Station.
Activities: Nature program, hiking, fishing.
Finding the campground: From the town of Forks, drive 14 miles south on U.S. Highway 101. Turn left (east) onto Hoh River Road and continue for 19 miles to the campground.

About the campground: Hoh Campground, in the Hoh Rain Forest, can be one of the wettest places on earth, but the surreal surroundings make this a very popular site. Visitors are surprised by how many shades of green can be found in this one place and by how big the plants grow here. There are two barrier-free loop trails nearby: one is a quarter-mile long, the other 1.25 miles. The Hall of Mosses Trail is a three-quarter-mile loop that begins and ends at the visitor center. The campground is open year-round.

32 Olympic National Park: Queets

Location: 75 miles north of Aberdeen on the Queets River in Olympic National Park.
Sites: 20 tent sites.
Facilities: Picnic tables, fire grills, vault toilets; no drinking water.
Fee per night: None.
Elevation: 350 feet.
Management: Olympic National Park, Queets Ranger Station.
Activities: Hiking, fishing.
Finding the campground: From Aberdeen, drive 61 miles north on U.S. Highway 101, passing the turnoff to Lake Quinault. Just past the Jefferson County line, look for the campground sign on the right. Turn right here onto Queets River Road, a dirt road, and drive 14 miles along the Queets River to the campground at the end of the road.

About the campground: The 2-acre Queets Campground is located as far into the Queets Rain Forest as you can drive. It is popular, nevertheless, for the rustic experience it offers. It is open from May 30 to September 30.

33 Olympic National Park: Sol Duc

Location: 40 miles southwest of Port Angeles on the Soleduck River in Olympic National Park.
Sites: 80 sites for tents or RVs no longer than 21 feet.
Facilities: Drinking water, picnic tables, fire grills, restrooms, dump station.
Fee per night: $.
Elevation: 1,700 feet.
Management: Olympic National Park, Soleduck Ranger Station.
Activities: Hiking, fishing, nature programs.
Finding the campground: From Port Angeles, drive west 28 miles on U.S. Highway 101. A few miles past Lake Crescent, turn left (southeast) onto Sol Duc River Road and continue for 12 miles to the campground.

About the campground: Sol Duc Campground is very popular because of its proximity to Sol Duc Hot Springs. The hot springs are fully developed and operated by a resort, so there is an admission fee. The mineral pools are like giant hot tubs. The campground is nicely set on the west side of the Soleduck River, and the spaces offer some privacy. The campground is open from May to late October, but minimal services are available in winter.

34 Olympic National Park: Staircase

Location: 17 miles northwest of Hoodsport on the North Fork Skokomish River in Olympic National Park.
Sites: 59 sites for tents or self-contained RVs no longer than 21 feet.
Facilities: Drinking water, picnic tables, fire grills, flush toilets, wheelchair-accessible facilities.
Fee per night: $.
Elevation: 820 feet.
Management: Olympic National Park, Staircase Ranger Station.
Activities: Hiking, fishing.
Finding the campground: From U.S. Highway 101 in the town of Hoodsport on Hood Canal, drive 17 miles west and then north on Washington Highway 119 (Lake Cushman Road). The campground is 1 mile north of Lake Cushman, where Lake Cushman Road becomes Forest Road 24.

About the campground: The hiking is splendid around this 8-acre campground, which sits on the North Fork Skokomish River. The name Staircase comes from the Staircase Rapids at the site. The campground is open year-round.

35 Schafer State Park

Location: 16 miles northwest of Elma on the East Fork Satsop River.
Sites: 47 developed tent sites, 6 RV sites with water and electrical hookups, 2 primitive tent sites.
Facilities: Drinking water, picnic tables, fire grills, dump station, toilets, coin-operated showers, firewood (fee), playground.
Fee per night: $ to $$.
Elevation: 235 feet.
Management: Washington State Parks and Recreation Commission.
Activities: Hiking, fishing, river floating, canoeing, kayaking.
Finding the campground: From Elma, drive 4 miles west on U.S. Highway 12 to the town of Satsop. Turn right (north) onto East Satsop Road and drive 12 miles to the campground.

About the campground: This nice, 119-acre, family campground features nearly a mile of shoreline on the East Fork Satsop River. The heavily wooded park was donated to the state by Schafer Brothers Logging Company. The park is open year-round, but facilities are limited in winter.

36 South Fork Hoh

Location: About 27 miles southeast of Forks on the South Fork Hoh River.
Sites: 3 sites for tents or self-contained RVs.
Facilities: Picnic tables, fire grills, tent pads, vault toilets; no drinking water.
Fee per night: None.
Elevation: 650 feet.

Management: Washington Department of Natural Resources, Olympic Region.
Activities: Hiking, fishing, boating, river rafting.
Finding the campground: From Forks, drive about 13 miles south on U.S. Highway 101. Turn left (east) at milepost 176 onto Upper Hoh Road. Drive 6.6 miles on paved road and ¡turn left onto H-1000 Road, which becomes one-lane gravel for the last few miles. The campground is on the right, 7.4 miles from the turn onto H-1000 Road.

About the campground: This campground is quite small and very remote, almost your own personal wilderness site. Open year-round, it is in the Olympic Experimental State Forest, also known as the Bert Cole State Forest. The Olympic National Park South Fork Trailhead is 2 miles beyond the campground.

37 Upper Clearwater

Location: About 66 miles north of Hoquiam on the Clearwater River.
Sites: 9 sites for tents or self-contained RVs.
Facilities: Undrinkable water, picnic tables, fire grills, tent pads, vault toilets, boat ramp.
Fee per night: None.
Elevation: 1,574 feet.
Management: Washington Department of Natural Resources, Olympic Region.
Activities: Fishing, hiking, boating.
Finding the campground: From Hoquiam, drive north on U.S. Highway 101 for about 50 miles. At milepost 147, midway between the towns of Amanda Park and Queets, turn north onto Hoh-Clearwater Mainline and drive for 12.9 miles. Turn right onto C-3000 Road, a one-lane gravel road, and continue for 3.2 miles to the campground on the right.

About the campground: This well-appointed yet primitive campground on the Upper Clearwater is in a nice section of the rain forest, not far from both Olympic National Forest and Olympic National Park. It is situated in the Olympic Experimental State Forest, also known as the Bert Cole State Forest, and is open year-round.

38 Western Lakes

Location: About 6 miles north of Naselle.
Sites: 3 primitive tent sites.
Facilities: Picnic tables, fire grills, tent pads, vault toilets; no drinking water.
Fee per night: None.
Elevation: 900 feet.
Management: Washington Department of Natural Resources, Central Region.
Activities: Hiking.
Finding the campground: From the junction of U.S. Highway 101 and Washington Highway 4, 5.5 miles northwest of Naselle, drive 3 miles south on WA 4 to milepost 3. Turn left (north) onto C-line Road. At the entrance to the Naselle

Youth Camp, take the left fork and drive for 2.9 miles. Turn left onto C-2600 Road and drive for 0.9 mile. At C-2650 Road, turn right and continue 0.3 mile to the campground. The road narrows to one lane and turns to gravel near the end.

About the campground: The Washington Department of Natural Resources knows how to build tiny, primitive campgrounds in the middle of nowhere, and this is one of the best and most private. The site is wooded, as are most, and is located near tiny Western Lakes. The campground is open year-round.

39 Willaby

Location: About 44 miles north of Aberdeen on Lake Quinault.
Sites: 22 sites for tents or RVs no longer than 16 feet.
Facilities: Drinking water, picnic tables, flush toilets, bathroom electricity, boat docks, boat ramp.
Fee per night: $$.
Elevation: 200 feet.
Management: Olympic National Forest, Quinault Ranger District.
Activities: Hiking, fishing, bicycling, boating, swimming.
Finding the campground: From Aberdeen, drive 42 miles north on U.S. Highway 101 to the Quinault turnoff (South Shore Road). Turn right (northeast) and drive 1.5 miles to the campground on the east shore of Lake Quinault.

About the campground: This wooded campground covers 7 acres in Olympic National Forest. The swimming is good, and there is a boat ramp. The beach is rocky, but the water is "warm" according to the local forest ranger—45 to 50 degrees F. Ouch! That is comparable to the temperature of Puget Sound. Nevertheless, the water is clean and brisk. The campground is open from mid-April to mid-September.

40 Willoughby Creek

Location: About 17 miles southeast of Forks on the Hoh River.
Sites: 3 sites for tents or self-contained RVs.
Facilities: Picnic tables, fire grills, tent pads, vault toilets; no drinking water.
Fee per night: None.
Management: Washington Department of Natural Resources, South Puget Sound Region.
Activities: Hiking, fishing.
Finding the campground: About 13 miles south of the town of Forks, between mileposts 178 and 179 on U.S. Highway 101, turn east onto Upper Hoh Road. Drive 3.5 miles to the campground on the right.

About the campground: It is hard to beat this 3-site campground, which charges nothing for a 14-day stay. Plan on a rainy and primitive experience with good fishing. This campground is in the Olympic Experimental State Forest, also known as the Bert Cole State Forest. It is open year-round.

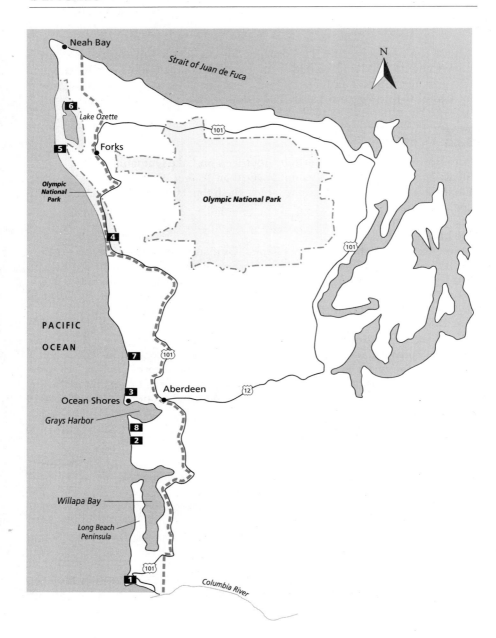

Neah Bay

Strait of Juan de Fuca

N

6

Lake Ozette

5

Forks

Olympic National Park

Olympic National Park

4

PACIFIC

OCEAN

101

7

101

Aberdeen

12

3

Ocean Shores

Grays Harbor

8

2

Willapa Bay

Long Beach Peninsula

101

1

Columbia River

BEACHES

	Group sites	RV sites	Total # of sites	Max. RV length	Hookups	Toilets	Showers	Drinking water	Dump station	Pets	Wheelchair	Recreation	Fee	Season	Can reserve	Stay limit
1 Fort Canby State Park	•	•	254	45	WES	F	•	•	•	•	•	HFB	$$–$$$		•	10
2 Grayland Beach State Park		•	63	40	WES	F	•	•		•	•	HFR	$$–$$$		•	10
3 Ocean City State Park	•	•	181	55	WES	F	•	•	•	•	•	HFRS	$$–$$$		•	10
4 Olympic Natl Park: Kaloch		•	177	21		F		•	•	•	•	HF	$$			14
5 Olympic Natl Park: Mora	•	•	95	21		F		•	•	•	•	HF	$$			14
6 Olympic Natl Park: Ozette		•	14	21		V		•		•		HFB				14
7 Pacific Beach State Park		•	64	45	E	F	•	•	•	•	•	FB	$$–$$$		•	10
8 Twin Harbors State Park		•	303	35	WES	F	•	•	•	•	•	FR	$$–$$$		•	10

Hookups: W = Water E = Electric S = Sewer
Toilets: F = Flush V = Vault P = Pit
Recreation: C = Bicycling/Mountain Biking H = Hiking S = Swimming F = Fishing B = Boating
O = Off-highway driving R = Horseback Riding
Maximum Trailer/RV Length given in feet. **Stay Limit** given in days.
Fee $ = less than $10; $$ = $10-$15; $$$ = $16–20; $$$$ = more than $20.
If no entry under **Season**, campground is open all year. If no entry under **Fee**, camping is free.

1 Fort Canby State Park

Location: About 3 miles southwest of Ilwaco on the Long Beach Peninsula.
Sites: 190 tent sites, 60 sites with hookups for RVs no longer than 45 feet, 4 primitive sites, cabins, yurts.
Facilities: Drinking water, picnic tables, fire grills, flush toilets, coin-operated showers, dump station, boat ramps, groceries, fishing gear, interpretive center, 4 miles of hiking trails.
Fee per night: $$ to $$$.
Elevation: Sea level.
Management: Washington State Parks and Recreation Commission.
Activities: Hiking, clam digging, surf fishing, beachcombing, seasonal whale watching, boating, interpretive center, nature program.
Finding the campground: From the town of Ilwaco on U.S. Highway 101, drive southwest on Fort Canby Road for 2.5 miles to the park.

About the campground: This is a mighty nice campground considering the rugged terrain and brutish winter weather. It was here, at Cape Disappointment, that Lewis and Clark finally reached the Pacific Ocean in 1805. The campsites are on the sea side of this 1,882-acre park. Lake O'Neil is nearby. The lake has 1.3 miles of shoreline, and the park itself includes 8 miles of shoreline on the Columbia River and Pacific Ocean. Trails lead through the park, to the beaches, to a pair of lighthouses (North Head and Cape Disappointment), and through old-growth forests. The Lewis and Clark Interpretive Center is open all year, and tours are available of the North Head Lighthouse. Fort Canby was first armed during the Civil War and was dedicated as a state park nearly 100 years later, in 1957. The Cape Disappointment area has been declared a National Historic District. The campground is open year-round. For a fee, you can make reservations by calling Reservations Northwest (see contact information on page 236).

2 Grayland Beach State Park

Location: About 20 miles southwest of Aberdeen.
Sites: 60 sites with full hookups for RVs no longer than 40 feet, 2 wheelchair-accessible sites, 3 primitive tent sites with a shared portable toilet.
Facilities: Drinking water, picnic tables, flush toilets, fire grills, coin-operated showers.
Fee per night: $$ to $$$.
Elevation: Sea level.
Management: Washington State Parks and Recreation Commission.
Activities: Hiking, fishing, clam digging, kite flying, horseback riding, beachcombing.
Finding the campground: From U.S. Highway 12 in Aberdeen, drive southwest for about 20 miles on Washington Highway 105. The campground is just south of Grayland.

About the campground: This state park features nearly 1.5 miles of wide, sandy beach. On a hot summer day, you would swear this was Southern California—until you touched the water, that is. It is a good 15 to 20 degrees colder here. Sand dunes stretch for a few miles to the south, and to the north there is a cranberry bog on the other side of the highway. This is a popular park, and families appreciate the large campsites, which are available year-round. For a fee, you can make reservations by calling Reservations Northwest (see contact information on page 236).

3 Ocean City State Park

Location: 17 miles west of Hoquiam, near Ocean Shores.
Sites: 149 tent sites, 3 primitive tent sites for hikers and bikers, 29 sites with full hookups for RVs no longer than 55 feet, 1 group site.
Facilities: Drinking water, picnic tables, restrooms, dump station, coin-operated showers.
Fee per night: $$ to $$$.
Elevation: Sea level.
Management: Washington State Parks and Recreation Commission.
Activities: Beachcombing, clam digging, fishing, horseback riding, kite flying, surfing, bird watching, mushroom picking, hiking, swimming.
Finding the campground: From U.S. Highway 101 in Hoquiam, head west on Washington Highway 109 for 16 miles. At the intersection with WA 115, turn left (south) and drive for 1 mile to the park entrance on the right.

About the campground: Ocean City State Park encompasses 170 acres, including 2,980 feet of coastline. The state's purchase of the land in 1960 ensured permanent public access to the beach. Regional Indians traditionally made regular, seasonal stops here to hunt for razor clams. Today, the park is popular because of its sandy beach, easy accessibility, and proximity to shopping and restaurants in the town of Ocean Shores, 2 miles south. The campground is open year-round. For a fee, you can make reservations by calling Reservations Northwest (see contact information on page 236).

4 Olympic National Park: Kalaloch

Location: 35 miles south of Forks in Olympic National Park.
Sites: 177 sites for tents or self-contained RVs no longer than 21 feet.
Facilities: Drinking water, picnic tables, fire grills, restrooms, wheelchair-accessible facilities, dump station.
Fee per night: $$.
Elevation: Sea level.
Management: Olympic National Park, Kalaloch Ranger Station.
Activities: Hiking, fishing, summer nature program.
Finding the campground: From the town of Forks, drive 35 miles south on U.S. Highway 101 to the campground.

About the campground: This is one of the few campgrounds on the Olympic Peninsula with access to Pacific beaches. Situated on a bluff above the beach, it is large enough that a walk around camp is an actual excursion. Some of the campsites feature an ocean view, and most are shielded from each other by scrub brush. Be prepared for wet weather, both fog and rain. The campground is open year-round. During the summer, there is an overflow area 3 miles to the south on a gravel lot close to the beach. It has restrooms but no other facilities.

5 Olympic National Park: Mora

Location: 14 miles west of Forks on the Quillayute River in Olympic National Park.
Sites: 94 sites for tents or self-contained RVs no longer than 21 feet, 1 group site.
Facilities: Drinking water, picnic tables, fire grills, restrooms, dump station.
Fee per night: $$.
Elevation: 50 feet.
Management: Olympic National Park.
Activities: Fishing, hiking, summer nature program.
Finding the campground: From the town of Forks, drive north for 2 miles on U.S. Highway 101. Turn left (west) on La Push Road (Washington Highway 110) and continue for 8 miles. Bear right onto Mora Road at the Y junction, following the signs for Mora Campground. Drive 4 miles to the campground.

About the campground: This is an isolated campground near the mouth of the Quillayute River. The nearby fishing community of La Push is home to the Quileute Indians. Mora Road continues past the campground to Rialto Beach, the only point between the Hoh River and Neah Bay with vehicle access to the coastline of Olympic National Park. The rocky headlands and offshore sea stacks are stark reminders of the wildness of this part of the coast. This stretch of the Pacific Ocean has been designated as the Quillayute Needles National Wildlife Refuge, a part of the Olympic Coast Marine Sanctuary. Nesting shorebirds and marine mammals find refuge here. The campground is open year-round.

6 Olympic National Park: Ozette

Location: 75 miles west of Port Angeles on Ozette Lake in Olympic National Park.
Sites: 14 sites for tents or self-contained RVs no longer than 21 feet.
Facilities: Drinking water, picnic tables, fire grills, vault toilets.
Fee per night: None.
Elevation: 40 feet.
Management: Olympic National Park, Lake Ozette Ranger Station.
Activities: Hiking, fishing, boating.
Finding the campground: From downtown Port Angeles, drive west on U.S. Highway 101 for 5 miles, bear right on Washington Highway 112, and drive another 49 miles. Two miles past the town of Sekiu, turn left (southwest) onto the Hoko-Ozette Road and drive 21 miles to Ozette, the campground, and a park ranger station.

About the campground: Open year-round, the campground is primitive, isolated, and very appealing because of the pristine lake. Cedar walkways lead 3 miles through dense forest to the beaches of the Pacific.

7 Pacific Beach State Park

Location: 29 miles northwest of Hoquiam in Pacific Beach, on the Long Beach Peninsula.
Sites: 33 sites for tents, 31 sites for RVs up to 45 feet long.
Facilities: Drinking water, restrooms, coin-operated showers, dump station.
Fee per night: $$ to $$$.
Elevation: Sea level.
Management: Washington State Parks and Recreation Commission.
Activities: Clam digging, freshwater and saltwater fishing, kite flying, beach-combing, bird watching, kayaking, surfing.
Finding the campground: From U.S. Highway 101 in Hoquiam, take Washington Highway 109 west for 16 miles. Turn north, still on WA 109, and drive for 13 miles to the park.

About the campground: The unusual in-town location of this park makes it very popular with campers who like the best of both worlds. It tends to stay full in the warm months. Originally a private campground, the state bought it to ensure public access to the beach. It was completely renovated in 1995. It covers

Open beaches and ocean breezes attract kite flyers to the Long Beach Peninsula

about 10 acres and features 2,300 feet of shoreline. Some of the sites have good ocean views. The campground is open year-round. For a fee, you can make reservations by calling Reservations Northwest (see contact information on page 236).

8 Twin Harbors State Park

Location: 19 miles southwest of Aberdeen, near Westport.
Sites: 249 tent sites (3 are wheelchair-accessible), 5 primitive sites, 49 sites with hookups for RVs up to 35 feet long.
Facilities: Drinking water, picnic tables, fire grills, restrooms, coin-operated showers, dump station, playground, clam-cleaning shed.
Fee per night: $$ to $$$.
Elevation: Sea level.
Management: Washington State Parks and Recreation Commission.
Activities: Surf fishing, clam digging, horseback riding, kite flying, beachcombing.
Finding the campground: From Aberdeen, take U.S. Highway 101 across the Chehalis River into South Aberdeen. Turn right (south) onto Washington Highway 105 and continue for 18 miles to the park. It is 3 miles south of Westport.

About the campground: Named for its location between Willapa Bay and Grays Harbor, this park was a U.S. Army training ground during the 1930s. The original park, created in 1937, had more than a half-mile of shoreline; the 12 miles of South Beach were added a piece at a time in 1973 and 1974. This is truly a beach-lover's paradise, and the sand dunes are especially appealing. There is even a Shifting Sands Nature Trail. The park is very popular, and the campsites are relatively densely packed. The campground is open year-round. For a fee, you can make reservations by calling Reservations Northwest (see contact information on page 236).

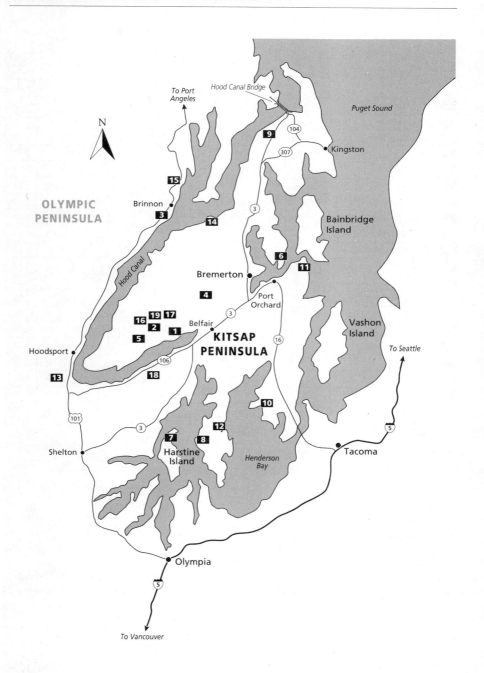

HOOD CANAL/KITSAP PENINSULA

	Group sites	RV sites	Total # of sites	Max. RV length	Hookups	Toilets	Showers	Drinking water	Dump station	Pets	Wheelchair	Recreation	Fee	Season	Can reserve	Stay limit
1 Belfair State Park		•	184	75	WES	F	•	•	•	•	•	HS	$$–$$$		•	10
2 Camp Spillman		•	6	21		V		•		•		HFC				7
3 Dosewallips State Park	•	•	130	60	WES	F	•	•	•	•		HF	$–$$		•	10
4 Gold Creek		•	6			V		•		•		HRC		May–Sep		7
5 Howell Lake		•	6	30		V		•		•		HBC				7
6 Illahee State Park	•	•	33	40		F	•	•	•	•	•	HB	$$–$$$	May–Labor Day		10
7 Jarrell Cove State Park	•	•	20	35		F	•	•		•	•	HFBS	$$–$$$	April–Labor Day		10
8 Joemma Beach State Park		•	24	35		V	•	•		•	•	FB	$$	Mem–Labor Day		10
9 Kitsap Memorial State Park	•	•	43	35	WE	F	•	•	•	•		HFB	$$			10
10 Kopachuck State Park	•	•	41	35		F	•	•	•	•		HFSB	$$–$$$			10
11 Manchester State Park	•	•	53	45		F	•	•	•	•		HFS	$$–$$$		•	10
12 Penrose Point State Park		•	84	35		F	•	•	•	•	•	HFB	$–$$		•	10
13 Potlatch State Park		•	37	60	WES	F	•	•	•	•	•	HFB	$$–$$$	May 1–Sep 3		10
14 Scenic Beach State Park	•	•	53	40		F	•	•	•	•	•	HFB	$$–$$$		•	10
15 Seal Rock		•	40	21		F	•	•		•	•	HFBS	$$	mid May–Sep		14
16 Tahuya River Horse Camp		•	9			V	•					HFR				7
17 Toonerville		•	4			V				•		HC				7
18 Twanoh State Park	•	•	62	35	WES	F	•	•		•	•	HFSB	$$–$$$			10
19 Twin Lakes		•	6			V				•		HFB				7

Hookups: W = Water   E = Electric   S = Sewer
Toilets: F = Flush   V = Vault   P = Pit
Recreation: C = Bicycling/Mountain Biking   H = Hiking   S = Swimming   F = Fishing   B = Boating
O = Off-highway driving   R = Horseback Riding
Maximum Trailer/RV Length given in feet. **Stay Limit** given in days.
Fee $ = less than $10; $$ = $10-$15; $$$ = $16–20; $$$$ = more than $20.
If no entry under **Season,** campground is open all year. If no entry under **Fee,** camping is free.

1   Belfair State Park

Location: 15 miles southwest of Bremerton on Hood Canal.
Sites: 137 tent sites, 47 sites with full hookups for RVs no longer than 75 feet.
Facilities: Drinking water, picnic tables, fire grills, restrooms, coin-operated showers, playground.
Fee per night: $$ to $$$.
Elevation: Sea level.
Management: Washington State Parks and Recreation Commission.
Activities: Beachcombing, swimming, hiking, kite flying, horseshoes, crabbing.
Finding the campground: From Bremerton on the Kitsap Peninsula, take Wash-

ington Highway 3 southwest for 12 miles to the town of Belfair. From there, drive 3 miles southwest on WA 300 to the campground.

About the campground: This 62-acre campground features 3,720 feet of shoreline on Hood Canal. A 300-foot swimming beach abuts an enclosed manmade saltwater basin, controlled by a tide gate. The beaches are closed to clam and oyster harvesting due to pollution at this end of the canal. Because of the many arrowheads found during the construction of park facilities, this beach was determined to have been a meeting place for many generations of Skokomish Indians. Two creeks run through the campground, Big Mission and Little Mission; salmon spawn in both during the fall. The park is open year-round. For a fee, you can make campground reservations by calling Reservations Northwest (see contact information on page 236).

2 Camp Spillman

Location: About 21 miles southwest of Bremerton on the Tahuya River.
Sites: 6 primitive sites for tents and small RVs no longer than 21 feet.
Facilities: Drinking water, picnic tables, fire grills, tent pads, vault toilets.
Fee per night: None.
Elevation: 390 feet.
Management: Washington Department of Natural Resources, South Puget Sound Region.
Activities: Hiking, fishing, mountain biking, trail biking.
Finding the campground: From Bremerton on the Kitsap Peninsula, take Washington Highway 3 southwest for 12 miles to the town of Belfair. From there, take WA 300 southwest for 3.5 miles. Turn right onto Belfair-Tahuya Road and drive 2 miles. Turn right onto Elfendahl Pass Road and drive 2.5 miles to Twin Lakes Road. Turn left and drive nearly a mile to the campground.

About the campground: This is a calm and remote wooded campground on the river. Trails in the area are inviting. The campground is open year-round.

3 Dosewallips State Park

Location: 24 miles north of Hoodsport on Hood Canal, near Brinnon.
Sites: 88 tent sites, 40 sites with full hookups for RVs no longer than 60 feet, 2 primitive sites, 2 group sites (one for 128 and one for 56 people).
Facilities: Drinking water, picnic tables, fire grills, restrooms, coin-operated showers, dump station.
Fee per night: $ to $$.
Elevation: Sea level.
Management: Washington State Parks and Recreation Commission.
Activities: Hiking, fishing, oyster harvesting and clam digging (when water quality permits), shrimping, wildlife watching.
Finding the campground: From Hoodsport, drive 24 miles north on U.S. Highway 101 to reach the park.

About the campground: This 425-acre park encompasses 5,500 feet of saltwater shoreline on Hood Canal and 5,400 feet of freshwater frontage on each bank of the Dosewallips River. The Dosewallips is the only glacier-fed river that flows into Hood Canal. It is clean and reputedly offers excellent fishing. The park beach is actually a large tidal flat with an abundance of clams and oysters. The beds open in January. Four miles of hiking trails wind up the steep hills that rise from the beach. Among the wildlife to be found here are deer, bald eagles, and a large seal population. An elk herd winters in the park. The fishing possibilities include steelhead trout in January and chum salmon in August. On the southeast side of the park, you can find old railroad beds—remnants from the logging heyday when logs were shipped by rail down the mountains to the water and then floated to mills and cargo ships. The campground is open year-round. For a fee, you can make reservations by calling Reservations Northwest (see contact information on page 236).

4 Gold Creek

Location: About 15 miles west of Bremerton on Gold Creek.
Sites: 6 sites for tents or self-contained RVs.
Facilities: Drinking water, picnic tables, fire grills, tent pads, vault toilets.
Fee per night: None.
Elevation: 340 feet.
Management: Washington Department of Natural Resources, South Puget Sound Region.
Activities: Hiking, horseback riding, mountain biking.
Finding the campground: From the Seabeck Highway, which runs between Bremerton and Seabeck, turn south onto Holly Road and drive 2.2 miles. Turn left onto Tahuya Lake Road NW and drive 1.3 miles. Turn left onto Gold Creek Road and drive 1.6 miles to the park entrance on the left.

About the campground: Located in the Green Mountain State Forest on the Kitsap Peninsula, this basic DNR campground is wooded and not heavily used. Hiking and trail riding are the main activities, and there are plenty of hills to climb. The campground is open from May to September.

5 Howell Lake

Location: 21 miles southwest of Bremerton on Howell Lake.
Sites: 6 sites for tents or self-contained RVs no longer than 30 feet.
Facilities: Drinking water, picnic tables, fire grills, tent pads, vault toilets, boat ramp.
Fee per night: None.
Elevation: 460 feet.
Management: Washington Department of Natural Resources, South Puget Sound Region.
Activities: Hiking, trail biking, mountain biking, boating.
Finding the campground: From Bremerton on the Kitsap Peninsula, take Wash-

ington Highway 3 southwest for 12 miles to the town of Belfair. From there, take WA 300 southwest for 3.5 miles. Turn right onto Belfair-Tahuya Road and continue 5.5 miles to the campground.

About the campground: This campground has all the elements for a relaxed vacation experience. There are trails through the woods and a boat ramp to get out on the little lake. The campground is open year-round.

6 Illahee State Park

Location: About 4 miles northeast of Bremerton on Port Orchard Bay.
Sites: 25 sites for tents or self-contained RVs no longer than 40 feet, 8 primitive overflow tent sites.
Facilities: Drinking water, picnic tables, fire grills, flush toilets, coin-operated showers, dump station, playground, ball field, fishing dock with 4 floats, concrete breakwater, 5 mooring buoys.
Fee per night: $$ to $$$.
Elevation: Sea level.
Management: Washington State Parks and Recreation Commission.
Activities: Hiking, boating, waterskiing, oyster harvesting, clam digging, scuba diving.
Finding the campground: From Bremerton on the Kitsap Peninsula, drive north on Washington Highway 303 for 2 miles through East Bremerton. Turn right onto Sylvan Way and drive nearly 2 miles to the park.

About the campground: This park on the outskirts of Bremerton covers 75 acres and features 1,800 acres of saltwater frontage on Port Orchard Bay. The campsites are on a bluff above a relatively rocky beach in a second-growth forest. The views across nearly a mile of water to Bainbridge Island are lovely. The campground is open from May 1 though Labor Day weekend.

7 Jarrell Cove State Park

Location: 17 miles northeast of Shelton on Harstine Island.
Sites: 20 sites for tents or self-contained RVs no longer than 35 feet.
Facilities: Drinking water, picnic tables, fire grills, restrooms, coin-operated showers, marine pump-out, 2 docks and moorage piers, 14 mooring buoys.
Fee per night: $$ to $$$.
Elevation: Sea level.
Management: Washington State Parks and Recreation Commission.
Activities: Hiking, fishing, boating, clam digging.
Finding the campground: From U.S. Highway 101 in Shelton, head northeast on Washington Highway 3 and drive 10 miles. Turn right onto Pickering Road. In about 3 miles, turn left and cross the bridge to Harstine Island. At the stop sign, turn left onto North Island Drive and continue 4 miles to the park.

About the campground: This wooded campground covers 43 acres and features 3,500 feet of saltwater shoreline on Pickering Passage. Swimming is possible, but the main attraction is boating in the protected cove. The site was named for the first woman settler on the island, Mrs. Philora Jarrell. The campground is open from April through Labor Day weekend.

8 Joemma Beach State Park

Location: About 28 miles west of Tacoma on Puget Sound.
Sites: 19 tent sites for tents or self-contained RVs no longer than 35 feet, 2 water trail sites, 3 primitive sites.
Facilities: Drinking water, picnic tables, fire grills, tent pads, vault toilets, coin-operated showers, large picnic shelter, boat ramp, 3 mooring buoys, large moorage dock (seasonal), camp host.
Fee per night: $$.
Elevation: Sea level.
Management: Washington State Parks and Recreation Commission.
Activities: Boating, clam digging, crabbing, fishing, beachcombing.
Finding the campground: You have to drive all the way around Henderson Bay and Carr Inlet to reach this park, but it is worth the drive. From Interstate 5 in Tacoma, drive 16 miles northwest on Washington Highway 16, crossing the Tacoma Narrows Bridge. Just before the town of Purdy, turn left onto WA 302 (Key Peninsula Highway). It is also called the Gig Harbor-Longbranch Road. Be sure to stay on WA 302 when it bears left in about 5 miles. Continue south to the town of Home. From the bridge in Home, continue south on Longbranch Road for 1.3 miles, turn right onto Whiteman Road, and drive 2.3 miles. Then turn right onto Bay Road and drive 1 mile to the camp on the right.

About the campground: This 122-acre park offers about 3,000 feet of saltwater frontage on Whiteman Cove. It was developed with help from the Olympia Outboard Motor Club and the Mission Creek Youth Camp. The oyster tracts off Whiteman Cove at Joemma Beach are operated by a local resident. The park is named for Joe and Emma Smith, who lived on the property from 1917 to 1932. This is a fine park for relaxation and exploration of Case Inlet. It is open from Memorial Day through Labor Day.

9 Kitsap Memorial State Park

Location: 19 miles north of Bremerton on Hood Canal.
Sites: 25 tent sites and 18 sites with water and electric hookups for RVs no longer than 35 feet.
Facilities: Drinking water, picnic tables, fire grills, dump station, flush toilets, playground, boat buoys, coin-operated showers, firewood (fee).
Fee per night: $$.
Elevation: Sea level.
Management: Washington State Parks and Recreation Commission.
Activities: Hiking, baseball, volleyball, fishing, marine recreation.
Finding the campground: From Bremerton on the Kitsap Peninsula, drive north on Washington Highway 3 for 19 miles. The entrance to the park is on the left 3 miles before you reach the Hood Canal Floating Bridge.

About the campground: Trails to the beach offer sweeping views of Hood Canal and the Olympic Peninsula. There is also a nice, 1-mile, wooded trail. Bottom fishing is supposed to be good. The campground is open year-round.

10 Kopachuck State Park

Location: 12 miles northwest of Tacoma on Puget Sound.
Sites: 41 sites for tents or self-contained RVs no longer than 35 feet.
Facilities: Drinking water, picnic tables, fire grills, restrooms, coin-operated showers, dump station, boat buoys, underwater marine park.
Fee per night: $$ to $$$.
Elevation: Sea level.
Management: Washington State Parks and Recreation Commission.
Activities: Hiking, fishing, clam digging, bird watching, swimming, boating, waterskiing, scuba diving.
Finding the campground: From Interstate 5 in Tacoma, take exit 132 and drive north on Washington Highway 16 for 7 miles. Look for the sign for Kopachuck State Park, turn left (west), and drive 5 miles to the camp on Henderson Bay.

About the campground: This 109-acre park has 5,600 feet of saltwater shoreline made mostly of fine gravel, as well as 1,500 feet of unguarded beach. There are numerous trails, some with views of Henderson Bay and the Olympic Mountains. The underwater marine reef is actually a barge that sank years ago. It is host to all kinds of marine life and is a very popular Puget Sound dive site. The campground is on the forested bluffs above Carr Inlet. This site was used for seasonal fishing and clam digging by the Puyallup and Nisqually tribes. It is open year-round.

11 Manchester State Park

Location: 35 miles northwest of Tacoma on Puget Sound, near Port Orchard.
Sites: 53 sites for tents or self-contained RVs up to 45 feet long.
Facilities: Drinking water, picnic tables, fire grills, restrooms, coin-operated showers, dump station.
Fee per night: $$ to $$$.
Elevation: Sea level.
Management: Washington State Parks and Recreation Commission.
Activities: Hiking, fishing, clam digging, scuba diving.
Finding the campground: From Interstate 5 in Tacoma, take exit 132 and head north on Washington Highway 16 toward Bremerton. Drive 24 miles and, just before reaching Port Orchard, take the WA 160/Southeast Sedgwick Road exit. Follow the signs for 11 miles to the park. Alternatively, from downtown Port Orchard, proceed east on Bay Street (Washington Highway 166) until it becomes Mile Hill Drive. Proceed for 3.2 miles on Mile Hill Drive until it ends at Colchester. Turn left (north) onto Colchester Drive Southeast and drive 3 miles north to the park, on the right.

About the campground: Manchester is a stop on the Cascadia Marine Trail, a sea kayaking route that stretches from Olympia north to Vancouver Island, British Columbia. The park covers 111 acres and offers 3,400 feet of saltwater shoreline on Rich Passage. Well off the beaten track for campers, the campground is usually not crowded. Yet, it is just 6 miles northeast of Port Orchard, a popular antique-shopping town. At the dawn of the 20th century, this site was a U.S. Coast Artillery Harbor Defense installation for the protection of Bremerton. During World War II, it was converted to a Navy fuel supply depot and Navy fire fighting station. In 1970, the state bought the land and converted it to a park. The Torpedo Warehouse remains to this day as a park attraction. The park is open year-round, with limited winter facilities. For a fee, you can make reservations by calling Reservations Northwest (see contact information on page 236).

12 Penrose Point State Park

Location: About 26 miles northwest of Tacoma on Carr Inlet.
Sites: 83 sites for tents or self-contained RVs no longer than 35 feet, 1 primitive tent site.
Facilities: Drinking water, picnic tables, dump station, flush toilets, coin-operated showers, 8 mooring buoys, 2.5 miles of hiking trails.
Fee per night: $ to $$.
Elevation: Sea level.
Management: Washington State Parks and Recreation Commission.
Activities: Fishing, clam digging, boating, hiking, beachcombing.
Finding the campground: You have to drive all the way around Henderson Bay and Carr Inlet to reach this park, but it is worth the drive. From Interstate 5 in Tacoma, take exit 132 and drive 16 miles northwest on Washington Highway 16. Just before the town of Purdy, turn left (west) onto WA 302 (Key Peninsula Highway). It is also called the Gig Harbor-Longbranch Road. Be sure to stay on WA 302 when it bears left in about 5 miles. Continue through the towns of Key Center and Home to Lakebay. Turn left (east) onto Cornwall Road KPS. Drive 1.25 miles and turn left (north) onto 158th Avenue KPS and into the park.

About the campground: This park was built out of a swamp that is now a large day-use area. A petroglyph etched into the rock in inner Mayo Cove indicates that Native Americans once occupied the area. The majority of the park is covered in natural forest and crisscrossed by trails. The beach is 1,700 feet long. The campground is open year-round. For a fee, you can make reservations by calling Reservations Northwest (see contact information on page 236).

13 Potlatch State Park

Location: 12 miles north of Shelton on Hood Canal, near Hoodsport.
Sites: 17 tent sites, 2 primitive sites, 18 drive-through sites with full hookups for trailers no longer than 60 feet.

Facilities: Drinking water, picnic tables, fire grills, restrooms, coin-operated showers, dump station, boat ramp, dock, 5 moorage buoys.
Fee per night: $$ to $$$.
Elevation: Sea level.
Management: Washington State Parks and Recreation Commission.
Activities: Hiking, fishing, clam digging, crabbing, scuba diving, boating.
Finding the campground: From Shelton, drive north on U.S. Highway 101 for 12 miles to the park.

About the campground: Potlatch covers 57 acres and features 9,570 feet of saltwater shoreline on Hood Canal. Skokomish and Twanoh Indians once gathered here to hold potlatches, or gift-giving ceremonies. Later, the cabins and hotel of Minerva Resort were built on the site. This is a terrific boaters' campground. The camping area is located across US 101 from the day-use area. The camp is open from May 1 to September 3.

14 Scenic Beach State Park

Location: About 9 miles northwest of Bremerton on Hood Canal.
Sites: 50 sites for tents or self-contained RVs no longer than 40 feet, 2 primitive tent sites, 1 primitive group site.
Facilities: Drinking water, picnic tables, fire grills, restrooms, showers, dump station, dock, boat ramp, horseshoe vault, volleyball courts, nature trail.
Fee per night: $$ to $$$.
Elevation: Sea level.
Management: Washington State Parks and Recreation Commission.
Activities: Hiking, fishing, boating, oyster harvesting.
Finding the campground: From Bremerton, drive north on Washington Highway 3 for about 5 miles. Before the town of Silverdale, take the Newberry Hill Road exit and drive west for 3 miles to the intersection with Seabeck Highway. Turn right (north) and proceed to the town of Seabeck, turning south when you reach Warrenville. Just past the Seabeck Elementary School, turn right onto Stavis Bay Road and drive 1 mile to the campground at the end of the road.

About the campground: This 88-acre campground, one of the loveliest in the state park system, features 1,500 feet of gravelly saltwater frontage and offers great views of the Olympic Mountains. It sits on the bluff in a forest of western redcedars, madrones, and western hemlocks. The park also is home to a 450-year-old Douglas-fir. This spot was originally developed as a home site and later converted to Scenic Beach Resort, offering cabins, campground, boat rentals, and picnic facilities. Birders should watch for varied thrushes and waterfowl, willow goldfinches and pileated woodpeckers. Orcas and pilot whales roam the waters. The campground is open year-round. For a fee, you can make reservations by calling Reservations Northwest (see contact information on page 236).

15 Seal Rock

Location: 27 miles north of Hoodsport on Hood Canal.
Sites: 40 sites for tents or self-contained RVs no longer than 21 feet.
Facilities: Drinking water, picnic tables, tent pads, flush toilets, nearby boat docks and ramp.
Fee per night: $$.
Elevation: Sea level.
Management: Olympic National Forest, Quilcene Ranger District.
Activities: Hiking, fishing, nature trails, clam digging, swimming, boating.
Finding the campground: From Hoodsport, drive 25 miles north via U.S. Highway 101 to the town of Brinnon. Continue 2 miles farther north to the campground.

About the campground: This 6-acre campground sits nicely on a rocky beach on Dabob Bay and is a natural for boaters. It is very popular, and all facilities are barrier-free. On the forested bluff is a nature trail through the woods. The campground is open from mid-May through September.

16 Tahuya River Horse Camp

Location: About 22 miles southwest of Bremerton on the Tahuya River, near Belfair.
Sites: 9 primitive sites for tents or self-contained RVs.
Facilities: Drinking water, picnic tables, fire grills, tent pads, vault toilets, horse trails.
Fee per night: None.
Elevation: 320 feet.
Management: Washington Department of Natural Resources, South Puget Sound Region.
Activities: Hiking, fishing, horseback riding, motorbiking.
Finding the campground: From Bremerton on the Kitsap Peninsula, take Washington Highway 3 southwest for 12 miles to the town of Belfair. From there, take WA 300 southwest for 3.5 miles. Turn right onto Belfair-Tahuya Road and continue 3.2 miles. Then turn right onto Spillman Road and drive 2.1 miles. Turn left and drive 0.8 mile to the campground.

About the campground: This way-out-of-the-way campground will appeal especially to hikers and trail riders, including both equestrians and dirt bikers. The rustic campsites are set along the river in the Tahuya State Forest. The campground is open year-round, but call the Department of Natural Resources (see contact information on page 235) to find out about seasonal closures.

17 Toonerville

Location: 21 miles southwest of Bremerton, near Belfair.
Sites: 4 sites for tents or self-contained RVs.
Facilities: Picnic tables, fire grills, tent pads, vault toilets; no drinking water.
Fee per night: None.
Elevation: 340 feet.
Management: Washington Department of Natural Resources, South Puget Sound Region.
Activities: Hiking, mountain biking, trail biking.
Finding the campground: From Bremerton on the Kitsap Peninsula, take Washington Highway 3 southwest for 12 miles to Belfair. From there, take WA 300 southwest for 3.5 miles. Turn right onto Belfair-Tahuya Road, drive 2 miles, and turn right onto Elfendahl Pass Road. Drive another 3.3 miles, past the Tahuya trailhead and through the intersection with Goat Ranch Road, to reach the campground.

About the campground: It is back to the basics at this campground, which does not even have a creek for distraction. Mostly used by hikers and trail riders, Toonerville may best serve as a base camp, unless you brought some good books to read. It is open year-round.

18 Twanoh State Park

Location: 21 miles northeast of Shelton on Hood Canal, near Belfair.
Sites: 62 sites, including 9 sites with full hookups for RVs no longer than 35 feet.
Facilities: Drinking water, picnic tables, fire grills, restrooms, coin-operated showers, store, playground, tennis court, horseshoe vaults, boat dock, 7 mooring buoys, marine pump-out, 2 boat ramps, 580 feet of swimming beach, kiddie wading pool.
Fee per night: $$ to $$$.
Elevation: Sea level.
Management: Washington State Parks and Recreation Commission.
Activities: Hiking, fishing, swimming, oyster harvesting, boating, waterskiing.
Finding the campground: From Shelton, drive north on U.S. Highway 101 for 10 miles and then turn right (east) onto Washington Highway 106. Continue for 11 miles to the park.

About the campground: Twanoh State Park covers 182 acres and features 3,167 feet of beautiful saltwater shoreline. It has good hiking trails, and fishermen appreciate the proximity of oysters, crabs, and perch. The park buildings were constructed by the Civilian Conservation Corps in the early 1930s and are still preserved in their original beauty. Because of the abundance of wildlife, early Indians here were among the few hunting and gathering societies in the world that produced wealth beyond their needs. The basis for their economy was fishing, and salmon was the main commodity. The campground is open year-round, with limited facilities in winter.

19 Twin Lakes

Location: About 23 miles southwest of Bremerton on Twin Lakes.
Sites: 6 primitive sites for tents or self-contained RVs.
Facilities: Picnic tables, fire grills, tent pads, vault toilets, boat ramp; no drinking water.
Fee per night: None.
Elevation: 315 feet.
Management: Washington Department of Natural Resources, South Puget Sound Region.
Activities: Hiking, fishing, boating.
Finding the campground: From Bremerton on the Kitsap Peninsula, take Washington Highway 3 southwest for 12 miles to the town of Belfair. From there, take WA 300 southwest for 3.5 miles. Turn right onto Belfair-Tahuya Road and continue 2 miles. Turn right onto Elfendahl Pass Road and drive 2.5 miles. At Twin Lakes Road, turn left and drive 2 miles, then turn right and drive one-half mile to the campground.

About the campground: This wooded campground in the Tahuya State Forest offers the height of privacy, and the fishing is supposed to be pretty good. Conditions are primitive, but the site is very nice. Call the Department of Natural Resources to find out about seasonal closures.

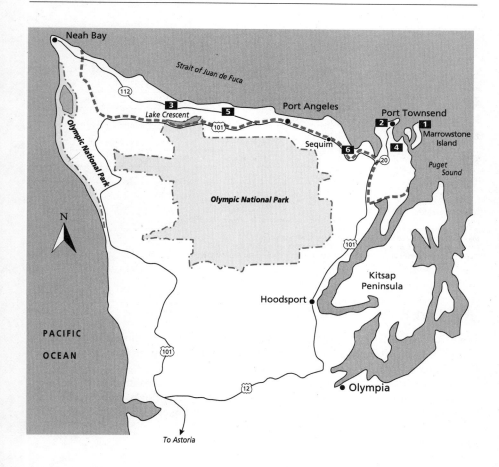

	Group sites	RV sites	Total # of sites	Max. RV length	Hookups	Toilets	Showers	Drinking water	Dump station	Pets	Wheelchair	Recreation	Fee	Season	Can reserve	Stay limit
1 Fort Flagler State Park	•	•	116	50	WE	F	•	•	•	•	•	HFBS	$$-$$$		•	10
2 Fort Worden State Park		•	83	50	WES	F	•			•	•	HFBSC	$-$$$		•	10
3 Lyre River		•	11			V	•			•		HF				14
4 Old Fort Townsend State Park	•	•	43	40		F	•	•	•	•		HF	$$-$$$	May 1–Labor Day		10
5 Salt Creek Recreation Area		•	92			F	•	•	•	•		HFSR	$-$$			14
6 Sequim Bay State Park	•	•	89	30	WES	F	•	•	•	•	•	HFB	$$-$$$		•	10

Hookups: W = Water   E = Electric   S = Sewer
Toilets: F = Flush   V = Vault   P = Pit
Recreation: C = Bicycling/Mountain Biking   H = Hiking   S = Swimming   F = Fishing   B = Boating
O = Off-highway driving   R = Horseback Riding
Maximum Trailer/RV Length given in feet.   **Stay Limit** given in days.
Fee $ = less than $10; $$ = $10-$15; $$$ = $16-20; $$$$ = more than $20.
If no entry under **Season**, campground is open all year. If no entry under **Fee**, camping is free.

1 Fort Flagler State Park

Location: About 19 miles southeast of Port Townsend on Marrowstone Island.
Sites: 102 tent sites, 14 sites with water and electric hookups for RVs no longer than 50 feet.
Facilities: Drinking water, picnic tables, fire grills, restrooms, coin-operated showers, dump station, store, cafe, 2 boat ramps, buoys, floats, underwater scuba diving park, fishing pier, American Youth Hostel, Cascadia Marine Trail campsite, 2 wheelchair-accessible vacation houses.
Fee per night: $$ to $$$.
Elevation: Sea level.
Management: Washington State Parks and Recreation Commission.
Activities: Hiking, bottom and salmon fishing, boating, beachcombing, scuba diving, clam digging, crabbing, sailboarding.
Finding the campground: Although the park is only 2 miles across Port Townsend Bay from Port Townsend, it is a 19-mile drive around the bay and across two islands. The road is paved the whole way. From Port Townsend, drive south on Washington Highway 20 for 5 miles and turn left (southeast) onto WA 19 (Rhody Road). In 3.5 miles, turn left (west) onto WA 116 to the town of Hadlock. From Hadlock stay on WA 116 for about 10 miles, crossing Indian Island and driving the length of Marrowstone Island to reach the park.

About the campground: Flagler was one of three forts built in the 1890s to defend the entrance to Puget Sound. (The others were Fort Worden and Fort Casey.) The fort's big artillery guns were scrapped after World War II, but replicas from the Philippines now stand in their place. There are other abandoned gun emplacements you can explore, as well as a lighthouse. The park covers 780 acres and is surrounded on three sides by Admiralty Inlet, with 3.6 miles of saltwater shoreline. This is definitely a complete park, almost luxurious, with activities to suit the whole family. The Marrowstone Field Station of the Bureau of U.S. Sports Fisheries and Wildlife is located on the beach just north of the camp. The campground is open year-round. For a fee, you can make reservations by calling Reservations Northwest (see contact information on page 236).

2 Fort Worden State Park

Location: In Port Townsend.
Sites: 80 sites for tents or self-contained RVs no longer than 50 feet, 3 primitive tent sites for campers who hike or bike in.
Facilities: Drinking water, picnic tables, firewood (fee), restroom, dock, 2 mooring floats, 9 mooring buoys, 2 boat ramps, underwater scuba park, 2 tennis courts, ball field, snack bar/grocery, restaurant (dinners, Sunday brunch), laundromat, 3 dormitories, youth hostel, 25 units of vacation housing, Cascadia Marine Trail campsite, Marine Science Center, 6 miles of hiking trails.
Fee per night: $ to $$$.
Elevation: Sea level.
Management: Washington State Parks and Recreation Commission.
Activities: Hiking, fishing, boating, sea kayaking, scuba diving, swimming, bicycling, kite flying.
Finding the campground: The park is within the city limits of Port Townsend at the north end of town. The directional signage from downtown is good.

About the campground: This big, magnificent year-round park encompasses 434 acres and offers 2 miles of saltwater shoreline on Admiralty Inlet and the Strait of Juan de Fuca. The fort is listed on both the State and National Register of Historic Places and has been designated a National Historic Landmark. The abandoned concrete bunkers and artillery vaults are a real curiosity. The old military buildings house conferences such as the Sea Kayak Symposium, held annually in September. The campground itself is very popular with sea kayakers and scuba divers. The sites are on a sandy peninsula that can get quite windy. Wildlife includes black-tailed deer, great blue herons, bald eagles, gray whales, and orcas. For a fee, you can make reservations by calling Reservations Northwest (see contact information on page 236).

3 Lyre River

Location: About 20 miles west of Port Angeles on the Lyre River.
Sites: 11 sites for tents or self-contained RVs.
Facilities: Drinking water, picnic tables, fire grills, tent pads, vault toilets, group shelter.
Fee per night: None.
Elevation: Near sea level.
Management: Washington Department of Natural Resources, Olympic Region.

Activities: Hiking, fishing, rockhounding.
Finding the campground: From Port Angeles, take U.S. Highway 101 west for 5 miles. Then turn right (west) onto Washington Highway 112 and continue driving about 15 miles. The paved entrance road is on the right, between mileposts 46 and 47.

About the campground: This primitive year-round campground is right on the Lyre River, not far from where it pours into the Strait of Juan de Fuca. A promontory forms a good catch-point for flotsam treasures from the strait, and the rockhounding is good here.

4   Old Fort Townsend State Park

Location: About 6 miles south of Port Townsend on Port Townsend Bay.
Sites: 40 sites for tents or self-contained RVs no longer than 40 feet, 3 primitive tent sites.
Facilities: Drinking water, picnic tables, fire grills, restrooms, coin-operated showers, playground, boat buoys, firewood (fee), dump station.
Fee per night: $$ to $$$.
Elevation: 150 feet.
Management: Washington State Parks and Recreation Commission.
Activities: Hiking, fishing, clam digging, historical walk.
Finding the campground: From downtown Port Townsend, drive south on Washington Highway 20 for 4.5 miles. Turn left (east) at the sign for the park and drive 1.5 miles. To get there from the junction of U.S. Highway 101 and WA 20 at the southern end of Discovery Bay, take WA 20 north for 9 miles toward Port Townsend. Turn right at the sign for the park and drive 1.5 miles to the park entrance.

About the campground: This 377-acre park sits above a 150-foot cliff, overlooking Port Townsend Bay, the islands of central Puget Sound, and the Cascade Mountains. The U.S. Army fort, built in 1856 from hand-hewn logs and clamshell plaster, was established to protect settlers in the area from Indians. This is a nice campground, not well known outside the area. There is a good beach below the bluffs. The park is open from May 1 through Labor Day.

5   Salt Creek Recreation Area

Location: 15 miles west of Port Angeles on Crescent Bay.
Sites: 92 sites for tents or self-contained RVs.
Facilities: Drinking water, picnic tables, toilets, showers, playground, firewood, dump station, swimming beach.
Fee per night: $ to $$.
Elevation: Sea level.
Management: Clallam County Parks, Salt Creek Recreation Area.
Activities: Hiking, fishing, swimming, horseshoes, beachcombing, horseback riding.

Finding the campground: From Port Angeles, take U.S. Highway 101 west for 5 miles. Then turn right (west) onto Washington Highway 112 and continue about 7 miles to Camp Hayden Road. Turn right (north) onto Camp Hayden Road and drive 3 more miles to the campground.

About the campground: Tongue Point, just west of the campground, juts into the Strait of Juan de Fuca toward Vancouver Island, about 12 miles away. Near-by Agate Bay is named for the treasures that can be found on local beaches. This is one of only a few campgrounds on the strait, and it is a good stopover for people driving around the Olympic Peninsula. It is open year-round.

6 Sequim Bay State Park

Location: 4 miles southeast of Sequim on Sequim Bay.
Sites: 26 sites with full hookups for RVs no longer than 30 feet, 60 developed sites for tents or self-contained RVs, 3 primitive tent sites.
Facilities: Drinking water, picnic tables, fire grills, restrooms, showers, play-ground, dump stations, boat ramp, docks, moorage camping, 2.5 miles of hiking trails.
Fee per night: $$ to $$$.
Elevation: Sea level.
Management: Washington State Parks and Recreation Commission.
Activities: Hiking, fishing, boating, clam digging, scuba diving, beach walking, marine life study, field and group sports, tennis, flora study, bird watching.
Finding the campground: The park is along U.S. Highway 101, 4 miles south-east of the town of Sequim.

About the campground: Sequim (pronounced "squim") is an Indian word meaning "quiet waters," and Sequim Bay truly is calm. That is due to a pair of naturally occurring and overlapping sand spits at the bay's entrance that force sailors to take a zigzag course into the bay from the Strait of Juan de Fuca. The park covers 92 acres and features nearly a mile of tidelands. It is in the rain shadow of the Olympic Mountains, which means that clouds release their precipitation mostly on the western slopes, forcing farmers on this side to irrigate. The bay is 5 miles long, so this park offers a lot of opportunity for safe recreation on the water. The campground is open year-round. For a fee, you can make reservations by calling Reservations Northwest (see contact information on page 236).

Western Region

One of the nation's largest inland waterways, Puget Sound, was sculpted by glaciers at the end of the last ice age. To the east lies the volcanic Cascade Range and its preeminent peaks: Mount Baker, Mount Rainier, Mount Adams, and Mount St. Helens. North Cascades National Park, in the northern part of the range, has one of the most extensive glacier systems in the contiguous states. Glaciers flow in all directions, supplying unbelievably beautiful mountain lakes and streams. The National Park Service wants to maintain the park in as natural a state as possible. As a consequence, the only traveler services along one 80-mile stretch of the North Cascades Highway are some occasional campgrounds.

Mount Rainier National Park and Mount St. Helens National Volcanic Monument each features terrain and activities appropriate to any level of interest. It would be tough to exhaust the rangers' and volunteers' knowledge of the areas, but if you do, they know where you can find out more. Be sure to take extra film and keep the camera ready, because the "photo-ops" are unlimited. Seeing is believing, and by camping in or near the parks you will gain a real sense of the spectacular scope and grandeur of this nearly-untouched part of the world.

Only serious hikers, packers, and skiers venture far beyond the few available roads through the wilderness. They soon learn just how primitive the Washington backcountry can be. For the rest of us, Washington offers 82 state parks with campgrounds and 51 more that are designated for day use only. There are hundreds of other publicly owned campgrounds in Washington. Their administration ranges from local municipalities to the Forest Service. These public agencies are guardians of these snowcapped peaks, glaciers, alpine lakes, cascading rivers, and conifer-blanketed hills and valleys that seem to go on forever.

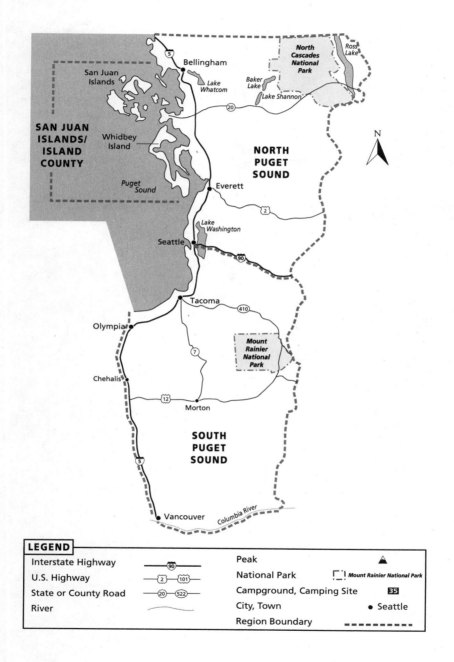

LEGEND

Interstate Highway	90	Peak	▲
U.S. Highway	2 101	National Park	Mount Rainier National Park
State or County Road	20 522	Campground, Camping Site	35
River		City, Town	● Seattle
		Region Boundary	▬ ▬ ▬ ▬

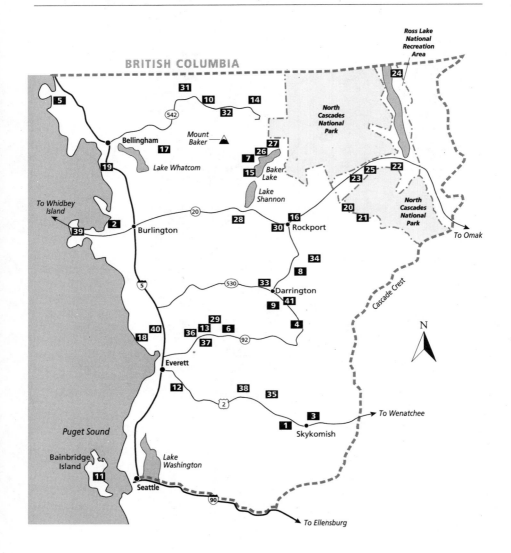

		Group sites	RV sites	Total # of sites	Max. RV length	Hookups	Toilets	Showers	Drinking water	Dump station	Pets	Wheelchair	Recreation	Fee	Season	Can reserve	Stay limit
1	Money Creek		•	17	21		V		•		•	•	HFS	$$		•	14
2	Bay View State Park	•	•	79	40	WE	F	•	•	•	•	•	HS	$$-$$$			10
3	Beckler River		•	27	21		V		•		•		HF	$$	Mem Day–Lab Day	•	14
4	Bedal		•	19			F				•	•	HFB		Jun–Sep		14
5	Birch Bay State Park	•	•	167		WE	F	•	•	•	•	•	HFB	$$-$$$		•	10
6	Boardman Creek		•	8			V				•		HF	$$	May 1–Sep 30		14
7	Boulder Creek	•		10			V				•		HF		mid May–mid Sep	•	14
8	Buck Creek		•	29	30		V				•		HF	$$	late May–Oct		14
9	Clear Creek		•	12			V				•		HF	$$	late May–Oct		14
10	Douglas Fir		•	30	26		V				•		HF	$$	May–Sep	•	14
11	Fay Bainbridge State Park		•	36	30		F	•	•	•	•		HFB	$$	Apr–Aug		10
12	Flowing Lake County Park		•	42	25	WE	F		•	•	•		FSB	$$	RVs all year/ Tents mid May–Sep		14
13	Gold Basin		•	93	31		F		•		•	•	HF	$$	mid May–Sep	•	14
14	Hannegan		•	O			V				•		H				14
15	Horseshoe Cove		•	34	34		F		•		•		HFBC	$$	May–Sep		14
16	Howard Miller Steelhead		•	59		WES	F	•	•	•	•		F	$$-$$$		•	14
17	Hutchinson Creek		•	11			V				•		HF				7
18	Kayak Point County Park		•	32		WE	F		•		•		HFBS	$$	May–late Sep		14
19	Larrabee State Park	•	•	98	60	WES	F	•	•	•	•	•	HFBC	$-$$$		•	10
20	Marble Creek		•	24	22		V				•		HF		mid May–mid Sep		14
21	Mineral Park			4			V				•		HF		mid-May–Sep		14
22	Northern Cascades Natl Park: Colonial Creek		•	162	32		F		•	•	•	•	HF	$$	mid-Apr–mid Oct/ 18 sites year-round		14
23	Northern Cascades Natl Park: Goodell Creek	•	•	21	22		V	•			•		F	$			14
24	Northern Cascades Natl Park: Hozomeen		•	122	22		V		•				HFB		late May–late Oct		14
25	Northern Cascades Natl Park: Newhalem Creek		•	128	32		F		•	•	•	•	HF	$$	mid May–mid Oct		14
26	Panorama Point		•	16	21		V		•				HFBC	$$	May–Sep	•	14
27	Park Creek		•	12	22		V				•		HFB	$$	mid May–early Sep	•	14
28	Rasar State Park		•	52			F	•	•	•	•		HF	$$-$$$		•	10
29	Red Bridge		•	16	31		F				•		HFS		late May–early Sep		14
30	Rockport State Park	•	•	65	45		F	•	•	•	•	•	HF	$$-$$$	Apr 1–mid Nov		10
31	Silver Lake Park	•	•	108		WE	F	•		•			BFSR	$$-$$$		•	14
32	Silver Fir		•	20	31		V	•			•		H	$$	May–Sep	•	14
33	Squire Creek County Park		•	30	25		F	•	•	•			HF	$$	mid-May–mid Sep		14

continued on following page

	Group sites	RV sites	Total # of sites	Max. RV length	Hookups	Toilets	Showers	Drinking water	Dump station	Pets	Wheelchair	Recreation	Fee	Season	Can reserve	Stay limit
34 Sulphur Creek		•	20	16		V				•		HF	$$	May 1–late Sep	•	14
35 Troublesome Creek		•	30	24		V				•		HF	$–$$	Mem Day–Lab Day	•	
36 Turlo		•	19	31		F	•			•		HFS	$$	mid May–late Sep	•	
37 Verlot		•	26	31		F	•			•		HFS	$$	mid May–late Sep	•	
38 Wallace Falls State Park			6			F	•			•		HFC	$$			10
39 Washington Park		•	70	70	WES	F	•	•	•	•		FBC	$$			
40 Wenberg State Park		•	75	50	WE	F	•	•	•	•	•	HFBS	$$–$$$		•	10
41 William C. Dearinger		•	12	25		V				•		FH				

Hookups: W = Water   E = Electric   S = Sewer
Toilets: F = Flush   V = Vault   P = Pit
Recreation: C = Bicycling/Mountain Biking   H = Hiking   S = Swimming   F = Fishing   B = Boating
O = Off-highway driving   R = Horseback Riding
Maximum Trailer/RV Length given in feet.   **Stay Limit** given in days.
Fee $ = less than $10; $$ = $10-$15; $$$ = $16–20; $$$$ = more than $20.
If no entry under **Season,** campground is open all year. If no entry under **Fee,** camping is free.

1 Money Creek

Location: 4 miles west of Skykomish on the Skykomish River.
Sites: 6 tent sites, 11 sites for tents or RVs no longer than 21 feet.
Facilities: Drinking water, picnic tables, vault toilets.
Fee per night: $$.
Elevation: 820 feet.
Management: Mount Baker-Snoqualmie National Forest, Skykomish Ranger District.
Activities: Hiking, fishing, swimming.
Finding the campground: From the town of Skykomish, drive 4 miles west on U.S. Highway 2 to the campground.

About the campground: Situated in the Mount Baker-Snoqualmie National Forest, across the Skykomish River from the highway and 46 miles east of Everett, this 13-acre campground is heavily forested with old-growth Douglas-fir. Freight trains run close by. The fishing is not bad, and the camp is a good base from which to hike the Cascade foothills. For a fee, you can make reservations by calling the National Recreation Reservation Service (see contact information on page 236).

2 Bay View State Park

Location: 7 miles west of Burlington on Padilla Bay.
Sites: 67 tent sites, 9 sites with water and electrical hookups for RVs no longer than 40 feet, 3 primitive sites.
Facilities: Drinking water, picnic tables, flush toilets, coin-operated showers, dump station.
Fee per night: $$ to $$$.
Elevation: Sea level.
Management: Washington State Parks and Recreation Commission.
Activities: Beach walking, swimming, sailboarding.
Finding the campground: From Interstate 5 in Burlington, take exit 231 and drive 7 miles west on Josh Wilson Road. In the town of Bay View, the road comes to a T junction with Bayview-Edison Road. Turn north onto Bayview-Edison Road, and the state park is right there. The entrance is on your right.

About the campground: This 25-acre park was formerly a baseball field, race-track, and local picnic area. It features a grassy expanse plus 1,300 feet of salt-water shoreline on Padilla Bay. The camping area is nestled on a hill above the road. To get to the gravel beach, you must walk through a highway underpass. This stretch of beach, part of the Padilla Bay National Estuarine Research Reserve, connects with the Padilla Bay Trail to form an 8-mile shoreline walk. The campground is open year-round.

3 Beckler River

Location: 2 miles northeast of Skykomish on the Beckler River.
Sites: 7 tent sites, 20 sites for tents or RVs up to 21 feet long.
Facilities: Drinking water, picnic tables, fire grills, vault toilets.
Fee per night: $$.
Elevation: 900 feet.
Management: Mount Baker-Snoqualmie National Forest, Skykomish Ranger District.
Activities: Hiking, fishing.
Finding the campground: From Skykomish, drive 1 mile east on U.S. Highway 2 and turn right (north) onto Forest Road 65. Drive 1 mile to the campground.

About the campground: Beckler River Campground is about 50 miles east of Everett. It occupies a very pleasant site that includes 12 forested acres on the river, where the fishing is reputed to be good. The campground is open from Memorial Day through Labor Day. For a fee, you can make reservations by calling the National Recreation Reservation Service (see contact information on page 236).

4 Bedal

Location: About 50 miles east of Everett on the Sauk River, near Darrington.
Sites: 19 sites for tents or self-contained RVs.
Facilities: Picnic tables, flush toilets, firewood; no drinking water.
Fee per night: None.
Elevation: 1,300 feet.
Management: Mount Baker-Snoqualmie National Forest, Darrington Ranger District.
Activities: Hiking, fishing, canoeing, kayaking.
Finding the campground: From Interstate 5 in Everett, take exit 194 and go east for 2 miles on U.S. Highway 2. Stay in the left lane over the causeway that crosses Ebey Island and go left onto Washington Highway 204 toward Lake Stevens. In another 2 miles, at WA 9, turn north and go 2 more miles to WA 92 (Mountain Loop Highway). Turn right onto WA 92 and continue for 8 miles into the town of Granite Falls. Head north out of town and then east on what is now the Mountain Loop Highway (County Road 92/Forest Road 7). Continue 36.5 miles to the campground. FR 7 becomes FR 20 at the 30-mile point, but it is still the Mountain Loop Highway. The last 6.5 miles are on a narrow gravel road, but it is well-graded.

About the campground: The Verlot Public Service Center, 11 miles east of Granite Falls, is a good place to check for local maps and get information on road conditions and campsite availability. The North and South Forks of the Sauk River meet at this 6-acre campground. Rustic and remote, it offers access to the Glacier Peak Wilderness and Henry M. Jackson Wilderness. The campground is open from June to early September.

The drive to Bedal is part of a Forest Service Scenic Byway that runs for 50 miles between Granite Falls and Darrington. The roadside woods are thick with second- and third-growth western hemlock, Douglas-fir, western redcedar, black cottonwood, red alder, vine and bigleaf maple, and some Sitka a spruce. These form a green canopy for nearly the entire route. With an average annual rainfall of 140 inches, this forest has no problem staying green. You may spot mountain goats on the upper slopes, as well as dogwood, trillium, and queen's cup on the forest floor.

5 Birch Bay State Park

Location: About 10 miles south of Blaine on Birch Bay.
Sites: 147 sites for tents or self-contained RVs, plus 20 sites with water and electrical hookups.
Facilities: Drinking water, picnic tables, fire grills, flush toilets, coin-operated showers, firewood, 2 dump stations.
Fee per night: $$ to $$$.
Elevation: Sea level.
Management: Washington State Parks and Recreation Commission.
Activities: Fishing, picnicking, hiking, clam digging, crabbing, bird watching,

waterskiing, beachcombing, scuba diving, sailboarding, kite flying, photography.

Finding the campground: From Interstate 5, 10 miles southeast of Blaine, take the Grandview exit (exit 270). Go west on Washington Highway 548 (Grandview Road) for about 7 miles. Turn right (north) onto Jackson Road. At 0.7 mile, turn left onto Helwig Road and into the park.

About the campground: A mile-long, sandy beach along Birch Bay is the major draw of this 200-acre, year-round park. Kayaking is popular, and there is a primitive boat ramp. The campground is nestled among tall cedars and hemlocks, and large fir stumps remain from logging done at the turn of the 20th century. Birch Bay was once inhabited by Semiahmoo, Lummi, and Nooksack Indians. In prehistoric days as well as today, an abundance of shellfish, migratory waterfowl, and salmon drew people to harvest these resources.

Terrell Creek Marsh is one of the few remaining saltwater/freshwater estuaries in northern Puget Sound. On the beach at the north end of the park is a natural sanctuary acquired through the Nature Conservancy under the condition that no development be permitted there. Residents include migratory waterfowl, bald eagles, and great blue herons. A half-mile nature trail skirts the marsh. Also inside the park are nearly 3 miles of freshwater shoreline on Terrell Creek. For a fee you can make reservations by calling Reservations Northwest. (See contact information on page 236).

6 | Boardman Creek

Location: About 30 miles east of Everett on the South Fork Stillaguamish River, near Granite Falls.
Sites: 8 sites for tents or self-contained RVs.
Facilities: Picnic tables, vault toilets, firewood; no drinking water.
Fee per night: $$.
Elevation: 1,470 feet.
Management: Mount Baker-Snoqualmie National Forest, Darrington Ranger District.
Activities: Hiking, fishing.
Finding the campground: From Interstate 5 in Everett, take exit 194 and go east for 2 miles on U.S. Highway 2. Stay in the left lane over the causeway that crosses Ebey Island and go left onto Washington Highway 204 toward Lake Stevens. In another 2 miles, at WA 9, turn north and go 2 more miles to WA 92 (Mountain Loop Highway). Turn right onto WA 92 and continue for 8 miles into the town of Granite Falls. Head north out of town and then east on what is now the Mountain Loop Highway (County Road 92/Forest Road 7). Continue for 16.5 miles to the campground.

About the campground: This campground on the South Fork Stillaguamish River is shady and roomy but always full in the summer. It is very popular because it offers easy access to the river. It is open from May 1 to September 30.

7 Boulder Creek

Location: 15 miles north of Concrete near Baker Lake.
Sites: 8 tent sites, 2 group sites.
Facilities: Picnic tables, fire grills, vault toilets; no drinking water.
Fee per night: None.
Elevation: 1,300 feet.
Management: Mount Baker-Snoqualmie National Forest, Mount Baker Ranger District.
Activities: Fishing, hiking.
Finding the campground: From the town of Concrete on Washington Highway 20, drive 9.5 miles north on County Road 25 and then 5.5 miles north on Forest Road 11.

About the campground: This 5-acre, wooded campground sits next to Boulder Creek, 1 mile west of Baker Lake. There are some good mountain views, especially of 10,778-foot Mount Baker. The camp is relaxing and makes a good base from which to explore the 9-mile-long lake or the nearby trails. The campground is open from mid-May to mid-September. For a fee, you can make reservations by calling the National Recreation Reservation Service (see contact information on page 236).

8 Buck Creek

Location: About 70 miles east of Everett on Buck Creek, near Darrington.
Sites: 29 sites for tents and self-contained RVs no longer than 30 feet.
Facilities: Picnic tables, vault toilets, firewood; no drinking water.
Fee per night: $$.
Elevation: 1,150 feet.
Management: Mount Baker-Snoqualmie National Forest, Darrington Ranger District.
Activities: Hiking, fishing.
Finding the campground: From Everett, drive north on Interstate 5 for 15 miles. Take exit 208 and drive east on Washington Highway 530 for 32 miles to the town of Darrington. Continue on WA 530, now heading north, for 7.5 miles. When the road forks, bear right onto Forest Road 26. It follows the Suiattle River for 15 miles to the campground.

About the campground: Situated on the western boundary of the Glacier Peak Wilderness, this campground is on Buck Creek not far from where it flows into the Suiattle River, which drains Huckleberry Mountain and Green Mountain. The real attraction, though, is the nearby wild and woolly Suiattle River and the steelhead that it hosts. Campground conditions are primitive, but then so is the wilderness. Call the Darrington Ranger District for current conditions (see contact information on page 235); there are occasional road washouts in winter. The campground is open from late May to October.

9 Clear Creek

Location: 50 miles east of Everett on the Sauk River, near Darrington.
Sites: 12 sites for tents or self-contained RVs.
Facilities: Picnic tables, fire grills, vault toilets, firewood; no drinking water.
Fee per night: $$.
Elevation: 650 feet.
Management: Mount Baker-Snoqualmie National Forest, Darrington Ranger District.
Activities: Hiking, fishing.
Finding the campground: From Everett, drive north on Interstate 5 for 15 miles. Take exit 208 and drive east on Washington Highway 530 for 32 miles to the town of Darrington. From there, turn south onto Forest Road 20 (Mountain Loop Highway), and drive 3 miles to the campground.

About the campground: This section of the Mountain Loop Highway is neither as thickly forested nor as populated as the section along the Stillaguamish River on the south side of the Boulder River Wilderness. But the highway is every bit as nice, the fishing is good, and trails lead into the wilderness. The campground, situated at the confluence of the Sauk River and Clear Creek in Mount Baker-Snoqualmie National Forest, is open from late May to October. For reservations, call Darrington Ranger District (see contact information on page 235).

10 Douglas Fir

Location: 33 miles east of Bellingham on the North Fork Nooksack River, near Glacier.
Sites: 30 sites for tents or self-contained RVs no longer than 26 feet.
Facilities: Drinking water, picnic tables, fire grills, vault toilets.
Fee per night: $$.
Elevation: 500 feet.
Management: Mount Baker-Snoqualmie National Forest, Mount Baker Ranger District.
Activities: Hiking, fishing.
Finding the campground: From Interstate 5 in Bellingham, drive 31 miles east on Washington Highway 542 (Mount Baker Highway) to the town of Glacier. The campground is 2 miles beyond Glacier on the left (north) side of WA 542.

About the campground: This little forested campground sits right on the North Fork Nooksack River a few miles from a spot where bald eagles congregate to feed on the salmon that migrate upriver to spawn. The rushing waters are a bit noisy, but a lot of campers like it that way. The campground is open from May through September. The Mount Baker Ski Area is about 15 miles up the highway, and the town of Glacier has a couple of very good restaurants. For a fee, you can make reservations by calling the National Recreation Reservation Service (see contact information on page 236).

11 Fay Bainbridge State Park

Location: On Bainbridge Island in Puget Sound, near Seattle.
Sites: 26 sites for tents or self-contained RVs no longer than 30 feet, 10 primitive sites for tents.
Facilities: Drinking water, picnic tables, fire grills, coin-operated showers, flush toilets, dump station, playground, firewood (fee), boat ramp, 2 mooring buoys.
Fee per night: $$.
Elevation: Sea level.
Management: Washington State Parks and Recreation Commission.
Activities: Hiking, fishing, scuba diving, boating, clam digging, crabbing, beach-combing.
Finding the campground: From the Seattle waterfront, take the Winslow Ferry to Bainbridge Island. Disembark at the town of Winslow and take Washington Highway 305 north for 4 miles. Turn right (northeast) onto Phelps Road Northeast and drive about 2 miles through Port Madison and around Point Monroe to the park.

About the campground: This 17-acre waterfront park on the northeastern shore of Bainbridge Island is the only park on the island with camping facilities. It features a sandy beach, kitchen shelters, and a boat ramp. A hiking trail winds past old bunkers and sword ferns under a canopy of coniferous trees. From the camping and day-use areas, there are scenic views of Puget Sound, the Cascade Range, and the Seattle metropolitan area. The campground is open from April through August; the park is open for day-use only during the rest of the year.

12 Flowing Lake County Park

Location: About 12 miles southeast of Everett on Flowing Lake, near Snohomish.
Sites: 10 sites for tents, 32 sites (with electrical and sewer hookups) for RVs no longer than 25 feet.
Facilities: Drinking water, picnic tables, flush toilets, dump station, firewood, playground; boat docks and launch nearby.
Fee per night: $$.
Elevation: 300 feet.
Management: Snohomish County Parks.
Activities: Swimming, sunbathing, boating, waterskiing, fishing.
Finding the campground: From Interstate 5 in Everett, take exit 194 and head east on U.S. Highway 2 for 10 miles. Turn left onto 100th Street Southeast (Westwick Road). Just after the French Creek Grange, bear left (north) as 100th Street becomes 171st Avenue Southeast. Continue to 48th Street Southeast and turn right (east). The park entrance is at the end of the road.

About the campground: This 38-acre county park is great for the whole family, including the dog (though it must be leashed). The park also gets a lot of day use from people who come to fish, picnic, or hike the trails. Entertainment is occasionally even provided in the amphitheater. The campground is open year-round for self-contained RVs and from mid-May to late September for other campers. The nearby town of Snohomish is well known in the state for its antique shops.

13 Gold Basin

Location: About 28 miles east of Everett on the South Fork Stillaguamish River, near the town of Granite Falls.
Sites: 10 sites for tents, 83 sites for tents or self-contained RVs no longer than 31 feet.
Facilities: Drinking water, picnic tables, flush toilets, firewood.
Fee per night: $$.
Elevation: 1,100 feet.
Management: Mount Baker-Snoqualmie National Forest, Darrington Ranger District.
Activities: Hiking, fishing.
Finding the campground: From Interstate 5 in Everett, take exit 194 and go east for 2 miles on U.S. Highway 2. Stay in the left lane over the causeway that crosses Ebey Island and go left (north) onto Washington Highway 204 toward Lake Stevens. In another 2 miles, turn north onto WA 9 and go 2 more miles to WA 92 (Mountain Loop Highway). Turn right onto WA 92 and continue for 8 miles into the town of Granite Falls. Drive north out of town and then east on what is now the Mountain Loop Highway (County Road 92/Forest Road 7). Continue 13.5 miles to the campground.

About the campground: The Boulder River Wilderness lies north of this 30-acre, riverside campground. Forest roads and nearby trails offer good access for hardy explorers, but be sure to get a map before taking off. The Verlot Public Service Center, 11 miles east of Granite Falls, is a good place to get local maps, as well as information on road conditions and campsite availability. Gold Basin is a large campground, and it is very popular, but only some of the campsites are on the river. There is a wheelchair-accessible interpretive trail. The campground is open from mid-May to early September. For a fee, you can make reservations by calling the National Recreation Reservation Service (see contact information on page 236).

14 Hannegan

Location: About 50 miles east of Bellingham on Ruth Creek.
Sites: No designated campsites.
Facilities: Vault toilet; no drinking water.
Fee per night: None.
Management: Mount Baker-Snoqualmie National Forest, Mount Baker Ranger District.
Activities: Hiking.
Finding the campground: From Interstate 5 in Bellingham, take exit 255 and

head northeast on Washington Highway 542 (Mount Baker Highway). Continue for about 46 miles and turn left (east) onto Forest Road 32 just before the bridge over the North Fork Nooksack River. Drive 5 miles to the campground at the end of FR 32.

About the campground: You can really rough it at the Hannegan Campground, which is really nothing more than a clearing in the woods. In winter, the access road is a cross-country ski trail. This beautiful woodsy spot is used mainly as a base camp for backpackers headed into the Mount Baker Wilderness and North Cascades National Park. Check for conditions and maps at the Glacier Public Service Center, which is a half-mile east of Glacier on Mount Baker Highway. The center is a joint operation of the Mount Baker-Snoqualmie National Forest and North Cascades National Park. The camp is open year-round.

15 Horseshoe Cove

Location: About 14 miles north of Concrete, on Baker Lake.
Sites: 8 sites for tents, 26 sites for tents or self-contained RVs no longer than 34 feet.
Facilities: Drinking water, picnic tables, flush toilets, boat ramp.
Fee per night: $$.
Elevation: 800 feet.
Management: Mount Baker-Snoqualmie National Forest, Mount Baker Ranger District.
Activities: Fishing, boating, waterskiing, hiking, mountain biking.
Finding the campground: From Washington Highway 20 in Concrete, drive 9.5 miles north on County Road 25 (Baker River Road), cross the Upper Baker Dam, and then drive a bit over 1 mile on Forest Road 1106 to its intersection with FR 11 (Baker Lake Road). Turn right and drive 1.5 miles on Baker Lake Road. Turn right onto FR 1118 and drive 1.5 miles to the campground.

About the campground: This busy lakeside campground appeals primarily to boaters, including those with personal watercraft. Baker Lake is 9 miles long and covers about 5,000 acres. The fishing is good, and the catch might include Dolly Varden trout, cutthroat trout, and kokanee salmon. The site is shady and the views of 10,778-foot Mount Baker are inspiring. The campground is open from May through September. For a fee, you can make reservations by calling the National Recreation Reservation Service (see contact information on page 236).

16 Howard Miller Steelhead

Location: 38 miles east of Burlington on the Skagit River, in the town of Rockport.
Sites: 10 tent sites, 49 RV sites with full hookups.
Facilities: Drinking water, picnic tables, restrooms, showers, dump station, clubhouse, Adirondack shelters, playground, boat ramp.

The campsites at Hutchinson Creek Campground, near Acme, are enveloped in a forest of evergreens, alders, and cottonwoods.

Fee per night: $$ to $$$.
Elevation: 500 feet.
Management: City of Rockport.
Activities: Fishing.
Finding the campground: From Interstate 5 in Burlington, take exit 230 and drive east on Washington Highway 20 (North Cascades Highway) for 38 miles to the town of Rockport. Turn right (south) onto WA 530. The campground is in 3 blocks on the right.

About the campground: This is a nice wooded and grassy site on the north bank of the Skagit River, a designated Wild and Scenic River. This is steelhead country, and the fishing is reputed to be good here. The campground is open year-round. For reservations, call the City of Rockport (see contact information on page 235).

17 Hutchinson Creek

Location: 24 miles northeast of Burlington on Hutchinson Creek.
Sites: 11 sites for tents or self-contained RVs.
Facilities: Tent pads, picnic tables, fire grills, vault toilets; no drinking water.
Fee per night: None.
Elevation: 150 feet.
Management: Washington Department of Natural Resources, Northwest Region.
Activities: Fishing, hiking.
Finding the campground: From Interstate 5 in Burlington, take exit 230 and head east on Washington Highway 20 (North Cascades Highway). Drive 6 miles, passing through Sedro Woolley, and turn left (north) onto WA 9. Continue 15 miles to Acme and cross the Nooksack River Bridge just north of town. Turn right onto Mosquito Lake Road, continue for 2.4 miles, and turn right at the campground sign onto a gravel one-lane access road which ends in 0.4 mile at the campground.

About the campground: This campground on Hutchinson Creek is one of just a few DNR campgrounds in rural Whatcom County. It is enveloped in a forest of evergreens, alders, and cottonwoods. The creek is supposed to offer good cutthroat fishing. The campsites are a bit close together, but rarely are more than a few of them occupied. The campground is open year-round. There is a grocery store in nearby Acme.

18 Kayak Point County Park

Location: 14 miles northwest of Marysville on Port Susan Bay.
Sites: 9 tent sites, 23 RV sites with partial hookups.
Facilities: Drinking water, picnic tables, restrooms, firewood, boat docks, boat ramps.
Fee per night: $$.
Elevation: Sea level.

Management: Snohomish County Parks.
Activities: Kayaking, boating, swimming, hiking, fishing, clam digging.
Finding the campground: From Interstate 5 in Marysville, take exit 199 and go west on Tulalip Road/Marine Drive for 14 miles through the Tulalip Indian Reservation. The park entrance is on the left.

About the campground: This 428-acre county park comes pretty close to being camping heaven. It is mostly wooded and has a 3,300-foot beach, so there is plenty of room to roam. It is on the southern end of Port Susan Bay, which is one of the most productive estuaries on Puget Sound, lush in its mix of organic matter on which intertidal animals thrive. The park has a 300-foot fishing pier. Keep an eye out for gray whales, which sometimes come within 100 feet of the pier. There are also seals and sea lions. Do not forget your kayak, and try your hand at clam digging. There is an 18-hole golf course nearby. The campground is open from May to late September.

19 Larrabee State Park

Location: About 5 miles south of Bellingham on Samish Bay.
Sites: 53 tent sites, 26 sites with full hookups for RVs no longer than 60 feet, 8 walk-in sites, 3 overflow sites, 8 primitive tent sites.
Facilities: Drinking water, picnic tables, fire grills, restrooms, dump station, coin-operated showers, firewood, band shell, boat ramp.
Fee per night: $ to $$$.
Elevation: Sea level.
Management: Washington State Parks and Recreation Commission.
Activities: Hiking, boating, freshwater and saltwater fishing, clam digging, mountain biking, waterskiing, crabbing, beachcombing, scuba diving.
Finding the campground: From Interstate 5 in Bellingham, take exit 250 and drive west on Old Fairhaven Parkway (Washington Highway 11) for just over a mile to a traffic light. Turn left (south) at the light onto 12th Street, which in 1 block becomes Chuckanut Drive. Follow it for about 5 miles to the park entrance on your right.

About the campground: Larrabee was the first state park created in Washington, in 1923. It covers 2,700 acres and features 8,000 feet of saltwater shoreline on Samish Bay and 6,700 feet of freshwater shoreline on Fragrance and Lost Lakes. An underpass allows access to the beach. The park occupies most of the west side of Chuckanut Mountain in Whatcom and Skagit Counties and stretches from sea level to an elevation of 1,940 feet. The mountain provides good views of the entire park and a whole lot more. A hiking trail leads to the summit and mountain bike routes, mostly on old logging roads, weave around its flanks. Wildlife you may see here includes black-tailed deer, bald eagles, and raccoons. Sea birds and sea mammals are commonly seen offshore.

Larrabee has a wonderful bandshell and a grassy amphitheater, which feature events as diverse as Air Force Band concerts and the awards ceremony for the 7-mile Chuckanut Foot Race, held each year in July. The 5.5-mile Interurban Trail, once an electric-train route between Bellingham and Sedro Woolley, connects the park with Bellingham. It is used a lot by hikers, bicyclists, and Chuckanut Foot Racers. The park's rocky beach, backed by a sandstone bluff, offers some of the best tidepooling around. For a fee, you can make reservations by calling Reservations Northwest (see contact information on page 236).

20 Marble Creek

Location: 55 miles east of Burlington on Marble Creek.
Sites: 24 sites for tents or self-contained RVs no longer than 22 feet.
Facilities: Picnic tables, fire grills, vault toilets; no drinking water.
Fee per night: None.
Elevation: 1,600 feet.
Management: Mount Baker-Snoqualmie National Forest, Mount Baker Ranger District.
Activities: Hiking, fishing.
Finding the campground: From Interstate 5 in Burlington, take exit 230 and drive east on Washington Highway 20 (North Cascades Highway) for 46 miles to Marblemount. Where the North Cascades Highway jogs left in Marblemount, turn right onto Cascade Road and cross the bridge over the Skagit River. Follow Cascade Road for 8 miles and then turn right (south) onto unpaved Forest Road 1530. Drive another mile to the campground.

About the campground: This campground is very primitive but in a beautiful wilderness setting. It is just inside the Mount Baker-Snoqualmie National Forest and not far from the trailhead for the Cascade Pass hiking trail. North Cascades National Park is less than a mile to the north. The campground is open from mid-May to mid-September.

21 Mineral Park

Location: About 62 miles east of Burlington on the Cascade River.
Sites: 4 tent sites.
Facilities: Picnic tables, fire rings, vault toilets; no drinking water.
Fee per night: None.
Elevation: 1,310 feet.
Management: Mount Baker-Snoqualmie National Forest, Mount Baker Ranger District.
Activities: Hiking, fishing.
Finding the campground: From Interstate 5 in Burlington, take exit 230 and head east on Washington Highway 20 for 46.6 miles. Turn east onto Cascade Road (County Road 3528) and drive 15 miles to the campground.

About the campground: Mineral Park is very small and very primitive, but those qualities make it very appealing. It is situated among the trees in Mount Baker-Snoqualmie National Forest, next to the Cascade River, which has fair fishing. Nearby trails lead into the Glacier Peak Wilderness. The campground is open from mid-May to mid-September.

22 North Cascades National Park: Colonial Creek

Location: 65 miles east of Sedro Woolley on Diablo Lake in North Cascades National Park.
Sites: 162 sites for tents or self-contained RVs no longer than 32 feet.
Facilities: Drinking water, restrooms, dump station, boat ramp.
Fee per night: $$.
Elevation: 1,200 feet.
Management: North Cascades National Park.
Activities: Fishing, hiking, summer nature programs.
Finding the campground: The campground is located 65 miles east of Sedro Woolley and 10 miles east of Newhalem on Washington Highway 20, the North Cascades Highway.

About the campground: Colonial Creek Campground occupies 28 acres on the south end of 5-mile-long Diablo Lake in the Ross Lake National Recreation Area, which is part of North Cascades National Park. Diablo is sandwiched between Ross Lake and Gorge Lake; all three lakes were created by hydroelectric dams operated by Seattle City Light. The campground is very pleasant, and the sites are set far enough from the highway that road noise is not a problem. The area is wooded and hilly, and some people swim a bit in the frigid water. The entire campground is open from mid-April to late October; 18 of the sites are open year-round.

23 North Cascades National Park: Goodell Creek

Location: 55 miles east of Sedro Woolley on the Skagit River in North Cascades National Park.
Sites: 21 sites for tents or self-contained RVs no longer than 22 feet.
Facilities: Drinking water, picnic tables, fire grills, vault toilets.
Fee per night: $.
Elevation: 600 feet.
Management: North Cascades National Park.
Activities: Fishing, river rafting.
Finding the campground: From Everett, head north on Interstate 5 and take exit 230. Drive northeast on Washington Highway 20 (North Cascades Highway) for 5 miles to Sedro Woolley and then continue east on WA 20 for another 55 miles. You will reach the campground just before the town of Newhalem.

About the campground: This 4-acre campground in the Ross Lake National Recreation Area and North Cascades National Park is at the confluence of Goodell Creek and the Wild and Scenic Skagit River. It is pristine, yet close to Newhalem and groceries. The easy river access makes this a popular site for river rafters. The campground is open year-round, but there are no services during the winter.

24 North Cascades National Park: Hozomeen

Location: 1 mile south of the Canadian border on Ross Lake in North Cascades National Park (accessible only from Canada).
Sites: 122 sites for tents or self-contained RVs no longer than 22 feet.
Facilities: Drinking water, picnic tables, fireplaces, vault toilets, boat ramp.
Fee per night: None.
Elevation: 1,600 feet.
Management: North Cascades National Park.
Activities: Fishing, boating, hiking.
Finding the campground: From the town of Hope, British Columbia, on the Trans-Canada Highway (Canada Highway 1), drive 40 miles south on Silver Skagit Road to the campground. Part of the drive goes through British Columbia's Manning Provincial Park. The road is dirt much of the way.

About the campground: This 4-acre campground is in the Ross Lake National Recreation Area and North Cascades National Park. Ross Lake itself extends into British Columbia. This is an area of great natural beauty, and since the road ends just a mile beyond the campground, there is very little traffic. Only people who are serious about camping travel this far to enjoy it. Fishing and boating are the main attractions. The campground is open from late May to late October.

25 North Cascades National Park: Newhalem Creek

Location: About 60 miles east of Burlington in North Cascades National Park.
Sites: 128 sites for tents or self-contained RVs up to 32 feet long.
Facilities: Drinking water, picnic tables, fire grills, restrooms, dump station.
Fee per night: $$.
Elevation: 980 feet.
Management: North Cascades National Park.
Activities: Fishing, hiking, summer campfire programs.
Finding the campground: From Interstate 5 in Burlington, take exit 230 and drive east on Washington Highway 20 (North Cascades Highway) for 60 miles to the town of Newhalem. The campground entrance is just before Newhalem; follow the campground signs beginning at milepost 120.

About the campground: This is a nice, relatively new campground in the Ross Lake National Recreation Area, which is part of North Cascades National Park. It is also near the Wild and Scenic Skagit River. An outstanding park visitor center is a short walk from the campground, which is open from mid-May to mid-October.

26 Panorama Point

Location: About 16 miles north of Concrete on Baker Lake.
Sites: 16 sites for tents or self-contained RVs up to 21 feet long.
Facilities: Drinking water, picnic tables, vault toilets.
Fee per night: $$.

Elevation: 800 feet.
Management: Mount Baker-Snoqualmie National Forest, Mount Baker Ranger District.
Activities: Hiking, fishing, boating, sailing, waterskiing, mountain biking.
Finding the campground: From the town of Concrete on Washington Highway 20, drive 9.5 miles north on County Road 25 (Baker River Road), cross the Upper Baker Dam, and then drive a bit over 1 mile on Forest Road 1106 to its intersection with FR 11 (Baker Lake Road). Turn right onto Baker Lake Road and drive just over 4 miles. The campground entrance is on the right.

About the campground: This national forest campground sits on a lovely point on the western shore of Baker Lake. The fishing is very good, with kokanee salmon, Dolly Varden trout, and cutthroat trout among the possibilities. The views of Mount Baker are outstanding, and the campground is neat and pleasant. It is open from May to mid-September. For a fee, you can make reservations by calling the National Recreation Reservation Service (see contact information on page 236).

27 Park Creek

Location: About 17 miles north of Concrete near Baker Lake.
Sites: 12 sites for tents or self-contained RVs no longer than 22 feet.
Facilities: Picnic tables, vault toilets, boat ramp (fee), docks; no drinking water.
Fee per night: $$.
Elevation: 800 feet.
Management: Mount Baker-Snoqualmie National Forest, Mount Baker Ranger District.
Activities: Hiking, fishing, boating.
Finding the campground: From the town of Concrete on Washington Highway 20, drive 9.5 miles north on County Road 25 (Baker River Road), cross the Upper Baker Dam, and then drive a bit over 1 mile on Forest Road 1106 to its intersection with FR 11 (Baker Lake Road). Turn right onto Baker Lake Road and drive 6 miles to the campground.

About the campground: This 9-acre campground is on Park Creek, not far from the western shore of Baker Lake. The camping is primitive, but the area is nice and woodsy. The campground is open from mid-May to early September. Reservations are required, and you can make them, for a fee, by calling the National Recreation Reservation Service (see contact information on page 236).

28 Rasar State Park

Location: 25 miles east of Burlington on the Skagit River, near Concrete.
Sites: 17 tent sites, 22 RV sites, 10 walk-in tent sites (including 3 four-person Adirondack shelters), 3 hiker-biker sites.
Facilities: Drinking water, picnic tables, restrooms, dump station.
Fee per night: $$ to $$$.

Elevation: 180 feet.
Management: Washington State Parks and Recreation Commission.
Activities: Hiking, fishing.
Finding the campground: From Interstate 5 in Burlington, take exit 230 and drive east on Washington Highway 20 (North Cascades Highway) for 23 miles. Turn right onto Lusk Road, drive half a mile, and turn left onto Capehorn Road. Drive 1.5 miles to the park.

About the campground: Rasar State Park encompasses 168 acres and fronts the Wild and Scenic Skagit River for nearly a mile. The state acquired most of the land in 1986 through a donation from the Rasar family. The acreage north of Capehorn Road was acquired from the Washington Department of Natural Resources in 1990. A wheelchair-accessible trail leads from the day-use area to the river, and there are interpretive trails through the park, which is open year-round. For a fee, you can make reservations by calling Reservations Northwest (see contact information on page 236).

29 Red Bridge

Location: About 32 miles east of Everett on the South Fork Stillaguamish River.
Sites: 2 tent sites, 14 sites for tents or self-contained RVs no longer than 31 feet.
Facilities: Picnic tables, flush toilets, firewood; no drinking water.
Fee per night: None.
Elevation: 1,300 feet.
Management: Mount Baker-Snoqualmie National Forest, Darrington Ranger District.
Activities: Hiking, fishing, swimming.
Finding the campground: From Interstate 5 in Everett, take exit 194 and go east for 2 miles on U.S. Highway 2. Stay in the left lane over the causeway that crosses Ebey Island and go left onto Washington Highway 204 toward Lake Stevens. In another 2 miles, at WA 9, turn north and drive 2 more miles to WA 92 (Mountain Loop Highway). Turn right onto WA 92 and continue for 8 miles to the town of Granite Falls. Drive north out of town and then east on what is now the Mountain Loop Highway (County Road 92/Forest Road 7). Continue 18 miles to the campground, which is on the right (south) side of the road.

About the campground: The Verlot Public Service Center, 11 miles east of Granite Falls, is a good place to get local maps and check road conditions and campsite availability. You can also learn about nearby remnants of the gold and silver mining that took place in this area at the turn of the 20th century: ghost towns, old mine tunnels, and overgrown railroad grades. The 6-acre campground is very popular, with its sunny patches between the trees. It offers access to the South Fork Stillaguamish River from both sides of its namesake bridge. A lot of people taking the scenic Mountain Loop Highway stop here to enjoy the river. The campground is open from late May to early September.

30 Rockport State Park

Location: 39 miles east of Burlington, near Rockport.
Sites: 3 primitive tent sites; 8 developed, walk-in tent sites; 65 sites with water and sewer hookups for RVs up to 45 feet long; 4 Adirondack shelters (capacity 8 each).
Facilities: Drinking water, picnic tables, fire grills, restrooms, showers, dump station, firewood.
Fee per night: $$ to $$$.
Elevation: 330 feet.
Management: Washington State Parks and Recreation Commission.
Activities: Hiking, fishing.
Finding the campground: Rockport State Park is on Washington Highway 20, 7 miles east of Concrete and 1 mile west of Rockport in Skagit County. From Interstate 5 in Burlington, take exit 230 and drive east on WA 20 (North Cascades Highway) for 38 miles to the town of Rockport. The park is 1 mile ahead on the left.

About the campground: This 457-acre state park is thickly wooded, mainly with old-growth Douglas-firs. It is above and across the highway from the Skagit River. The park is relatively new, yet the old-growth trees for which the park is noted reflect a unique history of ownership. Early in the 20th century, the parkland belonged to the Sound Timber Company, which for some reason did not log the timber. Instead, in July 1935, the company sold the land and timber to the state for $1. Recognizing the unique recreational and interpretive value of this tract of forest, the Washington State Parks and Recreation Commission acquired the land from the Washington Department of Natural Resources in 1961. The park was named for the nearby community of Rockport, which in turn was named for the many large rocks at a boat landing on the nearby Skagit River. The campground is open from April 1 to mid-November.

31 Silver Lake Park

Location: 30 miles northeast of Bellingham on Silver Lake, near the town of Maple Falls.
Sites: 27 tent sites, 53 RV sites with water and electrical hookups, 28-site horse camp.
Facilities: Drinking water, flush toilets, bunkhouse, overnight lodge, rental cabins, group shelters, day lodge, boat ramp, boat rentals.
Fee per night: $$ to $$$.
Elevation: 820 feet.
Management: Whatcom County Parks.
Activities: Boating, fishing, swimming, picnicking, horseback riding.
Finding the campground: From Interstate 5 in Bellingham, take exit 255 and head northeast on Washington Highway 542 (Mount Baker Highway). Drive 27 miles to the town of Maple Falls, turn left onto Silver Lake Road, and drive 3 miles to the park entrance.

About the campground: This is a wonderful, out-of-the-way county park used mainly by local people. The lake is stocked with rainbow and cutthroat trout, and the fishing is great. Each April, Silver Lake Park holds a 1-hour fishing derby for anglers of all ages. There is no entry fee. Registration is on derby day from 5 to 9 A.M., and prizes are awarded at 10 A.M. There is also a pancake breakfast from 6:30 A.M. to noon. The campground is open year-round. For reservations, call Whatcom County Parks (see contact information on page 235).

32 Silver Fir

Location: About 44 miles east of Bellingham on the North Fork Nooksack River, near Glacier.
Sites: 20 sites for tents or self-contained RVs no longer than 31 feet.
Facilities: Drinking water, picnic tables, fire grills, vault toilets.
Fee per night: $$.
Elevation: 600 feet.
Management: Mount Baker-Snoqualmie National Forest, Mount Baker Ranger District.
Activities: Hiking, cross-country skiing.
Finding the campground: From Interstate 5 in Bellingham, drive 31 miles northeast on Washington Highway 542 to Glacier. Continue another 12.5 miles east to the campground.

About the campground: This campground is mostly known as a day-use area for cross-country skiers in the winter, but in the summer it is a very pleasant wooded campground on the North Fork Nooksack River. Galena Creek feeds into the river nearby. Silver Fir is on the Mount Baker Scenic Byway, which continues on to the Mount Baker Ski Area and beyond to Artist Point. The road is paved the whole way, and there are some major trailheads at the end of it. The campground is open from May through September. For a fee, you can make reservations by calling the National Recreation Reservation Service (see contact information on page 236).

33 Squire Creek County Park

Location: 44 miles northeast of Everett on Squire Creek, near Darrington.
Sites: 30 sites with sewer hookups for tents or RVs no longer than 25 feet.
Facilities: Drinking water, picnic tables, restrooms, dump station, firewood, 2 large shelters with cook stoves.
Fee per night: $$.
Elevation: 400 feet.
Management: Snohomish County Parks.
Activities: Fishing, hiking
Finding the campground: From Everett, drive north on Interstate 5 for 15 miles. Take exit 208 and drive east on Washington Highway 530 for 29 miles through Arlington to the park, which is on the north (left) side of the highway just 3 miles before you reach Darrington.

About the campground: This Snohomish County park near Darrington occupies 28 acres in an old-growth forest on Squire Creek. The summer camping and fishing are good. Just 3 miles away in the Mount Baker-Snoqualmie National Forest, the 49,000-acre Boulder River Wilderness lies in a low-elevation valley that has never been logged. It is fairly rugged, but there are about 25 miles of trails. This lovely campground is open from mid-May to mid-September.

34 Sulphur Creek

Location: About 85 miles northeast of Everett on the Suiattle River, near Darrington.
Sites: 20 sites for tents or self-contained RVs up to 16 feet long.
Facilities: Picnic tables, fire grills, vault toilets; no drinking water.
Fee per night: $$.
Elevation: 1,300 feet.
Management: Mount Baker-Snoqualmie National Forest, Darrington Ranger District.
Activities: Fishing, hiking.
Finding the campground: From Everett, drive north on Interstate 5 for 15 miles. Take exit 208 and drive east on Washington Highway 530 for 32 miles to the town of Darrington. Continue on WA 530, now heading north, for another 7.5 miles. At the fork in the road, bear right onto Forest Road 26, which follows the Suiattle River for 30 miles to the campground.

About the campground: The Suiattle River is across the road from the campground, but access is easy. This is not a large campground, covering just 3 acres, and it is quite primitive. It features a horse camp and a trailhead for the Pacific Crest National Scenic Trail. The campground is open from May 1 to late September. For reservations, call the Darrington Ranger District (see contact information on page 235).

35 Troublesome Creek

Location: 48 miles east of Everett on the North Fork Skykomish River, near Index.
Sites: 24 sites for tents or self-contained RVs no longer than 24 feet, 6 walk-in tent sites.
Facilities: Picnic tables, fire grills, vault toilets; no drinking water.
Fee per night: $ to $$.
Elevation: 1,300 feet.
Management: Mount Baker-Snoqualmie National Forest, Skykomish Ranger District.
Activities: Hiking, fishing.
Finding the campground: From Interstate 5 in Everett, take exit 194 and drive southeast on U.S. Highway 2 for 36 miles to the town of Index. Turn northeast onto Index-Galena Road (Forest Road 63) and drive 12 miles to the campground.

About the campground: This 15-acre campground is remote, peaceful, and very basic. It sits nicely in the woods next to the North Fork Skykomish River, and the fishing is good. The campground is open from Memorial Day through Labor Day. For a fee, you can make reservations by calling the National Recreation Reservation Service (see contact information on page 236).

36 Turlo

Location: 24 miles east of Everett on the South Fork Stillaguamish River, near Granite Falls.
Sites: 19 sites for tents or self-contained RVs no longer than 31 feet.
Facilities: Drinking water, picnic tables, flush toilets, firewood.
Fee per night: $$.
Elevation: 900 feet.
Management: Mount Baker-Snoqualmie National Forest, Darrington Ranger District.
Activities: Hiking, fishing, swimming.
Finding the campground: From Interstate 5 in Everett, take exit 194 and go east for 2 miles on U.S. Highway 2. Stay in the left lane over the causeway that crosses Ebey Island and go left onto Washington Highway 204 toward Lake Stevens. In another 2 miles, at WA 9, turn north for 2 more miles to WA 92 (Mountain Loop Highway). Turn right onto WA 92 and continue for 8 miles to the town of Granite Falls. Drive north out of town and then east on what is now the Mountain Loop Highway (County Road 92/Forest Road 7). Continue 10 miles to the campground.

About the campground: The Verlot Public Service Center, 11 miles east of Granite Falls, is a good place to get local maps and information on road conditions and campsite availability. You can camp right on the river at Turlo, and there are hiking trails nearby. Late summer is a good time to visit, before the fall and winter rains start. This region gets 140 inches of rain a year. The campground is open from mid-May to late September. For a fee, you can make reservations by calling the National Recreation Reservation Service (see contact information on page 236).

37 Verlot

Location: 26 miles east of Everett on the South Fork Stillaguamish River, near Granite Falls.
Sites: 26 sites for tents or self-contained RVs up to 31 feet long.
Facilities: Drinking water, picnic tables, flush toilets, firewood.
Fee per night: $$.
Elevation: 900 feet.
Management: Mount Baker-Snoqualmie National Forest, Darrington Ranger District.
Activities: Hiking, fishing, swimming.
Finding the campground: From Interstate 5 in Everett, take exit 194 and go east for 2 miles on U.S. Highway 2. Stay in the left lane over the causeway that

crosses Ebey Island and go left onto Washington Highway 204 toward Lake Stevens. In another 2 miles, at WA 9, turn north for 2 more miles to WA 92 (Mountain Loop Highway). Turn right onto WA 92 and continue for 8 miles to the town of Granite Falls. Drive north out of town and then east on what is now the Mountain Loop Highway (County Road 92/Forest Road 7). Continue 11 miles to the campground.

About the campground: The Verlot Public Service Center is right next to this campground. It is a good place to get local maps and check road conditions and campsite availability. The shady, 6-acre campground sits nicely on the "Stilly," as the locals call the river, in the Mount Baker-Snoqualmie National Forest. Grocery shopping is available nearby. The campground is open from mid-May to late September. For a fee, you can make reservations by calling the National Recreation Reservation Service (see contact information on page 236).

38 Wallace Falls State Park

Location: About 28 miles east of Everett on the Wallace River, near Gold Bar.
Sites: 6 tent sites.
Facilities: Drinking water, picnic tables, fire grills, restrooms.
Fee per night: $$.
Elevation: 160 feet.
Management: Washington State Parks and Recreation Commission.
Activities: Hiking, fishing, berry picking, mushrooming, mountain biking.
Finding the campground: From Interstate 5 in Everett, take exit 194 (City Center/Stevens Pass) onto U.S. Highway 2 and drive 27 miles southeast to Gold Bar. Turn left onto First Street and go about a half-mile to McKenzie (Ley) Road. Turn right (east) and follow the signs to the park.

About the campground: The park has good hiking trails and primitive but adequate campsites. One fun trail is actually a railway abandoned by a logging company. A 7-mile loop trail leads to the spectacular falls, which cascade 265 feet over a series of cliffs and ledges. The 1,400-acre park also features 6,300 feet of freshwater shoreline on the Wallace River and Wallace Lake. The name Wallace is actually an anglicized version of a Skykomish Indian name, Kwayaylsh. Joe and Sarah Kwayaylsh, members of the Skykomish tribe, homesteaded near the present town of Startup (which was also named Wallace until 1901). Gold Bar, the town nearest the park, was named after the gravel bars in the Skykomish River, on which the Chinese railroad workers used to pan for gold. The campground is open year-round.

39 Washington Park

Location: About 21 miles west of Burlington on Rosario Strait, near Anacortes.
Sites: 70 sites for tents or RVs up to 70 feet long, including 46 with full (including cable TV) or water and electrical hookups.
Facilities: Drinking water, restrooms, showers, public phone, playground, recreation field, dump station, laundry room, boat ramp.

Fee per night: $$.
Elevation: Sea level.
Management: City of Anacortes.
Activities: Bicycling, boating, fishing.
Finding the campground: From Interstate 5 in Burlington, take exit 230 onto Washington Highway 20 and drive west for 18 miles to Anacortes, following signs for the ferries. At 12th Street, turn left and drive about 2 miles. Stay left on 12th Street at the ferry terminal and continue about a half-mile to the park.

About the campground: This 22-acre camp is on Fidalgo Head, a half-mile past the Washington State Ferries Terminal. The wooded sites are small but neat. The park features a 3.5-mile loop trail, part of which is along the shoreline. The beach is good for collecting little treasures and watching boat traffic coming and going. The campground is open year-round.

40 Wenberg State Park

Location: 9 miles northwest of Marysville on Lake Goodwin.
Sites: 65 tent sites, 10 sites with partial hookups for RVs no longer than 50 feet.
Facilities: Drinking water, picnic tables, restrooms, bathhouse, coin-operated showers, store, dump station, 2 playground units, summer concession stand, 2-lane concrete boat ramps, 2 swim/water-ski floats.
Fee per night: $$ to $$$.
Elevation: 120 feet.
Management: Washington State Parks and Recreation Commission.
Activities: Swimming, boating, waterskiing, freshwater fishing, hiking, sailboarding, sailing.
Finding the campground: From Interstate 5, 4 miles north of Marysville, take exit 206 west onto Washington Highway 531 and drive 5 miles to the campground.

About the campground: Wenberg covers 46 acres and features 1,140 feet of freshwater shoreline on Lake Goodwin, which is renowned for its cutthroat and rainbow trout fishing. The lake also holds smallmouth bass and perch up to 18 inches long. A former state legislator named Wenberg owned the land that became what was first a county park. There are some good hiking trails nearby as well as a half-mile of foot trails within the park. There is also a 465-foot unguarded swimming beach. The campground is open year-round. For a fee, you can make reservations by calling Reservations Northwest (see contact information on page 236).

41 William C. Dearinger

Location: About 60 miles east of Everett on the Sauk River, near Darrington.
Sites: 12 sites for tents or self-contained RVs up to 25 feet long.
Facilities: Picnic tables, fire grills, tent pads, vault toilets, firewood; no drinking water.
Fee per night: None.

Elevation: 620 feet.

Management: Washington Department of Natural Resources, Northwest Region.

Activities: Fishing, hiking, exploring historic mining districts.

Finding the campground: From Everett, drive north on Interstate 5 for 15 miles. Take exit 208 and drive east on Washington Highway 530 for 35 miles to Darrington. Continue on WA 530 as it turns north through town, and in a third-mile turn northeast onto Sauk Prairie Road. Drive 6 miles to a T junction, a half-mile past Inman Road. Turn left (west) at the T onto Zyman Road and stay with it for 0.7 mile as it turns north. Take the forest road that forks to the right and continue 4.5 miles to the campground.

About the campground: This secluded and little-known site, open year-round, is in the heart of the western Cascade Mountains. This was a gold and silver mining region around the turn of the 20th century, and evidence of this colorful history still remains.

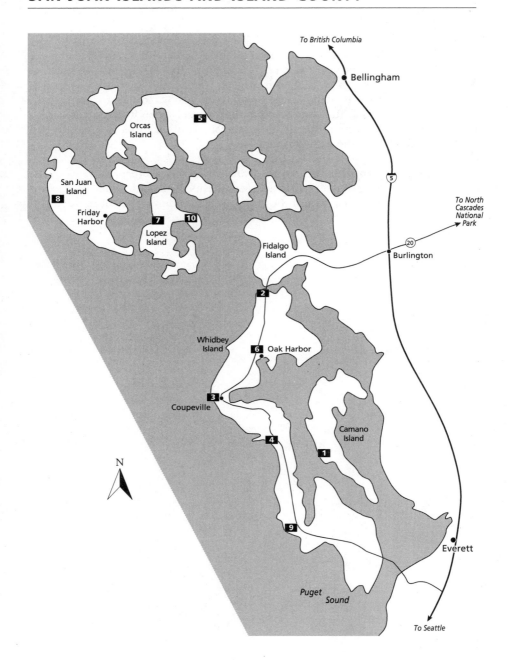

SAN JUAN ISLANDS AND ISLAND COUNTY

	Group sites	RV sites	Total # of sites	Max. RV length	Hookups	Toilets	Showers	Drinking water	Dump station	Pets	Wheelchair	Recreation	Fee	Season	Can reserve	Stay limit
1 Camano Island State Park	•	•	88	30			•	•	•	•	•	HFB	$–$$			10
2 Deception Pass State Park	•	•	251	50			•	•	•	•	•	HFBS	$–$$			10
3 Fort Casey State Park		•	38	40		F	•	•		•	•	HFB	$–$$			10
4 Fort Ebey State Park		•	53	70		F	•	•	•	•	•	HF	$–$$			10
5 Moran State Park		•	151	45		F	•	•		•	•	HFBS	$$–$$$		•	10
6 Oak Harbor City Beach Park		•	82		WE	F	•	•	•	•		FSB	$$			
7 Odlin County Park		•	30	35		P		•		•		FSB	$$		•	
8 San Juan County Park		•	20	25	WES	F		•		•		HFB	$–$$		•	
9 South Whidbey State Park	•	•	60	50		F	•	•	•	•	•	HFB	$–$$	late Feb–Oct		10
10 Spencer Spit State Park	•	•	45	20		F		•	•	•	•	F	$$	Mar–Oct	•	10

Hookups: W = Water   E = Electric   S = Sewer
Toilets: F = Flush   V = Vault   P = Pit   C = Chemical
Recreation: C = Bicycling/Mountain Biking   H = Hiking   S = Swimming   F = Fishing   B = Boating
O = Off-highway driving   R = Horseback Riding
Maximum Trailer/RV Length given in feet.   **Stay Limit** given in days.
Fee $ = less than $10; $$ = $10–$15; $$$ = $16–20; $$$$ = more than $20.
If no entry under **Season,** campground is open all year. If no entry under **Fee,** camping is free.

1 Camano Island State Park

Location: 34 miles northwest of Everett on Camano Island.
Sites: 87 sites for tents or self-contained RVs up to 30 feet long, 1 primitive tent site.
Facilities: Drinking water, picnic tables, fire grills, restrooms, coin-operated showers, dump station, playground, boat ramps, underwater park.
Fee per night: $ to $$.
Elevation: Sea level.
Management: Washington State Parks and Recreation Commission.
Activities: Hiking, boating, fishing, clam digging, nature study, scuba diving, bird watching, rock collecting.
Finding the campground: From Interstate 5, 15 miles north of Everett, take exit 212 and go west on Washington Highway 532 for 5 miles to Stanwood. Follow the signs for 14 miles to the park, on the west side of Camano Island.

About the campground: This quiet and wooded state park is 10 miles south of the town of Utsalady, which means "many berries." It covers 134 acres and features 6,700 feet of saltwater frontage on Saratoga Passage and Elger Bay. There are 4.5 miles of good hiking trails and 1.3 miles of beach. A half-mile nature trail leads though an old-growth forest that includes western redcedar and western hemlock. There is also a stand of old-growth Douglas-firs. On some trails, bridges take you over seasonal streams and deep ravines. The campground is open year-round.

2 Deception Pass State Park

Location: 18 miles west of Burlington on Whidbey and Fidalgo Islands.
Sites: 246 sites for tents or self-contained RVs up to 50 feet long, 5 primitive tent sites.
Facilities: Drinking water, picnic tables, fire pits, restrooms, showers, dump station, concession stand, boat ramp, boat rentals, buoys, floats, underwater park at Rosario Beach.
Fee per night: $ to $$.
Elevation: Sea level.
Management: Washington State Parks and Recreation Commission.
Activities: Fishing, hiking, swimming, scuba diving, boating.
Finding the campground: From Interstate 5 in Burlington, take exit 230 onto Washington Highway 20 and drive west for 12 miles. When the highway forks at Deans Corner, head south on WA 20 and drive 6 miles, crossing the bridge at Deception Pass, to reach the park on the right.

About the campground: This park straddles Deception Pass, encompassing 4,128 acres on the northern tip of Whidbey Island (in Island County) and the southern tip of Fidalgo Island (in Skagit County). The tide surges through the pass too swiftly for paddlers to navigate, but the rushing water provides a spectacle for onlookers on the 182-foot-high bridge that spans the pass. The state park features a few lakes, some old-growth Douglas-fir forests, marshland, sand dunes, and a few smaller islands. There are 35 miles of hiking trails and 1.5 miles of interpretive trail, as well as 15 miles of saltwater shoreline with rocky bluffs, coves, tidal flats, and sandy beaches. Black-tailed deer are common, and bald eagles nest in the treetops. The campground is open year-round, with limited services in winter.

3 Fort Casey State Park

Location: About 38 miles southwest of Burlington on Whidbey Island.
Sites: 35 sites for tents or self-contained RVs no longer than 40 feet, 3 primitive tent sites.
Facilities: Drinking water, picnic tables, fire grills, restrooms, flush toilets, coin-operated showers, lighthouse/interpretive center, historic bunkers, 2 boat ramps with grounding floats, underwater park.
Fee per night: $ to $$.
Elevation: Sea level.
Management: Washington State Parks and Recreation Commission.
Activities: Boating, fishing, scuba diving, hiking, driftwood collecting, clam digging.
Finding the campground: From Interstate 5 in Burlington, take exit 230 and drive west on Washington Highway 20 for about 38 miles, through Coupeville, to the park.

About the campground: Fort Casey State Park (including Keystone Spit) encompasses 411 acres and offers 7,000 feet of freshwater frontage on Crockett

Lake and 10,810 feet of saltwater shoreline on Admiralty Inlet. Established in the late 1890s as a U.S. Coast Guard artillery fort, Fort Casey was incorporated into Ebey's Landing National Historical Reserve by the National Park Service in 1980. Old gunnery fortifications are still in place. The beach on the west side of the campground is fine for walks and exploring. On occasion, you can see whales from both Fort Casey and Ebey's Landing. Pods of orcas that stray from their usual waters around the San Juan Islands are the most fun to see, but there are plenty of river otters, harbor seals, and California sea lions as well. Dolphins, minke whales, and humpback whales are less commonly sighted. In late spring and early summer you can see gray whales migrating from California to the Arctic. You can walk north along the beach for 4 miles to Fort Ebey (see below). The campground is open year-round.

4 Fort Ebey State Park

Location: About 10 miles southwest of Oak Harbor on Whidbey Island.
Sites: 50 sites for tents or self-contained RVs up to 70 feet long, 3 primitive sites for kayakers.
Facilities: Drinking water, picnic tables, fire grills, restroom, coin-operated showers, dump station.
Fee per night: $ to $$.
Elevation: Sea level.
Management: Washington State Parks and Recreation Commission.
Activities: Hiking, fishing, beachcombing.
Finding the campground: From Oak Harbor on Whidbey Island, drive 8 miles south on Washington Highway 20 to its intersection with Libbey Road. Turn right (west) onto Libbey Road, drive 1.2 miles, and turn left (south) onto Fort Ebey Road. Proceed for a quarter-mile on Fort Ebey Road to the park.

About the campground: You will find Fort Ebey on the bluffs high above the Strait of Juan de Fuca, where the strait flows into Admiralty Inlet. There are 24 picnic sites in the day-use area. The 645-acre park offers 3 miles of bluff trails and 1.5 miles of beach trails. Follow the curving boardwalk over the driftwood-strewn beach and look for Japanese glass fishing floats. Gun batteries and bunkers remain from the days when the fort was operational, and they are fun to explore. The park is a stop on the Cascadia Marine Trail. It features 8,000 feet of saltwater shoreline on Admiralty Inlet and 1,000 feet of freshwater frontage on Lake Pondilla. The campground is open year-round.

5 Moran State Park

Location: 15 miles from the ferry landing on Orcas Island in the San Juan Islands.
Sites: 136 sites for tents or self-contained RVs up to 45 feet long, 15 primitive hike-in/bike-in tent sites.
Facilities: Drinking water, picnic tables, fire grills, restrooms, showers, firewood, boat docks, fishing supplies, launching facilities (fee), boat rentals, envi-

ronmental learning center.
Fee per night: $$ to $$$.
Elevation: 800 feet.
Management: Washington State Parks and Recreation Commission.
Activities: Hiking, fishing, swimming, boating, picnicking.
Finding the campground: From the ferry landing on Orcas Island, take an immediate left onto Orcas to Olga Road and drive 15 miles around East Sound to the park.

About the campground: In 1920, Robert Moran, a shipbuilder and former mayor of Seattle, donated 2,600 acres on Orcas Island to the state for use as a park. Moran State Park has since grown to more than 5,000 acres, and it includes five lakes, 30 miles of foot trails, and 300 acres of old-growth forest. Most trails run through the woods, but you will find some paths with views of nearby islands. Among Moran's greatest attractions are the views from Mount Constitution (2,409 feet) and Little Summit Lookout (2,039 feet). You can drive, bike, or hike to either. A 52-foot tower at the top of Mount Constitution was patterned after watchtowers built in the Caucasus Mountains of Eastern Europe in the 12th century.

The park is open year-round but is busiest on summer weekends. Cold Springs is a particularly pleasant picnic spot. Dogs must be on a leash (8 feet in length or less) at all times, and they must be prevented from annoying other park visitors. Scooping is also required. You will find campsites on and across the road from Cascade Lake and at Mountain Lake. The latter is a reservoir, so swimming is not allowed. Fishing is permitted. For a fee, you can make reservations by calling Reservations Northwest (see contact information on page 236).

6 Oak Harbor City Beach Park

Location: In Oak Harbor on Whidbey Island.
Sites: 56 RV sites with water and electrical hookups, 26 overflow RV sites with no hookups.
Facilities: Drinking water, picnic tables, restrooms, coin-operated showers, dump station, playground, beach.
Fee per night: $$.
Elevation: Sea level.
Management: City of Oak Harbor.
Activities: Fishing, swimming, boating.
Finding the campground: Head south through the town of Oak Harbor on Washington Highway 20 and cross West Pioneer Way onto the continuation of 80 Southwest Street. The campground is on the left in 1 block.

About the campground: The swimming beach is the real attraction of this RV-only park. The campground is very pleasant and pretty busy throughout the summer. It is open year-round.

7 Odlin County Park

Location: 1 mile from the ferry landing on Lopez Island in the San Juan Islands.
Sites: 30 sites for tents or self-contained RVs up to 35 feet long.
Facilities: Drinking water, pit toilets, pier, float, boat ramp, mooring buoys, ball parks, covered cook shack.
Fee per night: $$.
Elevation: Sea level.
Management: San Juan County Parks.
Activities: Fishing, boating, swimming.
Finding the campground: The park is 1 mile south of the ferry landing, via Ferry Road, at the northwest end of Lopez Island.

About the campground: Odlin Park offers 80 acres of relaxation in a natural setting, as well as a mile of sandy beach on Upright Channel. You do not find many sandy beaches in the Northwest, and this is a nice one. Swim if you dare—the 50-degree F water feels mighty cold to most. Showers are available in nearby Lopez Village. The campground is open year-round. You can make reservations 7 to 60 days in advance by calling Odlin County Park on Wednesdays between 10 A.M. and 4 P.M. local time. A two-night minimum stay is required to make reservations. (See contact information on page 235.)

8 San Juan County Park

Location: 11 miles west of the Friday Harbor ferry landing on San Juan Island.
Sites: 20 sites, including 8 with full hookups for RVs no longer than 25 feet.
Facilities: Drinking water, flush toilets, boat ramp.
Fee per night: $ to $$.
Elevation: Sea level.
Management: San Juan County Parks.
Activities: Hiking, whale watching, fishing, boating.
Finding the campground: From the Washington State Ferry terminal at Friday Harbor, head southeast on Front Street. In 2 blocks, turn right (southwest) onto Spring Street. Near the western city limits, Spring Street becomes San Juan Valley Road. Turn left (south) onto Wold Road and then right (west) onto Bailer Hill Road, which becomes Westside Road and continues north up the coast. Once you pass Lime Kiln Point State Park, look for San Juan County Park Road and follow it into the park.

About the campground: This is the only county park on San Juan Island. It is located on Smallpox Bay on the west-central shore of the island. The campground is basic but pristine, and the views are outstanding. There are plenty of eagles and orcas to watch. The campground is open year-round. You can make reservations 7 to 60 days in advance in the summer by calling San Juan County Park on Wednesdays between 10 A.M. and 4 P.M. local time. (See contact information on page 235.)

9 South Whidbey State Park

Location: About 5 miles south of Greenbank on Whidbey Island.
Sites: 54 sites for tents or self-contained RVs no longer than 50 feet, 6 primitive tent sites.
Facilities: Drinking water, picnic tables, fire grills, restrooms, coin-operated showers, dump station, firewood (fee), amphitheater.
Fee per night: $ to $$.
Elevation: Sea level.
Management: Washington State Parks and Recreation Commission.
Activities: Hiking, saltwater fishing, boating, scuba diving, beachcombing, rock collecting, clam digging, bird watching, crabbing, driftwood collecting.
Finding the campground: From Washington Highway 525, almost 1 mile north of Greenbank, take Smugglers Cove Road west and south for about 4.5 miles to the campground on the right.

About the campground: This campground is a favorite. The 347-acre park has 4,500 feet of saltwater shoreline on Admiralty Inlet on the western shore of Whidbey Island. It offers a sandy beach and views of Puget Sound and the Olympic Mountains. There is a good loop trail through an old-growth cluster of western redcedar and Douglas-fir. Some of the trees are more than 250 years old. The campground is open from February 24 through October.

10 Spencer Spit State Park

Location: 3 miles south of the ferry landing on Lopez Island in the San Juan Islands.
Sites: 40 sites for tents or self-contained RVs no longer than 20 feet, including 15 walk-in sites; 3 primitive overflow sites; 2 sites with Adirondack shelters.
Facilities: Drinking water, picnic tables, fire grills, restrooms, dump station, 16 offshore moorage buoys.
Fee per night: $$.
Elevation: Sea level.
Management: Washington State Parks and Recreation Commission.
Activities: Saltwater fishing, clam digging, beachcombing, bird watching.
Finding the campground: From the ferry landing on Upright Head, on the north end of the island, go south on Ferry Road for just over a mile. Turn left (east) onto Port Stanley Road and continue nearly 2 miles around Swifts Bay to the park.

About the campground: Beach parks are a rarity on the rocky coast of Washington, especially in the "banana belt" San Juan Islands. This is an exceptionally nice one. The 130-acre park has 7,840 feet of saltwater shoreline on Lopez Sound. The park's main feature is a quarter-mile-long sand spit that contains a saltwater lagoon. The park also contains a midden, or archaeological remains of an early Indian campsite. The area is frequented by migratory birds, great blue herons, geese, and kingfishers. There are plenty of rabbits, deer, and raccoons. The campground is open from March through October. For a fee, you can make reservations by calling Reservations Northwest (see contact information on page 236).

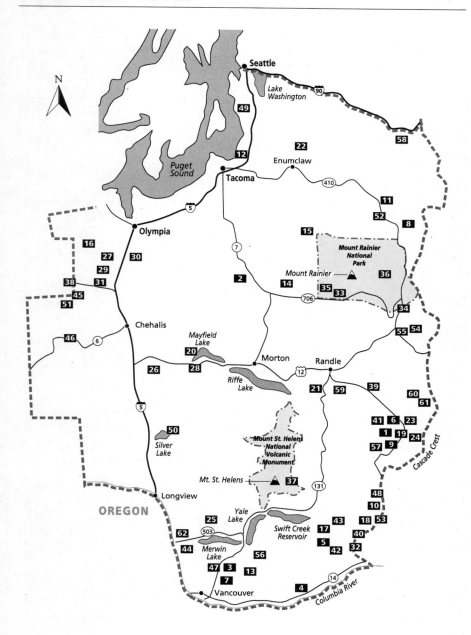

	Group sites	RV sites	Total # of sites	Max. RV length	Hookups	Toilets	Showers	Drinking water	Dump station	Pets	Wheelchair	Recreation	Fee	Season	Can reserve	Stay limit
1 Adams Fork		•	24	21		V	•			•		HFS	$	May–late Oct		14
2 Alder Lake		•	27	25		F	•			•		FBS				14
3 Battle Ground State Park	•	•	50	50		F	•	•	•	•	•	HFBSR	$–$$$		•	10
4 Beacon Rock State Park	•	•	35	50		F	•	•	•	•		HRBRC	$$–$$$			10
5 Beaver	•	•	26	25		P	•			•	•	HFS	$–$$$	mid Apr–late Sep	•	14
6 Cat Creek		•	5	16		P				•		HF	$	mid May–late Oct		14
7 Cold Creek		•	6			V	•			•		HFC				7
8 Corral Pass			20			V				•		HR		July–late Sep		14
9 Council Lake		•	9	16		P				•		HFSB	$	July–mid Sep		14
10 Cultus Creek		•	43	32		V	•			•	•	H	$–$$$	June–Sep	•	14
11 The Dalles		•	45	21		V	•			•		HF	$–$$	mid May–late Sep	•	14
12 Dash Point State Park	•	•	138	35	WE	F	•	•	•	•	•	HFS	$$–$$$		•	10
13 Dougan Creek		•	7			V	•			•		HF		mid May–mid Sep		7
14 Elbe Hills ORV Trailhead		•	3			P				•		O				7
15 Evans Creek			27			V	•			•		HFO		mid Jun–late Sep		14
16 Fall Creek		•	8			V				•		HRC		Apr–Oct		7
17 Falls Creek-Crest Horse Camp		•	6	15		P				•		HR		mid June–late Sep		14
18 Goose Lake		•	26	18		V				•		HFS	$	mid June–late Sep	•	14
19 Horseshoe Lake		•	10	16		P				•		HFBS		mid June–late Sep		14
20 Ike Kinswa State Park		•	103	60	WES	F	•	•	•	•	•	HFSB	$–$$$		•	10
21 Iron Creek		•	98	42		P	•			•		HF	$$–$$$	mid May–late Oct	•	14
22 Kanaskat-Palmer State Park	•	•	50	50	E	F	•	•	•	•		HFB	$$–$$$		•	10
23 Keene's Horse Camp		•	13	21		P				•		HR		July–late Sep		14
24 Killen Creek		•	8	21		P				•		HR		July–late Sep		14
25 Lake Merrill			11			V	•					HFB		May–Sep		7
26 Lewis and Clark State Park	•	•	27	60		F	•			•		HFR	$$			10
27 Margaret McKenny		•	32			P				•		HRC		Apr–Oct		14
28 Mayfield Lake County Park		•	54	40		F	•	•	•	•	•	FBS	$$	May–Sep	•	14
29 Middle Waddell		•	24			V				•		OC		Apr–Oct		14
30 Millersylvania State Park	•	•	193	45		F	•	•	•	•	•	HFBSC	$–$$		•	10
31 Mima Falls Trailhead		•	5			P	•			•		HRC		Apr–Oct		14
32 Moss Creek		•	18	32		P	•			•		F	$	mid May–late Sep	•	14
33 Mount Rainier National Park: Cougar Rock		•	200	30		F	•	•	•	•		HF	$$	mid May–late Oct	•	14
34 Mount Rainier National Park: Ohanapecosh		•	205	30		F	•	•	•	•		H	$$	mid May–mid Oct	•	14
35 Mount Rainier National Park: Sunshine Point		•	18	25		P	•			•	•	HRF	$$			14

continued on following page

#	Name	Group sites	RV sites	Total # of sites	Max. RV length	Hookups	Toilets	Showers	Drinking water	Dump station	Pets	Wheelchair	Recreation	Fee	Season	Can reserve	Stay limit
36	Mount Rainier National Park: White River		•	112	20		F	•	•		•	•	HFR	$	mid June–mid Sep		14
37	MSHNVM: Lower Falls RA		•	43	70		V		•		•	•	HR	$–$$	May–Sep		14
38	North Creek		•	5			V		•		•		HC		Apr–Oct		14
39	North Fork		•	33	31		V		•		•		HFC	$–$$$	mid May–late Sep	•	14
40	Oklahoma		•	23	22		P		•		•	•	F	$	mid May–mid Oct	•	14
41	Olallie Lake		•	5	22		P				•		FSB	$	July–late Sep		14
42	Panther Creek		•	33	25		P		•		•		HF	$–$$$	mid May–mid Oct	•	14
43	Paradise Creek		•	42	25		V		•		•	•	HF	$–$$$	mid May–mid Oct	•	14
44	Paradise Point State Park		•	79	45		F	•	•	•	•	•	HFB	$–$$		•	10
45	Porter Creek		•	14			V				•		HRC		Apr–Oct		14
46	Rainbow Falls State Park	•	•	50	32		F	•	•	•	•	•	HFSB	$–$$	Apr–Aug		10
47	Rock Creek		•	19			V		•		•	•	HFR				7
48	Saddle			12			P				•		HF		mid June–late Sep		14
49	Saltwater State Park	•	•	52	50		F	•	•	•	•	•	HFS	$$	late Mar–early Sep		10
50	Seaquest State Park	•	•	101	50	WES	F	•	•	•	•	•	HF	$–$$$		•	10
51	Sherman Valley		•	8			V		•		•		HC		Apr–Oct		14
52	Silver Springs		•	56	21		V		•		•		HF	$–$$	mid May–late Sep	•	14
53	Smokey Creek		•	3	22		P				•		H		June–late Sep		14
54	Soda Springs			6			V				•		H		mid June–early Sep		14
55	Summit Creek		•	6			P				•		H		mid June–early Sep		14
56	Sunset		•	16	22		P				•		HF	$			14
57	Takhlakh		•	54	21		V		•		•		HFB	$	mid June–late Sep	•	14
58	Tinkham		•	48	21		V		•		•	•	HF	$$	mid May–mid Sep	•	14
59	Tower Rock		•	22	22		V		•		•		F	$	mid May–late Sep		14
60	Walupt Horse Camp		•	6	18		V		•		•		FHR	$	Jun–Sep	•	14
61	Walupt Lake		•	44	22		V		•		•		HFSB	$-$$$	mid Jun–early Sep	•	14
62	Woodland		•	10			V		•		•	•			May–Sep		7

Hookups: W = Water   E = Electric   S = Sewer
Toilets: F = Flush   V = Vault   P = Pit
Recreation: C = Bicycling/Mountain Biking   H = Hiking   S = Swimming   F = Fishing   B = Boating
O = Off-highway driving   R = Horseback Riding
Maximum Trailer/RV Length given in feet. **Stay Limit** given in days.
Fee $ = less than $10; $$ = $10-$15; $$$ = $16-20; $$$$ = more than $20.
If no entry under **Season**, campground is open all year. If no entry under **Fee**, camping is free.

1 Adams Fork

Location: About 117 miles southeast of Olympia on the Cispus River.
Sites: 24 sites for tents or self-contained RVs no longer than 21 feet.
Facilities: Drinking water, picnic tables, vault toilets.
Fee per night: $.
Elevation: 2,600 feet.
Management: Gifford Pinchot National Forest, Randle Ranger District.
Activities: Hiking, fishing, swimming.
Finding the campground: From Interstate 5, 45 miles south of Olympia, take exit 68 and head east on U.S. Highway 12. Drive 48 miles to the town of Randle and turn south onto Washington Highway 131. Drive 1 mile, turn left (southeast) onto Forest Road 23 (Cispus Road), and drive 18 miles. Take the left fork, turning east onto FR 21, and drive 5 miles. Turn right (southeast) onto FR 56 and drive 0.1 mile to the campground.

About the campground: This campground on the Upper Cispus River is in an inspiring location: about 12 miles from the summit of Mount Adams. It is a fine place to kick back and refresh yourself, and there are plenty of trails for walking or hiking. The campground is open from May to late October.

2 Alder Lake

Location: 30 miles southeast of Tacoma on Alder Lake, near Eatonville.
Sites: 27 sites for tents or self-contained RVs no longer than 25 feet.
Facilities: Drinking water, picnic tables, fire grills, tent pads, flush toilets, boat ramp, dock.
Fee per night: None.
Elevation: 1,100 feet.
Management: Washington Department of Natural Resources, Central Region.
Activities: Fishing, boating, waterskiing, swimming.
Finding the campground: From Interstate 5 in Tacoma, take exit 134 and head south on Washington Highway 7. Drive 30 miles to the campground. From Eatonville, the campground is 6 miles south via WA 161 and WA 7.

About the campground: This 231-acre campground on the lakeshore is wooded and relatively peaceful but for the water-skiers, who start early in the morning. It is open year-round, with limited facilities in winter.

3 Battle Ground State Park

Location: About 19 miles northeast of Vancouver on Battle Ground Lake.
Sites: 15 primitive tent sites, 35 sites for tents or self-contained RVs no longer than 50 feet.
Facilities: Drinking water, fire grills, picnic tables, flush toilets, showers, dump station, store, firewood, restaurant, playground, unguarded swim beach, boat ramp, boat rentals, 5 miles of horse trails.

Fee per night: $ to $$$.
Elevation: 450 feet.
Management: Washington State Parks and Recreation Commission.
Activities: Hiking, swimming, boating, fishing, scuba diving, horseback riding, horseshoe pit, sports field, marina.
Finding the campground: From Interstate 5 in Vancouver, take exit 2 onto Washington Highway 500 and drive east for almost 5 miles. Turn north onto WA 503 and drive north for 9.5 miles to the town of Battle Ground. From there, follow the signs for 3 miles to the park.

About the campground: Battle Ground covers 280 acres and has 4,100 feet of freshwater shoreline on 28-acre Battle Ground Lake. The park is very popular because of its easy access to the lake. However, no motorboats are allowed. The campground is a nice mix of primitive and RV sites. It is open year-round. For a fee, you can make reservations by calling Reservations Northwest (see contact information on page 236).

4 Beacon Rock State Park

Location: 35 miles east of Vancouver on the Columbia River.
Sites: 33 sites for tents or self-contained RVs no longer than 50 feet, 2 primitive sites.
Facilities: Drinking water, picnic tables, fire grills, flush toilets, dump station, coin-operated showers, firewood (fee), playground, 2 boat ramps, dock.
Fee per night: $$ to $$$.
Elevation: Sea level.
Management: Washington State Parks and Recreation Commission.
Activities: Hiking, fishing, boating, rock climbing, horseback riding, mountain biking.
Finding the campground: From Interstate 5 in Vancouver, drive east on Washington Highway 14 for 35 miles.

About the campground: Just a mile east of the town of Skamania, Beacon Rock looms over the highway like a monolith from outer space. In fact, it is one of the largest monoliths in the nation. Serious hikers can take the steep 1-mile trail to the top of the rock (elevation 848 feet) for a fine view of this part of Columbia Gorge. The trail has a handrail, but people who suffer from vertigo will want to forego the climb. The rock is the remains of an ancient volcano. It was named by Lewis and Clark in 1805, and it marks the last of the rapids on the Columbia River and the beginning of tidal influence from the Pacific Ocean, 150 miles away. The park covers 4,500 acres on both sides of the highway, including 1.8 miles of shoreline on the Columbia River. There are 14 miles of hiking trails, 7 of them shared with equestrians and mountain bikers. Several creeks offer excellent fishing. The campground is open year-round but has limited facilities in winter.

The strong winds that blow through the Columbia Gorge make for some of the best and most challenging sailboarding in the country.

5 Beaver

Location: 59 miles northeast of Vancouver on the Wind River.
Sites: 26 sites for tents or self-contained RVs no longer than 25 feet.
Facilities: Drinking water, fire grills, picnic tables, pit toilets.
Fee per night: $ to $$$.
Elevation: 1,100 feet.
Management: Gifford Pinchot National Forest, Wind River Ranger District.
Activities: Hiking, fishing, swimming, berry and mushroom picking.
Finding the campground: From Interstate 5 in Vancouver, take exit 1 and head east on Washington Highway 14 for 47 miles to the town of Carson. Turn left (north) onto Wind River Road and drive 12 miles to the campground.

About the campground: This campground is remote yet easy to reach. It is shady, comfortable, cool, and right beside the Wind River. It is open from mid-April to late September. For a fee, you can make reservations by calling the National Recreation Reservation Service (see contact information on page 236).

6 Cat Creek

Location: 119 miles southeast of Olympia on the Cispus River, near Randle.
Sites: 5 sites for tents or self-contained RVs no longer than 16 feet.
Facilities: Picnic tables, fire grills, pit toilets, firewood; no drinking water.
Fee per night: $.

Elevation: 3,000 feet.
Management: Gifford Pinchot National Forest, Randle Ranger District.
Activities: Fishing, hiking.
Finding the campground: From Interstate 5, 45 miles south of Olympia, take exit 68 and head east on U.S. Highway 12 for 48 miles to the town of Randle. Turn right (south) onto Washington Highway 131, drive 1 mile, turn left (southeast) onto Forest Road 23 (Cispus Road), and drive 18 miles. Take the left fork and go east for 7 miles on Forest Road 21 to the campground.

About the campground: Located in Gifford Pinchot National Forest, this camp is only 12 miles from Mount Adams, and Mount St. Helens is to the west behind Blue Lake Ridge. The small, primitive campground is at the confluence of Cat Creek and the Cispus River. It is open from mid-May to late October.

7 Cold Creek

Location: About 25 miles northeast of Vancouver on Cold Creek.
Sites: 6 sites for tents or self-contained RVs.
Facilities: Drinking water, picnic tables, fire grills, tent pads, vault toilets, horse-loading ramp.
Fee per night: None.
Elevation: 640 feet.
Management: Washington Department of Natural Resources, Southwest Region.
Activities: Hiking, fishing, mountain biking.
Finding the campground: From Interstate 5, 5 miles north of Vancouver, take exit 9 and drive east on Northeast 179th Street for 5.5 miles. Turn right (south) onto Washington Highway 503 and drive 1.5 miles. Turn left (east) onto Northeast 159th Street and drive 2.5 miles. At a Y junction, bear left onto Rawson Road. At 2 miles, the pavement ends and the road becomes the L-1400 Road. Continue on it for 4 more miles, turn left onto L-1000 Road, and drive for 3.2 miles. Turn left onto L-1300 Road and go 0.8 mile to the campground.

About the campground: Situated in the Green Mountain State Forest, this basic DNR campground is wooded and not heavily used. Hiking and mountain biking are the main attractions, and there are plenty of hills to climb. The campground is open year-round.

8 Corral Pass

Location: 37 miles southeast of Enumclaw.
Sites: 20 tent sites.
Facilities: Picnic tables, fire grills, vault toilets, firewood, horse-loading ramp; no drinking water.
Fee per night: None.
Elevation: 5,700 feet.
Management: Mount Baker-Snoqualmie National Forest, White River Ranger District.

Activities: Hiking, horse packing.

Finding the campground: From Enumclaw, just east of Tacoma, drive 31 miles southeast on Washington Highway 410, turn left (east) onto Forest Road 7174, and drive 6 miles to the campground. The last 6 miles are on a winding dirt road that may be difficult for trailers and big RVs to negotiate.

About the campground: This 15-acre camp is both high and remote. It is near the western boundary of the Norse Peak Wilderness. The campground is quite rustic, but it is well suited as a base camp for explorations on foot or hoof. Trails head north and east from camp, which is open from July to late September.

9 Council Lake

Location: 126 miles southeast of Olympia on Council Lake, near Randle.
Sites: 9 sites for tents or self-contained RVs no longer than 16 feet.
Facilities: Picnic tables, pit toilets; no drinking water.
Fee per night: $.
Elevation: 4,300 feet.
Management: Gifford Pinchot National Forest, Randle Ranger District.
Activities: Hiking, fishing, swimming, boating.
Finding the campground: From Interstate 5, 45 miles south of Olympia, take exit 68 and head east on U.S. Highway 12. Drive 48 miles to the town of Randle and take Washington Highway 131 south. In 1 mile, turn southeast onto Forest Road 23 (Cispus Road) and drive 31 miles. Take the right fork, going west on FR 2334, and drive 1 mile to the campground.

About the campground: This campground is so close to Mount Adams that it is actually on the mountain's northern apron. It sits at the edge of Council Lake with easy access to hiking trails. It is a bit rustic, but comfortable. The campground is open from July to mid-September.

10 Cultus Creek

Location: 109 miles northeast of Vancouver on Cultus Creek, near the town of Trout Lake.
Sites: 43 sites for tents or self-contained RVs no longer than 32 feet.
Facilities: Drinking water, picnic tables, fire rings, vault toilets.
Fee per night: $ to $$$.
Elevation: 4,000 feet.
Management: Gifford Pinchot National Forest, Mount Adams Ranger District.
Activities: Hiking, berry picking, evening nature programs.
Finding the campground: From Interstate 5 in Vancouver, take exit 1 and head east on Washington Highway 14 for 66 miles. At Bingen, turn left (north) onto WA 141 and drive 25 miles to the town of Trout Lake. Continue through Trout Lake on WA 141 for 5.5 miles. The route becomes Forest Road 24 at the Skamania County line. Continue on FR 24 for 12.5 miles to the campground.

About the campground: This campground is located near both the Pacific Crest National Scenic Trail and the Indian Heaven Wilderness. The Big Lava Bed is a few miles to the south. This is high and dry country, so the forests are largely composed of pines. The campground is very pleasant and relaxing. Campground hosts are on site. The camp is open from June through September. For a fee, you can make reservations by calling the National Recreation Reservation Service (see contact information on page 236).

11 The Dalles

Location: 25 miles southeast of Enumclaw on Minnehaha Creek.
Sites: 19 tent sites, 26 sites for tents or self-contained RVs no longer than 21 feet.
Facilities: Drinking water, picnic tables, fire grills, vault toilets, firewood.
Fee per night: $ to $$.
Elevation: 2,400 feet.
Management: Mount Baker-Snoqualmie National Forest, White River Ranger District.
Activities: Hiking, fishing, hunting.
Finding the campground: From Enumclaw, just east of Tacoma, drive 25 miles southeast on Washington Highway 410 to the campground.

About the campground: This is a good-sized camp for being relatively primitive. Part of its appeal is the beauty of this valley along the White River and the stands of old-growth forest. The campground is nestled between Dalles and Huckleberry Ridges on the main entrance road to the east side of Mount Rainier National Park. The White River is just across the highway. The camp is open from mid-May to late September. For a fee, you can make reservations by calling the National Recreation Reservation Service (see contact information on page 236).

12 Dash Point State Park

Location: About 8 miles north of Tacoma on Puget Sound.
Sites: 110 tent sites, 28 sites with water and electrical hookups for RVs no longer than 35 feet.
Facilities: Drinking water, picnic tables, flush toilets, showers, dump station, playground.
Fee per night: $$ to $$$.
Elevation: Sea level.
Management: Washington State Parks and Recreation Commission.
Activities: Fishing, hiking, beachcombing, swimming, marine-life study.
Finding the campground: From Interstate 5 in Tacoma, take exit 136 and drive north for 2 blocks, passing Washington Highway 99 (Pacific Highway). Turn right onto WA 509 (East-West Road) and drive 8 miles to the park.

About the campground: Dash Point State Park straddles the line between King and Pierce Counties, which separates Tacoma from Federal Way. It covers 400 acres and has 3,300 feet of shoreline on Puget Sound's East Passage, plus 7.4

miles of hiking and mountain biking trails. The beach is a very popular place to walk and enjoy the views of Puget Sound. However, the water has been somewhat polluted by nearby industries, so clam digging is not recommended. This is basically an urban state park, and therefore very well used. The campground is open year-round. For a fee, you can make reservations by calling Reservations Northwest (see contact information on page 236).

13 Dougan Creek

Location: About 32 miles east of Washougal on Dougan Creek and the Washougal River.
Sites: 7 sites for tents or self-contained RVs.
Facilities: Drinking water, picnic tables, tent pads, fire grills, vault toilets.
Fee per night: None.
Elevation: 720 feet.
Management: Washington Department of Natural Resources, Southwest Region.
Activities: Hiking, fishing.
Finding the campground: From Interstate 5 in Vancouver, take exit 1 and head east on Washington Highway 14 for 16 miles to Washougal. Turn north onto Washougal River Road and follow it for 16.4 miles to the campground.

About the campground: This camp has a volunteer campground host on site. It is located at the confluence of Dougan Creek and the Washougal River. The campsites are nicely spaced within sight of the river. The campground is open from mid-May to mid-September.

14 Elbe Hills ORV Trailhead

Location: About 103 miles southeast of Olympia, near Elbe.
Sites: 3 primitive sites for tents or self-contained RVs.
Facilities: Picnic tables, tent pads, fire grills, pit toilets, group shelter; no drinking water.
Fee per night: None.
Elevation: 2,200 feet.
Management: Washington Department of Natural Resources, South Puget Sound Region.
Activities: Off-road driving.
Finding the campground: From Interstate 5, 45 miles south of Olympia, take exit 68 and drive 31 miles east on U.S. Highway 12 to the town of Morton. Then take Washington Highway 7 north for 17 miles to the town of Elbe. Turn right (east) at Elbe onto WA 706 and drive 6.3 miles. Turn left onto Stoner Road and drive for 3.1 miles. Keep right and continue 0.6 mile. Turn left for 0.1 mile to the campground.

About the campground: This camp is pretty basic, but its main purpose is to provide a base from which to access the 8 miles of trails maintained by the DNR for off-road-vehicle use. The campground is open year-round.

15 Evans Creek

Location: About 30 miles southeast of Tacoma on Evans Creek, near Buckley.
Sites: 27 tent sites.
Facilities: Drinking water, picnic tables, fire grills, vault toilets, firewood.
Fee per night: None.
Elevation: 3,400 feet.
Management: Mount Baker-Snoqualmie National Forest, White River Ranger District.
Activities: Hiking, fishing, off-road driving.
Finding the campground: From Interstate 5 in Tacoma, take exit 135 and drive east on Washington Highway 167 for 9 miles to Sumner. Then continue east for 12 miles on WA 410 to Buckley. From there, take WA 165 south for 19 miles. Take a left onto Forest Road 7920 and drive 1.5 miles to the campground.

About the campground: This is a 6-acre creekside campground in the Mount Baker-Snoqualmie National Forest. It is well into the foothills of Mount Rainier and offers plenty of opportunities for hiking and fishing. There are some trails for off-road driving nearby, so it is not entirely quiet. The campground is open from mid-June to late September.

16 Fall Creek

Location: About 20 miles southwest of Olympia on Fall Creek.
Sites: 8 primitive sites for tents or self-contained RVs.
Facilities: Picnic tables, tent pads, fire grills, vault toilets, horse-loading ramp; no drinking water.
Fee per night: None.
Elevation: 900 feet.
Management: Washington Department of Natural Resources, Central Region.
Activities: Hiking, horseback riding, mountain biking.
Finding the campground: From Interstate 5 just 1 mile south of Olympia, take exit 104 and drive northwest on U.S. Highway 101 for 4 miles. Turn south onto Delphi Road Southwest and drive for 6 miles, to the point where it becomes Waddell Creek Road Southwest. Continue for another 3 miles. At the intersection with Noschka Road, take C-line Road west for 3.3 miles. Turn south onto D-3000 Road and drive 2.4 miles. The site is on the right. Some of the road is unpaved.

About the campground: This is a nice, small, primitive campground on Fall Creek in the Black Hills southwest of Olympia. It is quieter than some of the other campgrounds in the vicinity because motorized vehicles are not allowed on the nearby trails. The campground is open from April through October.

17 Falls Creek-Crest Horse Camp

Location: 68 miles east of Vancouver.
Sites: 6 sites for tents or self-contained RVs no longer than 15 feet.
Facilities: Picnic tables, fire grills, pit toilets; no drinking water.
Fee per night: None.
Elevation: 2,300 feet.
Management: Gifford Pinchot National Forest, Mount Adams Ranger District.
Activities: Hiking, Horseback riding.
Finding the campground: From Interstate 5 in Vancouver, take exit 1 and head east on Washington Highway 14 for 47 miles to Carson. Turn left (north) onto the Wind River Road and drive 6 miles. Turn right onto Forest Road 65 (Panther Creek Road) and drive 15 miles to the campground.

About the campground: This camp for equestrians is close to the Pacific Crest National Scenic Trail and the Indian Heaven Wilderness in the Gifford Pinchot National Forest. The campground is open from mid-June to late September.

18 Goose Lake

Location: About 105 miles northeast of Vancouver on Goose Lake, near the town of Trout Lake.
Sites: 25 tent sites, 1 site for a tent or self-contained RV no longer than 18 feet.
Facilities: Picnic tables, fire rings, vault toilets; no drinking water.
Fee per night: $.
Elevation: 3,200 feet.
Management: Gifford Pinchot National Forest, Mount Adams Ranger District.
Activities: Hiking, fishing, swimming, berry picking.
Finding the campground: From Interstate 5 in Vancouver, take exit 1 and head east on Washington Highway 14 for 66 miles. At Bingen, turn north onto WA 141 and drive 25 miles to the town of Trout Lake. Continue through Trout Lake on WA 141 for 5.5 miles. WA 141 becomes Forest Road 24 at the Skamania County line. Continue on FR 24 even as it becomes FR 60 and drive west to Goose Lake. The distance from Trout Lake to Goose Lake is about 14 miles.

About the campground: This campground is set on the northern edge of the Big Lava Bed in Gifford Pinchot National Forest. It is a good, relaxed site at the edge of Goose Lake, and the fishing is fair. The campground is open from mid-June to late September. For a fee, you can make reservations by calling the National Recreation Reservation Service (see contact information on page 236).

19 Horseshoe Lake

Location: About 133 miles southeast of Olympia on Horseshoe Lake.
Sites: 10 sites for tents or self-contained RVs no longer than 16 feet.
Facilities: Picnic tables, pit toilets; no drinking water.
Fee per night: None.

Elevation: 4,200 feet.
Management: Gifford Pinchot National Forest, Randle Ranger District.
Activities: Hiking, fishing, boating (no gas motors), swimming, berry picking.
Finding the campground: From Interstate 5, 45 miles south of Olympia, take exit 68 and drive east on U.S. Highway 12 for 48 miles to the town of Randle. From there, take Washington Highway 131 south for 1 mile. Turn left (east) onto Forest Road 23 (Cispus Road) and drive 30 miles. At Takhlakh Lake, take a sharp left and head north on FR 2329. The road goes nearly all the way around Takhlakh Lake, but you should turn left (west) onto FR 78 after 7 miles. Drive 1.5 miles to the campground.

About the campground: This small, mid-altitude campground is very appealing, even though it is primitive. It sits right on the lakeshore, and trails from camp lead to nearby mountains, including Mount Adams. The campground is open from mid-June to late September.

20 Ike Kinswa State Park

Location: 64 miles southeast of Olympia on Mayfield Lake, near Mossyrock.
Sites: 2 primitive tent sites, 60 developed tent sites, 41 sites with full hookups for RVs no longer than 60 feet.
Facilities: Drinking water, picnic tables, fire grills, flush toilets, showers, dump station, store, cafe, playground, boat ramp.
Fee per night: $ to $$$.
Elevation: 1,300 feet.
Management: Washington State Parks and Recreation Commission.
Activities: Hiking, fishing, swimming, boating, waterskiing.
Finding the campground: From Interstate 5, 45 miles south of Olympia, take exit 68 and drive east on U.S. Highway 12 for 15 miles. Then turn left onto Washington Highway 122 and drive 4 miles to the campground.

About the campground: This campground offers 454 acres of fine scenery along Mayfield Lake and the Cowlitz and Tilton Rivers. In all, there are 8.7 miles of freshwater shoreline, including 400 feet of unguarded swimming beach. There are also 6 miles of hiking trails. Motorboat and ski traffic is heavy on Mayfield Lake, but the shore still attracts ospreys and eagles that nest in the Douglas-firs. The fishing is good, too. There are two fish hatcheries nearby. Paddlers can enjoy the quieter waters of the Tilton River, which flows through a gorge and features several small waterfalls. The campground is open year-round. For a fee, you can make reservations by calling Reservations Northwest (see contact information on page 236).

21 Iron Creek

Location: About 102 miles southeast of Olympia on the Cispus River, near Randle.
Sites: 98 sites for tents or self-contained RVs no longer than 42 feet.
Facilities: Drinking water, pit toilets.

Fee per night: $$ to $$$.
Elevation: 1,200 feet.
Management: Gifford Pinchot National Forest, Cowlitz Valley Ranger District.
Activities: Hiking, fishing.
Finding the campground: From Interstate 5, 45 miles south of Olympia, take exit 68 and head east on U.S. Highway 12 for 48 miles to the town of Randle. From there, go south on Washington Highway 131 (Woods Creek Road). In about a mile, it becomes Forest Road 25. Stay on FR 25 for 7.5 miles to the campground entrance on the left.

About the campground: This 32-acre campground is very popular because of its proximity to the east side of Mount St. Helens and its easy RV access. A Forest Service visitor center is nearby. The campground is open from mid-May to late October. For a fee, you can make reservations by calling the National Recreation Reservation Service (see contact information on page 236).

22 Kanaskat-Palmer State Park

Location: 36 miles east of Tacoma on the Green River, near Enumclaw.
Sites: 31 tent sites, 19 drive-through sites with electrical hookups for RVs no longer than 50 feet, 1 group site.
Facilities: Drinking water, picnic tables, flush toilets, coin-operated showers, dump station.
Fee per night: $$ to $$$.
Elevation: 885 feet.
Management: Washington State Parks and Recreation Commission.
Activities: Fishing, hiking, rafting, kayaking, nature study.
Finding the campground: From Interstate 5 in Tacoma, take exit 135 and drive east on Washington Highway 167 for 9 miles to Sumner. From there, take WA 410 east for 16 miles to Enumclaw. Turn north onto Farman Road and drive 11 miles to the park on the left.

About the campground: Located in the Green River Gorge Recreation Area, Kanaskat-Palmer covers nearly 300 acres and has 2.5 miles of river frontage. The Green River is known for its winter steelhead fishing (one of the state's top ten), as well as for summer rafting and kayaking. It also offers 3 miles of hiking trails. The campground has an on-site host. It is open year-round, with limited facilities in the winter. For reservations, call Reservations Northwest (see contact information on page 236).

23 Keene's Horse Camp

Location: About 132 miles southeast of Olympia on South Fork Spring Creek, near Randle.
Sites: 13 sites for tents or RVs no longer than 21 feet.
Facilities: Picnic tables, fire grills, pit toilets, horse corrals; no drinking water.
Fee per night: None.

Elevation: 4,200 feet.
Management: Gifford Pinchot National Forest, Randle Ranger District.
Activities: Hiking, horse packing.
Finding the campground: From Interstate 5, 45 miles south of Olympia, take exit 68 and head east on U.S. Highway 12 for 48 miles to Randle. From there, head south on Washington Highway 131 for 1 mile. Turn left (southeast) onto Forest Road 23 (Cispus Road) and drive 30 miles. At Takhlakh Lake, turn left onto FR 2329 and drive 8 miles. Then turn west onto FR 82 and drive 100 yards to the campground.

About the campground: Horse packers appreciate the accessibility of this campground in Gifford Pinchot National Forest. Trails lead right out of camp into the backcountry and high country. The Pacific Crest National Scenic Trail passes within a couple of miles of camp, which is located on South Fork Spring Creek on the northwest flank of Mount Adams. The campground is open from July to late September.

24 Killen Creek

Location: About 130 miles southeast of Olympia, near Randle.
Sites: 8 sites for tents or self-contained RVs no longer than 21 feet.
Facilities: Picnic tables, pit toilets; no drinking water.
Fee per night: None.
Elevation: 4,400 feet.
Management: Gifford Pinchot National Forest, Randle Ranger District.
Activities: Hiking, berry picking, horse packing.
Finding the campground: From Interstate 5, 45 miles south of Olympia, take exit 68 and head east on U.S. Highway 12 for 48 miles to Randle. From there, take Washington Highway 131 south for 1 mile. Turn left (southeast) onto Forest Road 23 (Cispus Road) and drive 30 miles. At Takhlakh Lake, take a sharp left and drive north on FR 2329 for 6 miles. The campground entrance is on the left.

About the campground: This very basic campground is a 3-mile hike from the Pacific Crest National Scenic Trail, which runs across the northwestern flank of Mount Adams. In fact, the campground sits practically on the border of the Mount Adams Wilderness. The campground is open from July to late September.

25 Lake Merrill

Location: About 34 miles northeast of Woodland on Merrill Lake.
Sites: 11 tent sites.
Facilities: Drinking water, picnic tables, tent pads, fire grills, vault toilets, boat ramp.
Fee per night: None.
Elevation: 1,640 feet.
Management: Washington Department of Natural Resources, Southwest Region.

Activities: Hiking, fishing, boating.
Finding the campground: From Interstate 5 in Woodland, take exit 21 and drive east on Washington Highway 503 for 23 miles. Turn left (north) onto Cougar Road (Forest Road 81) and go 5.5 miles to the campground on the left.

About the campground: The campground is pretty basic, but it is also usually pretty quiet. It sits in the woods on the shores of 2-mile-long Lake Merrill. The campground is open from May through September.

26 Lewis and Clark State Park

Location: About 13 miles southeast of Chehalis.
Sites: 25 sites for tents or self-contained RVs no longer than 60 feet, 2 group camps.
Facilities: Drinking water, picnic tables, fire grills, flush toilets, horseshoe pits, playground, corral/horseback riding area with stalls, loading ramps.
Fee per night: $$.
Elevation: 196 feet.
Management: Washington State Parks and Recreation Commission.
Activities: Hiking, fishing for children, nature program, wading, horseback riding.
Finding the campground: From Chehalis, drive 8 miles south on Interstate 5 and take exit 68. Drive east on U.S. Highway 12 for almost 3 miles and then turn right (south) onto Jackson Highway 99. The park is on your right in 1.5 miles.

About the campground: The Mount St. Helens crater is visible from this 620-acre park, which contains one of the last stands of lowland, old-growth forest in western Washington. A 1.5-mile interpretive trail and a 3.5-mile equestrian trail cut through the forest, and the park features a Mount St. Helens visitor center. A children's fishing pond is stocked with trout, and there is a natural wading pool. The park contains the first known home built by a white settler north of the Columbia River (in 1845), the John R. Jackson log cabin. The north spur of the Oregon Trail from the Cowlitz River Landing to Tumwater passed through the park. Cooling lava from Mount Rainier formed underground caverns here several thousand years ago. El Paso Natural Gas Company now uses these to store natural gas. The campground is open year-round, and there is an on-site host.

27 Margaret McKenny

Location: About 17 miles southwest of Olympia on Waddell Creek.
Sites: 25 primitive sites for tents or self-contained RV sites, 7 walk-in sites.
Facilities: Picnic tables, tent pads, pit toilets, campfire circle, horse-loading ramp; no drinking water.
Fee per night: None.
Elevation: 80 feet.
Management: Washington Department of Natural Resources, Central Region.
Activities: Hiking, horseback riding, mountain biking.

Finding the campground: From Interstate 5, 10 miles south of Olympia, take exit 95 and head west on Washington Highway 121 for 3 miles to Littlerock. Continue west for 1 mile and turn right onto Waddell Creek Road Southwest. Drive 2.5 miles, turn left, and drive 0.2 mile to the campground.

About the campground: Close to the Mima Mounds Natural Area Preserve, this primitive, forested campground sits on the bank of Waddell Creek in Capitol State Forest. There are several inviting trails nearby. The campground is open from April through October.

28 Mayfield Lake County Park

Location: 25 miles southeast of Centralia on Mayfield Lake.
Sites: 54 sites for tents or self-contained RVs no longer than 40 feet.
Facilities: Drinking water, restrooms, showers, dump station.
Fee per night: $$.
Elevation: 215 feet.
Management: Mayfield Lake County Park.
Activities: Fishing, swimming, boating, waterskiing.
Finding the campground: From Interstate 5, 14 miles south of Centralia, take exit 68 and head east on U.S. Highway 12 for 11 miles to the campground.

About the campground: This lakeside campground, though slightly primitive, is popular. So reservations are recommended. The sites are wooded and cool, and access to the lake is easy. The campground is open from May to September. For reservations, call Mayfield Lake County Park (see contact information on page 235).

29 Middle Waddell

Location: About 17 miles southwest of Olympia on Waddell Creek.
Sites: 24 sites for tents or self-contained RVs.
Facilities: Picnic tables, fire grills, tent pads, vault toilets; no drinking water.
Fee per night: None.
Elevation: 75 feet.
Management: Washington Department of Natural Resources, Central Region.
Activities: Mountain biking, motorbiking.
Finding the campground: From Interstate 5, 10 miles south of Olympia, take exit 95 and drive west on Washington Highway 121 for 3 miles to Littlerock. Continue west for 1 mile and turn right onto Waddell Creek Road Southwest. Drive 3 miles, turn left, and drive 0.1 mile to the campground.

About the campground: If the noise of motorcycles does not bother you, or if you are a motorcycle enthusiast yourself, then this wooded campground in Capitol State Forest will suit you just fine. The campground is open from April through October.

30 Millersylvania State Park

Location: About 10 miles south of Olympia on Deep Lake.
Sites: 135 tent sites, 52 sites for RVs no longer than 45 feet, 4 primitive tent sites, 2 group sites (capacity 40, 20 people).
Facilities: Drinking water, picnic tables, fire grills, flush toilets, showers, playground, dump station, boat ramp, environmental learning center.
Fee per night: $ to $$.
Elevation: 210 feet.
Management: Washington State Parks and Recreation Commission.
Activities: Hiking, fishing, boating, swimming, mountain biking.
Finding the campground: From Interstate 5, 6 miles south of Olympia, take exit 99 and head east on 93rd Avenue for just over 1 mile to Tilley Road Southwest. Turn right onto Tilley Road Southwest and drive about 3 miles to the park entrance on the right.

About the campground: It is hard to believe that this 842-acre park, which features 3,300 feet of frontage on Deep Lake, was acquired for a total cost of $251. The state purchased it in five parcels, the first in 1921 and the last in 1952. It was once owned by John H. Miller, a former general in the Austrian army and a bodyguard of the Austrian emperor. The Miller family stipulated that the land should go to the state for use as a park upon the death of the last remaining family member. The park was developed by the Civilian Conservation Corps in the mid-1930s. This excellent park is big and uncrowded. It features old-growth forest crisscrossed by 6.6 miles of hiking trails, including a fitness trail that is wheelchair-accessible. Some old buildings constructed by the CCC of logs and Tenino sandstone lend the park some real charm. Wildlife you may see here includes foxes, black-tailed deer, coyotes, red-tailed hawks, wood ducks, and porcupines. The raccoons can be clever in their pursuit of an easy meal, so seal your food containers and do not leave food lying around. The campground is open year-round. For reservations, call Reservations Northwest (see contact information on page 236).

31 Mima Falls Trailhead

Location: About 18 miles southwest of Olympia, near Littlerock.
Sites: 5 primitive sites for tents or self-contained RVs.
Facilities: Drinking water, picnic tables, fire grills, tent pads, pit toilets, horse-loading ramp.
Fee per night: None.
Elevation: 80 feet.
Management: Washington Department of Natural Resources, Central Region.
Activities: Hiking, horseback riding, mountain biking.
Finding the campground: From Olympia, drive south on Interstate 5 for 11 miles. Take exit 95 and drive west on Washington Highway 121 for 3 miles to Littlerock. Continue on WA 121 for 1 mile, turn left onto Gate Mima Road Southwest, and drive for 1.5 miles to Bordeaux Road Southwest. Turn right and drive for three-quarters of a mile to Marksman Street Southwest, where you turn right

and drive for two-thirds of a mile. Turn left and go about 200 yards to the campground.

About the campground: This is a very quiet and peaceful site. The Mima Mounds Natural Area Preserve is about a mile to the northwest, and the trail to it is excellent. The campground is open from April through October.

32 Moss Creek

Location: 58 miles east of Vancouver on the White Salmon River.
Sites: 18 sites for tents or self-contained RVs no longer than 32 feet.
Facilities: Drinking water, fire rings, picnic tables, pit toilets.
Fee per night: $.
Elevation: 1,400 feet.
Management: Gifford Pinchot National Forest, Mount Adams Ranger District.
Activities: Fishing.
Finding the campground: From Interstate 5 in Vancouver, take exit 1 and drive east on Washington Highway 14 for 50 miles to Cook. Turn left (north) onto Cook-Underwood Road (County Road 1800) and drive 8 miles to the campground. The name of the route changes to Willard Road and then Oklahoma Road along the way.

About the campground: This wooded 7-acre campground in Gifford Pinchot National Forest is rarely full. It sits nicely on the White Salmon River, not far from the Big Lava Bed, which can be reached via Forest Road 66. The campground is open from mid-May to late September. For a fee, you can make reservations by calling the National Recreation Reservation Service (see contact information on page 236).

33 Mount Rainier National Park: Cougar Rock

Location: About 115 miles southeast of Olympia in Mount Rainier National Park.
Sites: 200 sites for tents or self-contained RVs no longer than 30 feet.
Facilities: Drinking water, picnic tables, flush toilets, dump station.
Fee per night: $$.
Elevation: 3,180 feet.
Management: Mount Rainier National Park.
Activities: Recreation program, hiking, trout fishing.
Finding the campground: From Interstate 5, 45 miles south of Olympia, take exit 68 and head east on U.S. Highway 12 for 31 miles to Morton. Take Washington Highway 7 north for 17 miles to the town of Elbe. Turn east at Elbe onto WA 706 and drive 14 miles to the park's southwest entrance. The campground is about 8 miles inside the park. Part of the drive is on gravel road.

About the campground: This is a fine, rustic, mid-altitude campground, and it is easier to get to than most camps in the park. It is not far from the Paradise Visitor Center. It packs a lot of campsites onto 60 acres, but they are nicely laid out, and besides, the main appeal is to have a place to park your gear while you go hiking. The campground is open from mid-May to late October. For reservations, write or call Mount Rainier National Park (see contact information on page 235).

34 Mount Rainier National Park: Ohanapecosh

Location: 121 miles southeast of Olympia on the Ohanapecosh River in Mount Rainier National Park.
Sites: 205 sites for tents or self-contained RVs no longer than 30 feet.
Facilities: Drinking water, picnic tables, flush toilets, dump station, interpretive center.
Fee per night: $$.
Elevation: 1,914 feet.
Management: Mount Rainier National Park.
Activities: Hiking.
Finding the campground: From Interstate 5, 45 miles south of Olympia, take exit 68 and drive east on U.S. Highway 12 for 72 miles to Washington Highway 123. Turn left (north) onto WA 123 and drive 4 miles to the campground's entrance. The park's through road begins 1 mile farther north.

About the campground: Hiking is the main appeal of Ohanapecosh, with arguably the best day hikes in the state right outside the tent flap or RV door. You

More than 14,000 feet high, Mount Rainier is covered by a permanent snowpack.

can walk among 1,000-year-old western redcedars and Douglas-firs, over a thundering gorge, and to the base of a giant waterfall. The campground itself is huge and is one of the best in Washington despite its size. The shady sites are spaced to give campers plenty of room. The river is relatively noisy, so you may not want to camp right next to it. The campground is open from mid-May to mid-October. Reservations are required from July through Labor Day and can be made by calling the National Park Reservation Service (see contact information on page 236).

35 Mount Rainier National Park: Sunshine Point

Location: About 104 miles southeast of Olympia in Mount Rainier National Park.
Sites: 18 sites for tents or self-contained RVs no longer than 25 feet.
Facilities: Drinking water, picnic tables, pit toilets.
Fee per night: $$.
Elevation: 2,230 feet.
Management: Mount Rainier National Park.
Activities: Hiking, backpacking, campfire and evening interpretive programs, interpretive walks, fishing, horseback riding.
Finding the campground: From Interstate 5, 45 miles south of Olympia, take exit 68 and head east on U.S. Highway 12 for 30 miles. At Morton, turn north onto Washington Highway 7 and drive 17 miles to Elbe. From there, turn east onto WA 706 and drive 12 miles to the park's southwest entrance. The campground is a quarter-mile beyond the entrance.

About the campground: This campground is near the Nisqually entrance to Mount Rainier National Park. It is the only campground in the park that is open year-round. The park encompasses 378 square miles. The hiking trails are generally accessible beginning in mid- to late June or early July, depending on snow depths. Saddle and pack stock are permitted on more than 100 miles of trails. However, bicycles are not permitted on any park trails, and the park roads are uncomfortably narrow for bicycling. All locations and facilities in Mount Rainier National Park are open from July 1 through Labor Day. Most locations are accessible from Memorial Day to July and from Labor Day into October. From November or December through May, snow limits vehicle access to the 18-mile stretch of road between the Nisqually entrance and Paradise.

36 Mount Rainier National Park: White River

Location: 48 miles southeast of Enumclaw on the White River in Mount Rainier National Park.
Sites: 112 sites for tents or self-contained RVs no longer than 20 feet.
Facilities: Drinking water, picnic tables, fire grills, flush toilets, dump station.
Fee per night: $.
Elevation: 4,400 feet.
Management: Mount Rainier National Park.

Activities: Hiking, backpacking, campfire and evening interpretive programs, interpretive walks, fishing, horseback riding.
Finding the campground: From Enumclaw, take Washington Highway 410 east for 43 miles to the park's northeast entrance. The campground is 5 miles beyond the entrance.

About the campground: This campground is in a beautiful setting on the White River. It is large and comfortable, with reasonable privacy from other sites. But it is often crowded with climbers and backpackers, because the campground is a trailhead for the backcountry. No bicycles are allowed on park trails, and the park roads are uncomfortably narrow for bicycling. The campground is open from mid-June to mid-September.

37 Mount St. Helens National Volcanic Monument: Lower Falls Recreation Area

Location: 53 miles east of Woodland on the Lewis River in Mount St. Helens National Volcanic Monument.
Sites: 43 sites for tents or self-contained RVs no longer than 70 feet.
Facilities: Drinking water, composting toilets.
Fee per night: $ to $$.
Elevation: 1,300 feet.
Management: Mount St. Helens National Volcanic Monument.
Activities: Hiking, horseback riding.
Finding the campground: From Interstate 5 in Woodland, take exit 21 and drive east on Washington Highway 503 for 32 miles. WA 503 becomes Forest Road 90 at the Skamania County line. Continue east on FR 90 for 21 miles to the campground.

About the campground: This campground is nestled in tall firs on the Lewis River in the Gifford Pinchot National Forest. It is close to three very beautiful waterfalls. They are accessible via the Lewis River Trail, which includes a wheelchair loop. The area is sometimes incorrectly referred to as Lower Lewis River Falls Recreation Area. Several other trails pass nearby as they crisscross the east flank of Mount St. Helens. The campground is open from May through September.

38 North Creek

Location: About 43 miles southwest of Olympia on Cedar Creek.
Sites: 5 primitive sites for tents or self-contained RVs.
Facilities: Drinking water, picnic tables, fire grills, tent pads, vault toilets.
Fee per night: None.
Elevation: 370 feet.
Management: Washington Department of Natural Resources, Central Region.
Activities: Hiking, mountain biking.
Finding the campground: From Interstate 5, 25 miles south of Olympia, take

exit 88 and drive west on U.S. Highway 12 for 12 miles to Oakville. Continue for another 2.5 miles west on US 12 to Cedar Creek Road (D-Line Road). Turn right (east) and drive for 3.9 miles. The campground is on the right.

About the campground: This small, rustic DNR campground sits at the confluence of Cedar and North Creeks, well shaded by the forest canopy. There are plenty of trails for hiking and mountain biking. The campground is open from April through October.

39 North Fork

Location: 105 miles southeast of Olympia on the Cispus River.
Sites: 33 sites for tents or self-contained RVs no longer than 31 feet.
Facilities: Drinking water, picnic tables, vault toilets.
Fee per night: $ to $$$.
Elevation: 1,500 feet.
Management: Gifford Pinchot National Forest, Cowlitz Valley Ranger District.
Activities: Hiking, fishing, mountain biking.
Finding the campground: From Interstate 5, 45 miles south of Olympia, take exit 68 and head east on U.S. Highway 12 for 48 miles to Randle. From there, take Washington Highway 131 south for 1 mile. Turn left (southeast) onto Forest Road 23 (Cispus Road) and drive 11 miles to the campground.

About the campground: The backcountry is easy to reach from this riverside campground in Gifford Pinchot National Forest. The campsites are reasonably spaced, and there is plenty to do given the hiking trails and bike paths. The fishing is rumored to be OK, too. The campground is open from mid-May to late September. For reservations, call the National Recreation Reservation Service (see contact information on page 236).

40 Oklahoma

Location: 64 miles east of Vancouver on the Little White Salmon River.
Sites: 23 sites for tents or self-contained RVs no longer than 22 feet.
Facilities: Drinking water, fire rings, picnic tables, pit toilets.
Fee per night: $.
Elevation: 1,700 feet.
Management: Gifford Pinchot National Forest, Mount Adams Ranger District.
Activities: Fishing.
Finding the campground: From Interstate 5 in Vancouver, take exit 1 and drive east on Washington Highway 14 for 50 miles to Cook. Turn left (north) onto Cook-Underwood Road (County Road 1800) and drive 14 miles to the campground. The name of the route changes to Willard Road and then Oklahoma Road along the way.

About the campground: This 12-acre campground on the upper reaches of the Little White Salmon River in Gifford Pinchot National Forest is a bit rustic, but its shady riverbank location makes up for a lot. The campground is open from mid-May to mid-October. For a fee, you can make reservations by calling the National Recreation Reservation Service (see contact information on page 236).

41 Olallie Lake

Location: About 126 miles southeast of Olympia on Olallie Lake.
Sites: 5 sites for tents or self-contained RVs no longer than 22 feet.
Facilities: Picnic tables, pit toilets; no drinking water.
Fee per night: $.
Elevation: 4,200 feet.
Management: Gifford Pinchot National Forest, Randle Ranger District.
Activities: Fishing, boating, swimming.
Finding the campground: From Interstate 5, 45 miles south of Olympia, take exit 68 and head east on U.S. Highway 12 for 48 miles to the town of Randle. From there, head south on Washington Highway 131. In 1 mile, turn left (southeast) onto Forest Road 23 (Cispus Road) and drive 30 miles. At Takhlakh Lake, take a sharp left and head north on FR 2329 for 1 mile. Then continue north on FR 5601 for a half-mile to the campground.

About the campground: This campground is especially quiet because gas-powered motors are prohibited on Olallie Lake. This is an alpine lake, fed by glacier streams from Mount Adams. The campground is rustic, but very nicely situated in Gifford Pinchot National Forest. It is open from July to late September.

42 Panther Creek

Location: About 58 miles east of Vancouver on Panther Creek, near Carson.
Sites: 33 sites for tents or self-contained RVs no longer than 25 feet.
Facilities: Drinking water, picnic tables, pit toilets.
Fee per night: $ to $$$.
Elevation: 1,000 feet.
Management: Gifford Pinchot National Forest, Wind River Ranger District.
Activities: Hiking, fishing, berry and mushroom picking.
Finding the campground: From Interstate 5 in Vancouver, take exit 1 and head east on Washington Highway 14 for 47 miles to Carson. Turn left (north) onto the Wind River Road and drive 9 miles. Then turn right onto Forest Road 6517. Drive 1.5 miles to FR 65 (Panther Creek Road) and turn left (north) to the campground just ahead.

About the campground: Just a hair's breadth away from the Pacific Crest National Scenic Trail, this campground in Gifford Pinchot National Forest is a nice fishing camp on Panther Creek. The campground is open from mid-May to mid-October. For a fee, you can make reservations by calling the National Recreation Reservation Service (see contact information on page 236).

43 Paradise Creek

Location: 67 miles east of Vancouver on the Wind River.
Sites: 42 sites for tents or self-contained RVs no longer than 25 feet.
Facilities: Drinking water, picnic tables, fire grills, vault toilets.
Fee per night: $ to $$$.
Elevation: 1,500 feet.
Management: Gifford Pinchot National Forest, Wind River Ranger District.
Activities: Hiking, fishing.
Finding the campground: From Interstate 5 in Vancouver, take exit 1 and head east on Washington Highway 14 for 47 miles to Carson. Turn left (north) onto the Wind River Road and drive 20 miles to the camp.

About the campground: This campground is in the deep, thick woods of Gifford Pinchot National Forest, at the confluence of Paradise Creek and the Wind River. Several trails lead out of the campground, one of which climbs to the scenic Lava Butte. The campground is open from mid-May to mid-October. For a fee, you can make reservations by calling the National Recreation Reservation Service (see contact information on page 236).

44 Paradise Point State Park

Location: About 15 miles north of Vancouver on the East Fork Lewis River, near Woodland.
Sites: 70 sites for tents or self-contained RVs no longer than 45 feet, 9 primitive tent sites.
Facilities: Drinking water, fire grills, picnic tables, flush toilets, showers, dump station, primitive boat ramp.
Fee per night: $ to $$.
Elevation: 40 feet.
Management: Washington State Parks and Recreation Commission.
Activities: Hiking, fishing, boating.
Finding the campground: From Vancouver, drive 15 miles north on Interstate 5. Take the Paradise Point State Park exit and follow the signs to the campground. The park is adjacent to the freeway.

About the campground: This 88-acre campground has more than a mile of freshwater shoreline on the East Fork Lewis River. The fishing is good and the river access is easy. There are two hiking trails that pass through camp. This is mainly a layover for I-5 travelers, but it is a comfortable camp. It is open year-round. For a fee, you can make reservations by calling Reservations Northwest (see contact information on page 236).

45 Porter Creek

Location: 50 miles southwest of Olympia on Porter Creek.
Sites: 14 primitive sites for tents or self-contained RVs.
Facilities: Picnic tables, fire grills, tent pads, vault toilets, horse-loading ramps;

no drinking water.
Fee per night: None.
Elevation: 170 feet.
Management: Washington Department of Natural Resources, Central Region.
Activities: Hiking, horseback riding, trail biking, motorbiking.
Finding the campground: From Interstate 5, 25 miles south of Olympia, take exit 88 and head west on U.S. Highway 12 west for 21 miles to Porter. Turn right (northeast) onto Porter Creek Road and drive for 3.4 miles. At a 4-way intersection, continue straight on B-line Road for 0.6 mile to the campground on the left.

About the campground: Capitol State Forest is rife with trails, and several connect with this campground, which is within the state forest boundary. The camp is pretty rustic but shady and comfortable. It is on the bank of Porter Creek and is open from April through October.

46 Rainbow Falls State Park

Location: 17 miles west of Chehalis on the Chehalis River.
Sites: 47 sites for tents or self-contained RVs no longer than 32 feet, 3 primitive tent sites, 1 group site (capacity 17 people).
Facilities: Drinking water, picnic tables, flush toilets, showers, dump station, playground, recreation field.
Fee per night: $ to $$.
Elevation: 290 feet.
Management: Washington State Parks and Recreation Commission.
Activities: Hiking, fishing, swimming, kayaking.
Finding the campground: From Interstate 5 in Chehalis, take exit 77 and drive 17 miles west on Washington Highway 6 to the park entrance.

About the campground: This 850-acre state park has 3,400 feet of shoreline on the Chehalis River. There are plenty of hiking trails, some through old-growth forest, and the pool beneath the falls is a delight for both swimmers and anglers. Bear, elk, deer, and grouse live in the surrounding area. The campground is open from April through August.

47 Rock Creek

Location: About 24 miles northeast of Vancouver on Rock Creek.
Sites: 19 sites for tents or self-contained RVs.
Facilities: Drinking water, picnic tables, fire grills, tent pads, vault toilets, horse-loading ramp.
Fee per night: None.
Elevation: 1,050 feet.
Management: Washington Department of Natural Resources, Southwest Region.
Activities: Hiking, fishing, horseback riding.
Finding the campground: From Interstate 5, 5 miles north of Vancouver, take

exit 9 and drive east on Northeast 179th Street for 5.5 miles. Turn right onto Washington Highway 503 and drive 1.5 miles. Turn left onto Northeast 159th Street. Drive 2.5 miles and then, at a Y junction, take the left turn onto Rawson Road. After 2 miles, the pavement ends and the route becomes the L-1400 Road. Continue on it for another 4 miles, turn left onto L-1000 Road, and drive for 3.7 miles. Turn left onto L-1200 Road and go 0.2 mile to the camp entrance on the right.

About the campground: Situated in the Yacolt Burn State Forest, this basic DNR campground is wooded and not heavily used. Hiking and trail riding are the main activities, and there are plenty of hills to climb. There is a campground host on site. The campground is open year-round.

48 Saddle

Location: About 115 miles northeast of Vancouver near the Mosquito Lakes.
Sites: 12 tent sites.
Facilities: Picnic tables, fire rings, pit toilets; no drinking water.
Fee per night: None.
Elevation: 4,200 feet.
Management: Gifford Pinchot National Forest, Mount Adams Ranger District.
Activities: Hiking, fishing, huckleberry picking.
Finding the campground: From Interstate 5 in Vancouver, take exit 1 and head east on Washington Highway 14 for 66 miles. At Bingen, turn north onto Washington Highway 141 and drive 25 miles to the town of Trout Lake. Continue through town on WA 141 for 5.5 miles. The route becomes Forest Road 24 at the Skamania County line. Continue on FR 24 for 18 miles to the campground.

About the campground: This primitive campground is way out there in Gifford Pinchot National Forest, but it is worth the drive. It is on the Pacific Crest National Scenic Trail. Forest roads in this area are good, and the scenery is magnificent. The region is dotted with lakes. Mosquitoes are a problem though— Mosquito Creek feeds nearby Big Mosquito Lake. The campground is open from mid-June to late September.

49 Saltwater State Park

Location: 19 miles south of downtown Seattle on East Passage, near Des Moines.
Sites: 52 sites for tents or self-contained RVs no longer than 50 feet.
Facilities: Drinking water, picnic tables, fire grills, flush toilets, dump station, showers, playground, firewood, scuba rinse station, 3 buoys.
Fee per night: $$.
Elevation: Sea level.
Management: Washington State Parks and Recreation Commission.
Activities: Hiking, scuba diving, clam digging.
Finding the campground: From Interstate 5, 15 miles south of downtown Seattle, take exit 149 and head west on Washington Highway 516 for 2 miles.

Turn south onto WA 509 (Marine View Drive) and go 2 more miles to the park at 8th Place South.

About the campground: Because of the unusual underwater park, which features a sunken barge and a tire reef, this campground is a favorite of scuba divers. On shore, the park covers 90 acres, including a quarter mile of shoreline and 150 feet of unguarded beach. There are 2 miles of hiking trails, with some good views of the Olympic Mountains and the islands in Puget Sound. The original park facilities were built by the Civilian Conservation Corps in the 1930s, and later McSorely Creekbed was actually moved north to enlarge the parking area and extend the beach. The campground is open from late March through early September.

50 Seaquest State Park

Location: 62 miles south of Olympia, near Silver Lake.
Sites: 76 standard campsites, 16 sites (with full hookups) for RVs no longer than 50 feet, 8 primitive walk-in sites, 1 group site with 3 Adirondack shelters (capacity 50 people).
Facilities: Drinking water, picnic tables, flush toilets, showers, playground, horseshoe pits, ball field, dump station.
Fee per night: $ to $$$.
Elevation: 485 feet.
Management: Washington State Parks and Recreation Commission.
Activities: Hiking, horseshoes, fishing.
Finding the campground: From Interstate 5 in Castle Rock, 57 miles south of Olympia, take exit 49 and head east on Washington Highway 504 for 5 miles to the park.

About the campground: Seaquest State Park, which is nowhere near the sea, encompasses 475 acres, including more than a mile of shoreline on freshwater Silver Lake and 116 acres of wetland. The Mount St. Helens National Volcanic Monument Interpretive Center is located across WA 504 from the entrance to Seaquest. The state park is lovely and offers all the amenities, including 8 miles of hiking trails. It is used mostly as a base camp for people visiting Mount St. Helens. Area wildlife includes marmots, pikas, red-tailed hawks, Steller's jays, whiskey jacks, black-tailed deer, and sometimes a black bear. Trout, salmon, and spiny-ray fish await anglers. The campground, which is just across the highway from Silver Lake, is open year-round. For reservations, call Reservations Northwest (see contact information on page 236).

51 Sherman Valley

Location: About 46 miles southwest of Olympia on Cedar Creek.
Sites: 5 primitive sites for tents or self-contained RVs, 3 walk-in sites.
Facilities: Drinking water, picnic tables, fire grills, tent pads, vault toilets.
Fee per night: None.

Elevation: 370 feet.
Management: Washington Department of Natural Resources, Central Region.
Activities: Hiking, mountain biking.
Finding the campground: From Interstate 5, 25 miles south of Olympia, take exit 88 and head west on U.S. Highway 12 for 12 miles to Oakville. Then go another 2.5 miles west on US 12 to Cedar Creek Road (D-Line Road). Turn right (east) and continue for 1.6 miles. Then take the fork on the right. Continue 4.5 miles to the campground on the right.

About the campground: This rustic campground along Porter Creek in Capitol State Forest is mainly a hiking and mountain biking destination. Horses are not permitted on the trails. The campground is very peaceful, shady, and small. It is open from April through October.

52 Silver Springs

Location: 32 miles southeast of Enumclaw on the White River.
Sites: 16 tent sites, 40 sites for tents or self-contained RVs no longer than 21 feet.
Facilities: Drinking water, picnic tables, fire grills, vault toilets, firewood, grocery store.
Fee per night: $ to $$.
Elevation: 2,600 feet.
Management: Mount Baker-Snoqualmie National Forest, White River Ranger District.
Activities: Hiking, fishing.
Finding the campground: From Enumclaw, east of Tacoma, head southeast on Washington Highway 410 and drive 32 miles to the campground.

About the campground: This 25-acre campground in old-growth forest is on the White River just a few miles north of Mount Rainier National Park. It is on the east side of the Sourdough Mountains, just a bit over 5 miles from the park's northeast entrance to Sunrise. A good trail leads from camp to Crystal Mountain, a popular ski area, and to the Pacific Crest National Scenic Trail. The campground is open from mid-May to late September. For a fee, you can make reservations by calling the National Recreation Reservation Service (see contact information on page 236).

53 Smokey Creek

Location: About 104 miles northeast of Vancouver on Smokey Creek.
Sites: 3 sites for tents or self-contained RVs no longer than 22 feet.
Facilities: Picnic tables, pit toilets; no drinking water.
Fee per night: None
Elevation: 3,700 feet.
Management: Gifford Pinchot National Forest, Mount Adams Ranger District.
Activities: Hiking, berry picking.
Finding the campground: From Interstate 5 in Vancouver, take exit 1 and head

east on Washington Highway 14 for 66 miles to Bingen. Turn left (north) onto Washington Highway 141 and drive 25 miles to the town of Trout Lake. Continue through town on WA 141 for 5.5 miles to the Skamania County line, where the route becomes Forest Road 24. Continue on FR 24 for 7 miles to the campground.

About the campground: This campground is near the Indian Heaven Wilderness in Gifford Pinchot National Forest. It is really small, and since it is not used much, you will probably have it all to yourself. Hiking trails in the area are good, and the campground is next to Smokey Creek. It is open from June to late September.

54 Soda Springs

Location: About 127 miles southeast of Olympia on Summit Creek.
Sites: 6 primitive tent sites.
Facilities: Picnic tables, vault toilets; no drinking water.
Fee per night: None.
Elevation: 3,200 feet.
Management: Gifford Pinchot National Forest, Packwood Ranger District.
Activities: Hiking.
Finding the campground: From Interstate 5, 45 miles south of Olympia, take exit 68 and head east on U.S. Highway 12. Drive 75 miles and turn left (north) onto Forest Road 45 (10 miles past Packwood). In a bit less than half a mile, FR 4510 takes off to the left (north). Take it, and continue for 7 miles to the campground at the end of the road.

About the campground: Soda Springs is used mainly as a base camp for backpacking and hiking into the William O. Douglas Wilderness. Horses are not allowed in the wilderness area. The camp is primitive, but it sits alongside Summit Creek in Gifford Pinchot National Forest. It is open from mid-June to early September.

55 Summit Creek

Location: About 123 miles southeast of Olympia on Summit Creek.
Sites: 6 primitive sites for tents or self-contained RVs.
Facilities: Picnic tables, pit toilets; no drinking water.
Fee per night: None.
Elevation: 2,400 feet.
Management: Gifford Pinchot National Forest, Packwood Ranger District.
Activities: Hiking.
Finding the campground: From Interstate 5, 45 miles south of Olympia, take exit 68 and head east on U.S. Highway 12. Drive 75 miles and turn left (north) onto Forest Road 45 (10 miles past Packwood). In a bit less than half a mile, FR 4510 takes off to the left (north). Take it, and continue for 3 miles to the campground.

About the campground: This campground is attractive and rustic at the same time. It sits next to Summit Creek in Gifford Pinchot National Forest and is used mainly as a base camp for hikers and backpackers. The campground is open from mid-June to early September.

56 Sunset

Location: About 32 miles northeast of Vancouver on the East Fork Lewis River.
Sites: 10 sites for tents or self-contained RVs no longer than 22 feet, 6 walk-in sites.
Facilities: Drinking water, picnic tables, pit toilets.
Fee per night: $.
Elevation: 1,000 feet.
Management: Gifford Pinchot National Forest, Mount St. Helens National Volcanic Monument.
Activities: Hiking, fishing, huckleberry picking.
Finding the campground: From Interstate 5, 5 miles north of Vancouver, take exit 9 and drive north and then east on Washington Highway 502 for 8 miles to the town of Battle Ground. Turn left (north) onto WA 503 and drive for 5.2 miles. Then turn right (east) onto Lucia Falls Road. Follow it as it goes south for 1 mile and east for 6 miles to Moulton. At Moulton, turn right (southeast) onto County Road 12 and follow it for 7 miles to the campground.

About the campground: The campground is worth the drive. It is just inside the western boundary of Gifford Pinchot National Forest, right beside the East Fork Lewis River. Jack Mountain is 1 mile to the north, and the drainage rivers and creeks east of the campground offer some good hikes and fishing. The campground is open year-round.

57 Takhlakh

Location: 126 miles southeast of Olympia on Takhlakh Lake.
Sites: 54 sites for tents or self-contained RVs no longer than 21 feet.
Facilities: Drinking water, picnic tables, vault toilets, boat ramp.
Fee per night: $.
Elevation: 4,500 feet.
Management: Gifford Pinchot National Forest, Randle Ranger District.
Activities: Hiking, canoeing, fishing, berry picking.
Finding the campground: From Interstate 5, 45 miles south of Olympia, take exit 68 and head east on U.S. Highway 12. Drive 48 miles to the town of Randle and take Washington Highway 131 south. In 1 mile, turn left (southeast) onto Forest Road 23 (Cispus Road) and drive for 30 miles. Turn left (northeast) onto FR 2329 and drive 2 miles to the campground.

About the campground: This shoreside campground in Gifford Pinchot National Forest is well designed, pleasant, and quiet due to a prohibition on boats with gas motors. There are great views of Mount Adams. The campground is open from mid-June to late September. For reservations, call the Randle Ranger District (see contact information on page 235).

58 Tinkham

Location: About 44 miles southeast of Seattle on the Snoqualmie River.
Sites: 48 sites for tents or self-contained RVs no longer than 21 feet.
Facilities: Drinking water, picnic tables, vault toilets, firewood.
Fee per night: $$.
Elevation: 1,300 feet.
Management: Mount Baker-Snoqualmie National Forest, North Bend Ranger District.
Activities: Hiking, fishing.
Finding the campground: From Interstate 5 in Seattle, head east on Interstate 90 and drive 42 miles. Take exit 42. Turn right onto Forest Road 55 and drive 1.5 miles southeast to the campground.

About the campground: This riverside campground is pleasant enough, except it sits close to the interstate highway. The hiking is terrific though. The very popular Alpine Lakes Wilderness starts just north of the highway. The campground is open from mid-May to mid-September. For a fee, you can make reservations by calling the National Recreation Reservation Service (see contact information on page 236).

59 Tower Rock

Location: 104 miles southeast of Olympia on the Cispus River.
Sites: 22 sites for tents or self-contained RVs no longer than 22 feet.
Facilities: Drinking water, picnic tables, vault toilets.
Fee per night: $.
Elevation: 1,100 feet.
Management: Gifford Pinchot National Forest, Randle Ranger District.
Activities: Fishing.
Finding the campground: From Interstate 5, 45 miles south of Olympia, take exit 68 and head east on U.S. Highway 12. Drive 48 miles to the town of Randle and take Washington Highway 131 south. In 1 mile, turn (left) southeast onto Forest Road 23 (Cispus Road) and drive for 6.5 miles. Turn right (south) onto FR 28 and drive 1.5 miles to FR 76. Turn left (west) and drive 2 miles to the campground.

About the campground: This is a good-sized campground on the Cispus River, with more room than most. Fishing is the primary activity here. The campground is open from mid-May to late September.

60 Walupt Horse Camp

Location: About 128 miles southeast of Olympia, near Walupt Lake.
Sites: 6 sites for tents or self-contained RVs no longer than 18 feet.
Facilities: Drinking water, picnic tables, vault toilets.
Fee per night: $.
Elevation: 3,930 feet.
Management: Gifford Pinchot National Forest, Packwood Ranger District.
Activities: Fishing, horse packing, hiking.
Finding the campground: From Interstate 5, 45 miles south of Olympia, take exit 68 and head east on U.S. Highway 12. Drive 62.5 miles to Forest Road 21, which you reach 2.5 miles before you get to Packwood. Turn right (southeast) onto FR 21 and drive 16.5 miles. Then turn left (east) onto FR 2160 and drive 3.5 miles to the campground. For about the last 20 miles, the road is gravel.

About the campground: This camp is very popular with equestrians because of the close proximity of trails that lead into the nearby Goat Rocks Wilderness. There are 85 miles of pack trails. The campground, located in Gifford Pinchot National Forest, is open from June through September. Reservations are required and can be made, for a fee, by calling the National Recreation Reservation Service (see contact information on page 236).

61 Walupt Lake

Location: 128 miles southeast of Olympia on Walupt Lake.
Sites: 8 tent sites, 36 sites for tents or self-contained RVs no longer than 22 feet.
Facilities: Drinking water, picnic tables, vault toilets, boat ramp.
Fee per night: $ to $$$.
Elevation: 3,900 feet.
Management: Gifford Pinchot National Forest, Packwood Ranger District.
Activities: Hiking, fishing, swimming, canoeing, boating (trolling motors only).
Finding the campground: From Interstate 5, 45 miles south of Olympia, take exit 68 and head east on U.S. Highway 12. Drive 62.5 miles to Forest Road 21, which you reach 2.5 miles before you get to Packwood. Turn right (southeast) onto FR 21 and drive 16.5 miles. Then turn left (east) onto FR 2160 and drive 4 miles to the campground. About the last 20 miles is on gravel road.

About the campground: Walupt Lake may seem tough to reach, but it is well worth it. The campground is on the lakeshore, and access to the water is easy. Lots of hikers stay here because of the nearby trails. One trail begins in the campground and leads to the Goat Rocks Wilderness. The campground is open from mid-June to early September. For a fee, you can make reservations by calling the National Recreation Reservation Service (see contact information on page 236).

62 Woodland

Location: About 24 miles north of Vancouver, just outside Woodland.
Sites: 10 sites for tents or self-contained RVs.
Facilities: Drinking water, picnic tables, fire grills, tent pads, vault toilets, firewood, playground.
Fee per night: None.
Elevation: 160 feet.
Management: Washington Department of Natural Resources, Southwest Region.
Activities: Children's play.
Finding the campground: From Interstate 5 in Woodland, take exit 21 and drive east on Washington Highway 503 for 1 block. Turn right onto East CC Street and cross the bridge over the Lewis River. Just south of the bridge, turn right onto County Road 1 and drive 0.3 mile. Turn left onto CR 38 and drive 2.5 miles to the campground on the left.

About the campground: This is a cozy campground close to I-5, with a playground for the kids. There is not much to do here, but it is a good stopover for through travelers. The campground is open from May to September.

Eastern Region

The part of Washington east of Wenatchee is getting popular both for desert camping and lake sports between Wenatchee and Spokane and for mountain sports up north in the Colville National Forest. Be sure to take your own camping and sports gear to eastern Washington. Amenities like bike shops, ski rentals, and outfitters are still few and far between.

The Columbia River winds through this region like a dropped bootlace, flowing in all directions of the compass. Because of all the hydroelectric dams, vast sections of the river are actually lakes.

Southeastern Washington, including the Palouse hills south of Spokane, actually comprises the northern end of the Great Basin. Its surface was formed by vast lava flows. No trees have grown in the region for several million years. The average annual rainfall is less than 12 inches, but it adds up quickly to form the mighty Columbia River, whose drainage basin blankets 260,000 square miles that range over 10 degrees of latitude. In the extreme southeast are the relatively modest Blue Mountains. The Columbia Plateau extends eastward across the southern two-thirds of the state from the volcanic Cascade Mountains to and beyond the border with Idaho. Indians of the plateau lived as hunters and gatherers for 10,000 years in this land of strong contrasts. Their encyclopedic knowledge of the different environments was their main survival tool.

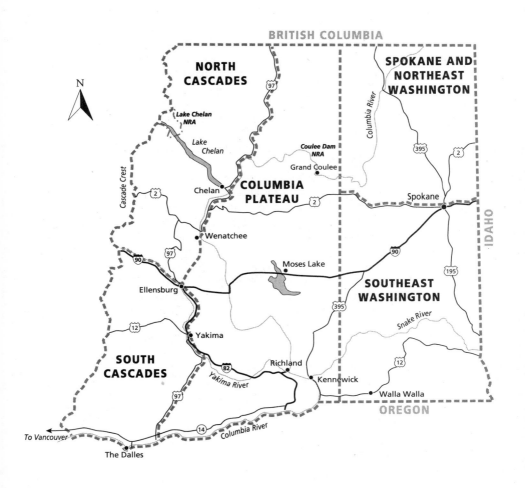

BRITISH COLUMBIA

NORTH CASCADES

SPOKANE AND NORTHEAST WASHINGTON

Lake Chelan NRA

Lake Chelan

Coulee Dam NRA

Grand Coulee

Columbia River

Chelan

COLUMBIA PLATEAU

Spokane

Wenatchee

Moses Lake

Ellensburg

SOUTHEAST WASHINGTON

Snake River

Yakima

SOUTH CASCADES

Richland

Yakima River

Kennewick

Walla Walla

OREGON

IDAHO

To Vancouver

The Dalles

Columbia River

Cascade Crest

N

LEGEND

Interstate Highway	90
U.S. Highway	2 101
State or County Road	20 522
River	

Peak	▲
National Park	⌐¬ _Mount Rainier National Park_
Campground, Camping Site	35
City, Town	● Seattle
Region Boundary	▬ ▬ ▬ ▬

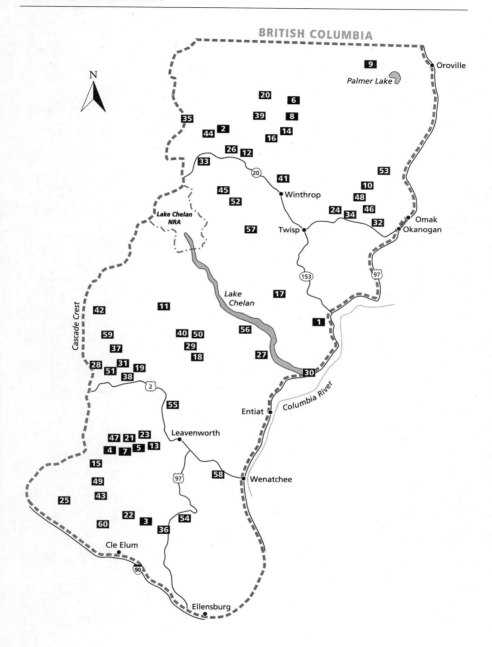

	Group sites	RV sites	Total # of sites	Max. RV length	Hookups	Toilets	Showers	Drinking water	Dump station	Pets	Wheelchair	Recreation	Fee	Season	Can reserve	Stay limit
1 Alta Lake State Park	•	•	189	45	W	F	•	•	•	•	•	HFSB	$–$$$			10
2 Ballard			7			V				•		HF		June–Sep or Oct		14
3 Beverly		•	16	21		P				•		HF		Jun–mid Nov		14
4 Blackpine Creek Horse Camp		•	14	21		V	•			•		HR	$	mid May–late Oct		14
5 Bridge Creek	•	•	7			V	•			•		HF	$	mid Apr–late Oct	•	14
6 Camp 4			5			V				•		HFR	$	June–late Sep		14
7 Chatter Creek	•	•	13	21		V	•			•		HF	$	May–late Oct	•	14
8 Chewuch			4			V				•		HFRC	$	June–late Sep		14
9 Chopaka Lake		•	16			V	•			•		HFBRC				14
10 Conconully State Park		•	81	60	W	F	•	•	•	•		HFBS	$–$$$			10
11 Cottonwood		•	25	21		P	•			•		HF	$	June–Sep		14
12 Early Winters		•	13	24		V	•			•		HFC	$	June–Sep or Oct		14
13 Eightmile	•	•	46	21		V	•			•		HF	$	mid Apr–late Oct	•	14
14 Falls Creek		•	7	18		V	•			•		HFSR	$	June–late Sep		14
15 Fish Lake			15			V				•		HFB		July–Oct		14
16 Flat		•	12	15		V				•		HF	$	June–late Sep		14
17 Foggy Dew		•	13			V				•		HFC	$	late May–early Sep		14
18 Fox Creek			16			V	•			•		HFC	$	May–mid Oct		14
19 Glacier View		•	20	16		P	•			•		HFBS	$	May–Sep		14
20 Honeymoon		•	6	22		V				•		HF	$	June–late Sep		14
21 Ida Creek		•	10	21		V	•			•		HF	$	May–Oct		14
22 Indian Camp		•	9			P				•		HF				7
23 Johnny Creek		•	65	30		V	•			•		HF	$	May–late Oct		14
24 J.R.		•	6	16		V	•			•		HFC	$	late May–early Sep	•	14
25 Kachess	•	•	184	32		P	•	•		•	•	HFSBC	$$	late May–mid Sep	•	14
26 Klipchuck		•	46	34		FV	•					HFC	$	June–late Sep		14
27 Lake Chelan State Park		•	144	30	WES	F	•	•	•	•	•	HFBS	$$–$$$	Apr–Oct	•	10
28 Lake Creek			8			P				•		HF		May–early Nov		14
29 Lake Creek II			18			V	•			•		HF	$	May–mid Oct		14
30 Lakeshore RV Park		•	160		WES	F	•	•		•		FBS	$$–$$$	Feb–Nov	•	
31 Lake Wenatchee State Park	•	•	197	60		F	•	•	•	•	•	HFBSCR	$–$$		•	10
32 Leader Lake		•	16			P				•		HF				7
33 Lone Fir		•	27	21		V	•			•		HF	$	June–late Sep		14
34 Loup Loup		•	25	21		V	•			•		HFC	$	May–Sep		14
35 Meadows			14			V				•		H	$	mid July–late Sep		14
36 Mineral Springs	•	•	13	21		V	•			•		HF	$	late May–early Sep		14
37 Napeequa Crossing		•	5	30		P				•		HF		mid May–late Oct		14

continued on following page

	Group sites	RV sites	Total # of sites	Max. RV length	Hookups	Toilets	Showers	Drinking water	Dump station	Pets	Wheelchair	Recreation	Fee	Season	Can reserve	Stay limit
38 Nason Creek		•	70	31		F	•			•		HFSB	$$	May–late Oct		14
39 Nice			4			V				•		HF	$	Jun–late Sep		14
40 North Fork	•	•	10			P	•			•		HF	$	mid May–late Sep		14
41 Pearrygin Lake State Park	•	•	85	60	WES	F	•	•	•	•		HFSB	$$–$$$	Apr–Oct	•	10
42 Phelps Creek			7			P				•		HFR		mid June–mid Oct		14
43 Red Mountain			15			P				•		HF	$	mid May–mid Nov		14
44 River Bend		•	5	16		V				•		HFR	$	June–late Sep		14
45 Roads End		•	4			V				•		HF	$	May–early Sep		14
46 Rock Creek		•	6			V	•			•		HF				7
47 Rock Island		•	22	21		V	•			•		HF	$	May–late Oct		14
48 Rock Lakes		•	8			V				•		HF				7
49 Salmon La Sac	•	•	126	21		F	•			•		HFR	$$	late May–late Sep	•	14
50 Silver Falls		•	30	21		V	•			•		HF	$	Mem Day–Sep		14
51 Soda Springs			5			P				•		HF		May–late Oct		14
52 South Creek		•	6	30		V				•		HFR	$	late May–early Sep		14
53 Sugarloaf		•	5	21		V				•		FB		mid May–mid Sep		14
54 Swauk		•	23	21		P				•		HF	$	mid Apr–late Sep		14
55 Tumwater	•	•	85	30		F	•			•		HF	$	May–mid Oct	•	14
56 Twenty-Five Mile Creek State Park	•	•	87	45	WES	F	•	•	•	•		HFSBC	$$–$$$	early Apr–late Oct	•	10
57 War Creek		•	11	21		V	•			•		HF	$	May–Sep		14
58 Wenatchee River County Park		•	79		WES	F	•	•	•	•		F	$$–$$$			
59 White River Falls			5			P				•		HF		June–mid Oct		14
60 Wish Poosh		•	39	21		F	•			•		HFSB	$$	mid May–mid Sep		14

Hookups: W = Water   E = Electric   S = Sewer
Toilets: F = Flush   V = Vault   P = Pit
Recreation: C = Bicycling/Mountain Biking   H = Hiking   S = Swimming   F = Fishing   B = Boating
O = Off-highway driving   R = Horseback Riding
Maximum Trailer/RV Length given in feet. **Stay Limit** given in days.
Fee $ = less than $10; $$ = $10-$15; $$$ = $16–20; $$$$ = more than $20.
If no entry under **Season,** campground is open all year. If no entry under **Fee,** camping is free.

1 Alta Lake State Park

Location: About 65 miles northeast of Wenatchee on Alta Lake, near Chelan.
Sites: 148 tent sites, 32 RV sites with water and electrical hookups, 9 group sites.
Facilities: Drinking water, picnic tables, fire grills, flush toilets, coin-operated showers, 2 boat ramps, bathhouse, boat dock, dump station.
Fee per night: $ to $$$.
Elevation: 1,150 feet.
Management: Washington State Parks and Recreation Commission.
Activities: Hiking, fishing, swimming, scuba diving, boating, waterskiing, bird watching, snowmobiling, cross-country skiing.
Finding the campground: From Washington Highway 285, 2 miles north of Wenatchee, head north on U.S. Highway 97 (or use US 97A—the two routes converge after following opposite banks of the Columbia River) for 58 miles to its junction with WA 153. Turn left (northwest) onto WA 153 and drive 2 miles to Alta Lake Road. Then turn left (southwest) and drive 2.5 miles to the park.

About the campground: This 180-acre state park lies in a pine forest at the eastern edge of the Okanogan National Forest. It offers most of the usual amenities as well as 300 feet of beach and a 0.6-mile hiking trail. There is even a golf course nearby. The campground is open year-round.

2 Ballard

Location: 22 miles northwest of Winthrop near the Methow River.
Sites: 7 tent sites.
Facilities: Picnic tables, fire grills, vault toilets; no drinking water.
Fee per night: None.
Elevation: 2,600 feet.
Management: Okanogan National Forest, Methow Valley Visitor Center.
Activities: Hiking, fishing.
Finding the campground: From Winthrop, drive west for 13 miles on Washington Highway 20 to the Mazama turnoff on your right. At Mazama, a half-mile from the turnoff, turn left (northwest) onto Mazama Road toward Harts Pass and drive 8 miles to the campground on the left.

About the campground: Hiking trails abound here, and the river is close by for trout fishing. This campground in Okanogan National Forest borders on primitive, but it is serviceable. It is open from June through September or October, depending on the weather.

3 Beverly

Location: About 108 miles southeast of Seattle on the North Fork Teanaway River, near Cle Elum.
Sites: 13 tent sites, 3 sites for tents or self-contained RVs no longer than 21 feet.
Facilities: Picnic tables, fire grills, pit toilets; no drinking water.

Fee per night: None.
Elevation: 3,200 feet.
Management: Wenatchee National Forest, Cle Elum Ranger District.
Activities: Hiking, fishing.
Finding the campground: From Interstate 5 in Seattle, take exit 164 and drive east on I-90 for 85 miles. Take exit 85 and cross the freeway to Cle Elum and Washington Highway 970. Turn right (east) onto WA 970 and continue 7 miles to Teanaway Road. Turn left (north) onto Teanaway Road and drive for about 7 miiles along the Teanaway River. At Casland, turn north onto North Fork Teanaway Road, which becomes Forest Road 9737. Follow FR 9737 to the campground, about 9 miles from Casland. The last 9 miles are unpaved.

About the campground: This is a good base camp for hikers, because trails lead from here into the Alpine Lakes Wilderness. The 5-acre campground is primitive but peaceful, and it offers good fishing opportunities. It is open from June to mid-November.

4 Blackpine Creek Horse Camp

Location: 18 miles west of Leavenworth on Icicle Creek.
Sites: 14 sites for tents or self-contained RVs no longer than 21 feet.
Facilities: Drinking water, fire grills, picnic tables, vault toilets, firewood, riding facilities.
Fee per night: $.
Elevation: 3,000 feet.
Management: Wenatchee National Forest, Leavenworth Ranger District.
Activities: Horseback riding, hiking.
Finding the campground: From U.S. Highway 2 at the west end of Leavenworth, turn south onto Icicle Road and drive 18 miles south and west to the campground. The last mile is unpaved.

About the campground: Blackpine sits at the confluence of Blackpine Creek and Icicle Creek, at the end of Icicle Road in the Wenatchee National Forest. Since this rustic camp is close to the boundary of the Alpine Lakes Wilderness and has facilities for horses, it serves well as a base camp for pack trips. The campground is open from mid-May to late October.

5 Bridge Creek

Location: 9 miles west of Leavenworth on Icicle Creek.
Sites: 6 tent sites, 1 group site.
Facilities: Drinking water, fire grills, picnic tables, vault toilets, firewood.
Fee per night: $.
Elevation: 1,900 feet.
Management: Wenatchee National Forest, Leavenworth Ranger District.
Activities: Hiking, fishing.
Finding the campground: From U.S. Highway 2 at the west end of Leavenworth, turn south onto Icicle Road and drive 9 miles to the campground.

About the campground: This small, primitive camp is nestled in the shady canyon formed by Icicle Creek in the Wenatchee National Forest. It is close to some hiking trails that access the Alpine Lakes Wilderness. The campground is open from mid-April to late October. You can make group reservations only by calling the USDA National Reservation Line (see contact information on page 236).

6 Camp 4

Location: 17 miles north of Winthrop on the Chewuch River.
Sites: 5 tent sites.
Facilities: Picnic tables, fire grills, vault toilets; no drinking water.
Fee per night: $.
Elevation: 2,384 feet.
Management: Okanogan National Forest, Methow Valley Visitor Center.
Activities: Hiking, fishing, horse packing.
Finding the campground: Drive 6 miles north out of Winthrop on Eastside Chewuch Road. At the junction with West Chewuch Road (Forest Road 51), turn right (north) and drive 11 miles to the campground.

About the campground: Camp 4 is actually the third camp along this stretch of the Chewuch River. It is smaller than the other two (Falls Creek and Chewuch, see below) and a bit more rustic. The fourth is Thirtymile, about 11 miles farther at the end of the road. Between the two are trailheads for trails leading into the Pasayten Wilderness. There are amenities for horses at the trailheads, including corrals, hitching rails, truck docks, and watering troughs. The campground is open from June to late September.

7 Chatter Creek

Location: 15 miles west of Leavenworth on Icicle Creek.
Sites: 3 sites for tents or self-contained RVs no longer than 21 feet, 9 tent sites, 1 group site.
Facilities: Drinking water, fire grills, picnic tables, vault toilets.
Fee per night: $.
Elevation: 2,800 feet.
Management: Wenatchee National Forest, Leavenworth Ranger District.
Activities: Hiking, fishing.
Finding the campground: From U.S. Highway 2 at the west end of Leavenworth, turn south onto Icicle Road and drive 15 miles south and west to the campground.

About the campground: This small campground sits at the confluence of Chatter Creek and Icicle Creek, slightly downstream from where Trout Creek enters the Icicle. The fishing and hiking possibilities seem infinite here below steep Icicle Ridge, the top of which forms the southern boundary of the of the northern section of the Alpine Lakes Wilderness in the Chiwaukum Mountains. Trails lead north and south from camp into the wilderness area. The campground is open from May to late October. You can make reservations for groups only by calling the USDA National Reservation Line (see contact information on page 236).

8 Chewuch

Location: 14 miles north of Winthrop on the Chewuch River.
Sites: 4 tent sites.
Facilities: Picnic tables, fire grills, vault toilets; no drinking water.
Fee per night: $.
Elevation: 2,278 feet.
Management: Okanogan National Forest, Methow Valley Visitor Center.
Activities: Hiking, fishing, mountain biking, horse packing.
Finding the campground: From Winthrop, head north on Eastside Chewuch Road for 6 miles. At the junction with West Chewuch Road (Forest Road 51), turn right (north) and drive 8 miles to the campground.

About the campground: Chewuch is the second of three campgrounds along this stretch of the Chewuch River. It is rustic here in the ponderosa pine forest, but the fishing is good and some hiking trails lead into the mountains from here. The sites on the river are particularly nice. About 6 miles farther up the road are some trailheads into the Pasayten Wilderness, with horse amenities at the roadside, including corrals, hitching rails, truck docks, and watering troughs. The campground is open from June to late September.

9 Chopaka Lake

Location: About 57 miles north of Okanogan on Chopaka Lake, near Oroville.
Sites: 16 sites for tents or self-contained RVs.
Facilities: Drinking water, picnic shelters, vault toilets, boat ramp.
Fee per night: None.
Elevation: 2,880 feet.
Management: Bureau of Land Management, Wenatchee Resource Area.
Activities: Hiking, bicycling, boating, climbing, educational programs, fishing, horseback riding.
Finding the campground: From Okanogan, drive north on U.S. Highway 97 for 24 miles and turn left (north) onto Tonasket-Oroville Westside Road. Drive nearly 11 miles along the Okanogan River, through Tonasket. Bear left (west) on Loomis-Oroville Road and drive 11 miles to Loomis. From the Loomis grocery store, go north for 2.1 miles on Loomis-Oroville Road. Turn left onto Toats Coulee Road, go 1.4 miles, turn right onto a steep one-lane road, and continue 3.4 miles. Stay left and go another 1.7 miles. Turn right and go 2 miles to the campground. This last 2-mile section is unpaved.

About the campground: Chopaka Lake and the campground that bears its name are nestled on top of Chopaka Mountain in the rolling, sage-covered Okanogan uplands of eastern Washington. The lake is surrounded by open fields of grass and sagebrush intermixed with dense forests of Douglas-fir and ponderosa pine. The campground covers only 10 acres, but the 5,500-acre Chopaka Mountain Wilderness Study Area is right outside your tent flap. Area wildlife includes bears, mountain goats, and deer. In the basalt canyon of Douglas Creek, songbirds and raptors perch in the cottonwoods, and the road paralleling the creek passes beaver ponds and cascading pools. Only canoes, kayaks, and small boats are permitted on the lake. There are hiking trails in the Chopaka Mountain Wilderness Study Area, but no vehicles, including mountain bikes, are permitted there. The campground is open year-round.

10 Conconully State Park

Location: About 22 miles northwest of Omak on Conconully Lake.
Sites: 71 tent sites, 10 sites with water hookups for RVs no longer than 60 feet, 2 hiker/biker sites.
Facilities: Drinking water, fire grills, picnic tables, flush toilets, showers, firewood, dump station, playground, wading pool, gravel boat ramp.
Fee per night: $ to $$$.
Elevation: 2,300 feet.
Management: Washington State Parks and Recreation Commission.
Activities: Fishing, boating, swimming, hiking, cross-country skiing, snowmobiling.
Finding the campground: From U.S. Highway 97 in Omak, drive west on Kermel Road for 6 miles to Conconully Road. Turn right (north) and continue about 16 miles north to the park.

About the campground: The 80-acre park is tucked between Conconully Lake and Conconully Reservoir in the eastern foothills of the North Cascades. It has a mile of shoreline within its boundaries, providing access to the 4-mile-long lake and large reservoir. Together the bodies of water have a surface area of 760 acres. The name Conconully comes from Conconulp, the Indian name for this valley. It meant "money hole" and referred to the valley's large beaver population. Beaver skins were as good as cash at the Fort Okanogan store. This is also the site of the original mining town of Conconully, which was washed out by a flood. It grew back and now has two general stores, a gas station, and several restaurants. The park has a good nature trail and a road, Sinlahekin Road, that skirts the lake. Anglers will find rainbow trout, cutthroat trout, and smallmouth bass. The campground is open year-round, but service is limited in winter.

11 Cottonwood

Location: 54 miles northwest of Wenatchee on the Entiat River, near Entiat.
Sites: 25 sites for tents or self-contained RVs no longer than 21 feet.
Facilities: Drinking water, fire grills, picnic tables, pit toilets.
Fee per night: $.
Elevation: 3,100 feet.
Management: Wenatchee National Forest, Entiat Ranger District.

Activities: Hiking, fishing.
Finding the campground: From Washington Highway 285, 2 miles north of Wenatchee, head north on U.S. Highway 97A for 15 miles. Just before you reach the town of Entiat, turn left (northwest) onto County Road 371 (Entiat River Road). Continue 38.5 miles to the campground, making sure you stay on the paved road that becomes Forest Road 51 and then FR 317. The pavement ends at the campground.

About the campground: The Entiat River drains both the Chelan and Entiat mountain ranges. Cottonwood Campground sits where Shetipo Creek joins the river from the south. This is about as far into the backcountry as you can get on a paved road, and the 9-acre campground provides good access to the Glacier Peak Wilderness. The campground is open from June through September.

12 Early Winters

Location: 15 miles northwest of Winthrop on Early Winters Creek.
Sites: 7 tent sites, 6 sites for tents or self-contained RVs no longer than 24 feet.
Facilities: Drinking water, picnic tables, fire grills, vault toilets.
Fee per night: $.
Elevation: 2,130 feet.
Management: Okanogan National Forest, Methow Valley Visitor Center.
Activities: Hiking, fishing, mountain biking.
Finding the campground: From Winthrop, drive northwest on Washington Highway 20 for 15 miles to the campground on the left.

About the campground: This campground sits at the confluence of Early Winters Creek and the Methow River. It is pretty, comfortable, and spacious—a good place to spend a few days. The campground is open from June through September or October, depending on the weather.

13 Eightmile

Location: 8 miles west of Leavenworth on Icicle Creek.
Sites: 45 sites for tents or self-contained RVs no longer than 21 feet, 1 group site.
Facilities: Drinking water, fire grills, picnic tables, vault toilets.
Fee per night: $.
Elevation: 1,800 feet.
Management: Wenatchee National Forest, Leavenworth Ranger District.
Activities: Hiking, fishing.
Finding the campground: From U.S. Highway 2 at the west end of Leavenworth, turn south onto Icicle Road and drive 8 miles south and west to the campground.

About the campground: This campground on Icicle Creek, the first in a string of seven national forest campgrounds in Icicle Canyon, is the trailhead for some choice backpacking routes south into the Alpine Lakes Wilderness. Nearby Mountaineer Creek was so-named for a good reason. The campground nestles at the bottom of a steep canyon, so it is in shade much of the day. It is open from mid-April to late October. In winter, the access road is closed, but walk-in campers are welcome. You can make group reservations only by calling the USDA National Reservation Line (see contact information on page 236).

14 Falls Creek

Location: 11 miles north of Winthrop on the Chewuch River.
Sites: 7 sites for tents or self-contained RVs no longer than 18 feet.
Facilities: Drinking water, picnic table, vault toilets.
Fee per night: $.
Elevation: 2,100 feet.
Management: Okanogan National Forest, Methow Valley Visitor Center.
Activities: Hiking, fishing, swimming, horse packing.
Finding the campground: From Winthrop, head north on Eastside Chewuch Road for 6 miles. At the junction with West Chewuch Road (Forest Road 51), turn right (north) and drive 5 miles to the campground.

About the campground: Located at the confluence of Falls Creek and the Chewuch River, this campground is fairly good sized and the sites are roomy, shady, and clean. From camp, you can hike a quarter-mile to the falls on Falls Creek. About 9 miles farther up the road from camp are some trailheads for trails leading into the Pasayten Wilderness. There are horse amenities beside the road, including corrals, hitching rails, truck docks, and watering troughs. The campground is open from June to late September.

15 Fish Lake

Location: About 109 miles southeast of Seattle on Tucquala Lake, near Cle Elum.
Sites: 15 tent sites.
Facilities: Picnic tables, fire grills, vault toilets; no drinking water.
Fee per night: None.
Elevation: 3,400 feet.
Management: Wenatchee National Forest, Cle Elum Ranger District.
Activities: Hiking, fishing, boating.
Finding the campground: From Interstate 5 in Seattle, take exit 164 and head east on I-90 for 80 miles. Take exit 80 (4 miles west of Cle Elum) and go north on Bullfrog Road, which intersects with Washington Highway 903 in about 3 miles. Take WA 903 north through Roslyn and Ronald, driving about 5 miles to Salmon la Sac Road (Forest Road 4330) near the southern end of Cle Elum Lake. Take it north along the east side of the lake for 21 miles to the campground. The road is rough and gravel for the last few miles.

About the campground: This one is out in the boonies for sure, just 6 miles south of the point at which King, Chelan, and Kittitas Counties intersect and 3 miles east of the Pacific Crest National Scenic Trail. The 2-acre camp is set nicely on the north end of mile-long Tucquala Lake where the Cle Elum River drains into it. The campground is basic and usually used by hikers as a base camp. It is open from July to October.

16 Flat

Location: 11 miles north of Winthrop on Eightmile Creek.
Sites: 12 sites for tents or self-contained RVs no longer than 15 feet.
Facilities: Picnic tables, fire grills, vault toilets; no drinking water.
Fee per night: $.
Elevation: 2,858 feet.
Management: Okanogan National Forest, Methow Valley Visitor Center.
Activities: Hiking, fishing.
Finding the campground: From Winthrop, head north on Eastside Chewuch Road for 6 miles. At the junction with West Chewuch Road (Forest Road 51), turn right (north) and drive 2.5 miles to the intersection with Eightmile Creek Road (FR 5130). Turn left (northwest) and drive 2.5 miles to the campground. The road is paved all the way.

About the campground: You can pull a trailer to this camp with no problem. That means it is probably more popular than the camps farther upriver. But it is a nice camp just the same. Eightmile Creek offers some good fishing, and a nearby trail heads up Eightmile Ridge to Lamb Butte. The campground is open from June to late September.

17 Foggy Dew

Location: 32 miles south of Winthrop on Foggy Dew Creek.
Sites: 13 sites for tents or self-contained RVs.
Facilities: Picnic tables, fire grills, vault toilets; no drinking water.
Fee per night: $.
Elevation: 2,300 feet.
Management: Okanogan National Forest, Methow Valley Visitor Center.
Activities: Hiking, fishing, mountain biking, trail biking, cross-country skiing, snowmobiling.
Finding the campground: From Winthrop, drive south on Washington Highway 20 East for 11 miles to the WA 153 turnoff. Take the turnoff to the right and drive 15 miles to Gold Creek Road (Forest Road 4340). Turn right (west) and drive 6 miles to the campground.

About the campground: This camp is still about 8 miles shy of Sawtooth Ridge above Lake Chelan, but it feels like it is deep in the wilderness. It is a good-sized campground, though primitive. Foggy Dew Creek flows into the North Fork Gold Creek here, and there are lots of trails nearby that lead to upcountry lakes. In the winter, the area is open to cross-country skiers and snowmobilers during the day. The campground is open from late May to early September.

18 Fox Creek

Location: 42 miles north of Wenatchee on the Entiat River, near Entiat.
Sites: 16 tent sites.
Facilities: Drinking water, fire grills, picnic tables, vault toilets.
Fee per night: $
Elevation: 2,000 feet.
Management: Wenatchee National Forest, Entiat Ranger District.
Activities: Hiking, fishing, mountain biking, cross-country skiing, snowmobiling.
Finding the campground: From Washington Highway 285, 2 miles north of Wenatchee, head north on U.S. Highway 97A for 15 miles. Just before the town of Entiat, turn left (northwest) onto County Road 371 (Entiat River Road). Continue 25 miles to the campground, making sure you stay on the paved road that becomes Forest Road 51.

About the campground: Nestled on the west side of the Entiat River, the campground is about halfway between Tommy and Fox Creeks. It is quiet and wooded, like all the Forest Service campgrounds along the Entiat. It is open from May to mid-October.

19 Glacier View

Location: About 25 miles northwest of Leavenworth on Lake Wenatchee.
Sites: 16 tent sites, 4 sites for tents or self-contained RVs no longer than 16 feet.
Facilities: Drinking water, fire grills, picnic tables, pit toilets, boat ramp.
Fee per night: $.
Elevation: 1,866 feet.
Management: Wenatchee National Forest, Lake Wenatchee Ranger District.
Activities: Hiking, fishing, boating, waterskiing, swimming.
Finding the campground: From U.S. Highway 2, midway between Stevens Pass (20 miles) and Leavenworth (16 miles), turn north at Coles Corner onto Washington Highway 207 and drive 3.5 miles toward Lake Wenatchee. Turn left (west) onto Cedar Brae Road (County Road 413/Forest Road 6607) and drive 5 miles to the campground.

About the campground: This is a pleasant, sunny little campground, well away from the hubbub of Lake Wenatchee State Park at the other end of the lake. Many of the campsites are walk-ins on the lakeshore. The campground is open from May through September.

20 Honeymoon

Location: About 18 miles north of Winthrop on Eightmile Creek.
Sites: 6 sites for tents or self-contained RVs no longer than 22 feet.
Facilities: Picnic tables, fire grills, vault toilets; no drinking water.
Fee per night: $.
Elevation: 3,280 feet.

Management: Okanogan National Forest, Methow Valley Visitor Center.
Activities: Hiking, fishing.
Finding the campground: From Winthrop, head north on Eastside Chewuch Road for 6 miles. At the junction with West Chewuch Road (Forest Road 51), turn right (north) and drive 2.5 miles to the intersection with Eightmile Creek Road (FR 5130). Turn left (northwest) and drive 9 miles to the campground. The road turns to gravel well before the camp.

About the campground: Small and quaint, this campground is the perfect spot for a rustic honeymoon. A forest ranger and his bride thought so, too, and that is how it got its name. The campground is open from June to late September.

21 Ida Creek

Location: 13 miles west of Leavenworth on Icicle Creek.
Sites: 5 tent sites, 5 sites for tents or self-contained RVs no longer than 21 feet.
Facilities: Drinking water, fire grills, picnic tables, vault toilets.
Fee per night: $.
Elevation: 2,360 feet.
Management: Wenatchee National Forest, Leavenworth Ranger District.
Activities: Hiking, fishing.
Finding the campground: From U.S. Highway 2 at the west end of Leavenworth, turn south onto Icicle Road and drive 13 miles south and west to the campground.

About the campground: This small camp is on the north side of Icicle Creek, between the confluences of Ida and Big Slide Creeks. It is in the bottom of a canyon, so it is shady much of the day. The campground is open from May to late October.

22 Indian Camp

Location: About 106 miles southeast of Seattle on the Middle Fork Teanaway River, near Cle Elum.
Sites: 9 small sites for tents or self-contained RVs.
Facilities: Picnic tables, fire grills, pit toilets; no drinking water.
Fee per night: None.
Elevation: 2,780 feet.
Management: Washington Department of Natural Resources, Southeast Region.
Activities: Hiking, fishing.
Finding the campground: From Interstate 5 in Seattle, take exit 164 and head east on I-90 for 85 miles. Take exit 85 and cross the freeway to Cle Elum and Washington Highway 970. Turn right (east) onto WA 970 and continue 7 miles to Teanaway Road. Turn left (north) onto Teanaway Road and drive about 7 miles along the Teanaway River. In Casland, head west on West Fork Teanaway Road for 0.6 mile to Middle Fork Teanaway Road. Turn right (north) and drive 4 miles to the campground on your left. Toward the end, the road becomes one-lane gravel.

About the campground: This camp is not well known, but it is in a lovely, sunny setting along the Middle Fork Teanaway River. Conditions are primitive. The campground is open year-round.

23 Johnny Creek

Location: 11 miles west of Leavenworth on Icicle Creek.
Sites: 13 tent sites, 52 sites for tents or self-contained RVs no longer than 30 feet.
Facilities: Drinking water, fire grills, picnic tables, vault toilets.
Fee per night: $.
Elevation: 2,300 feet.
Management: Wenatchee National Forest, Leavenworth Ranger District.
Activities: Hiking, fishing.
Finding the campground: From U.S. Highway 2 at the west end of Leavenworth, turn south onto Icicle Road and drive 11 miles south and west to the campground.

About the campground: This camp sits in the bottom of Icicle Canyon where Johnny Creek drains into Icicle Creek from the north and Victoria Creek drains in from the south. It is a large campground compared to others along the creek, and it is close to a few trails into the Alpine Lakes Wilderness. The campground is open from May to late October. The access road is closed in winter, but walk-in campers are welcome.

24 J.R.

Location: 22 miles east of Winthrop on Frazier Creek.
Sites: 6 sites for tents or self-contained RVs no longer than 16 feet.
Facilities: Drinking water, picnic tables, vault toilets.
Fee per night: $.
Management: Okanogan National Forest, Methow Valley Visitor Center.
Elevation: 3,900 feet.
Activities: Hiking, fishing, mountain biking, cross-country skiing, snowmobiling.
Finding the campground: From Winthrop, drive south on Washington Highway 20 East for 22 miles to the campground.

About the campground: Located in Okanogan National Forest near the Loup Loup Summit, this rustic campground on Frazier Creek offers a lot of recreational opportunities. Trails head into the forest across the highway, and the Methow Wildlife Area is just 3 miles west. The campground is open from late May to early September. For reservations, call the Methow Valley Visitor Center (see contact information on page 235).

25 Kachess

Location: 67 miles southeast of Seattle on Kachess Lake, near Cle Elum.
Sites: 133 tent sites, 50 sites for tents or self-contained RVs no longer than 32 feet, 1 group site.
Facilities: Drinking water, picnic tables, fire grills, pit toilets, dump stations, boat ramp, barrier-free nature trail.
Fee per night: $$.
Elevation: 2,253 feet.
Management: Wenatchee National Forest, Cle Elum Ranger District.
Activities: Hiking, fishing, swimming, boating, waterskiing, mountain biking.
Finding the campground: From Interstate 5 in Seattle, take exit 164 and drive east on I-90 for 62 miles. Take exit 62 off I-90 and turn northeast onto Forest Road 49. Drive 5 miles to the campground.

About the campground: This 92-acre campground is immense by Forest Service standards, and it was certainly well planned with spacious sites. It is very popular with families and with boaters, too. Kachess Lake is 10 miles long. Things quiet down by the end of August, and that is also a good time for hiking the many trails in the area. The Alpine Lakes Wilderness is 4 miles northeast of camp via Forest Road 4948. The campground is open from late May to mid-September. For reservations, call the National Recreation Reservation Service (see contact information on page 236).

26 Klipchuck

Location: 19 miles northwest of Winthrop on Early Winters Creek.
Sites: 6 tent sites, 40 sites for tents or self-contained RVs no longer than 34 feet.
Facilities: Drinking water, picnic tables, flush and vault toilets.
Fee per night: $.
Elevation: 2,900 feet.
Management: Okanogan National Forest, Methow Valley Visitor Center.
Activities: Hiking, fishing, mountain biking.
Finding the campground: From Winthrop, drive west on Washington Highway 20 West for 18 miles to Forest Road 300. Turn right (north) and drive 1 mile to the campground.

About the campground: This campground is one of the nicest around. Its spacious sites nestle in a pine forest on Early Winters Creek. The trees are majestic. Watch out for rattlesnakes, which are occasionally seen in the area. There are nearby hiking trails for all abilities. The campground is open from June to late September.

27 Lake Chelan State Park

Location: 39 miles north of Wenatchee on Lake Chelan, near the town of Chelan.
Sites: 127 tent sites, 17 sites with full hookups for RVs no longer than 30 feet.
Facilities: Drinking water, restrooms, showers, some wheelchair-accessible facilities, playground, bathhouse, boat ramp and dock, water-ski floats, dump station, store, restaurant, ice.
Fee per night: $$ to $$$.
Elevation: 1,099 feet.
Management: Washington State Parks and Recreation Commission.
Activities: Hiking, boating, swimming, fishing, waterskiing, sailboarding, jet skiing, scuba diving, skin diving.
Finding the campground: From Washington Highway 285, 2 miles north of Wenatchee, head north on U.S. Highway 97A for 31 miles to South Lakeshore Road on Lake Chelan. Turn left (northwest) and drive 6 miles to the campground.

About the campground: This state park covers 127 acres and has over a mile of waterfront on Lake Chelan, including 300 feet of sandy beach. A lot of recreational boaters and anglers use the park as a base. So if you prefer a quiet setting, look elsewhere. If noise and hubbub do not bother you, this park is ideal for all the activities it affords. Families love it. The campground is open from April through October. The boat ramp is open all year. For reservations, call either Reservations Northwest or the National Recreation Reservation Service (see contact information on page 236).

28 Lake Creek

Location: 37 miles northwest of Leavenworth on the Little Wenatchee River.
Sites: 8 tent sites.
Facilities: Picnic tables, fire grills, pit toilets; no drinking water.
Fee per night: None.
Elevation: 2,230 feet.
Management: Wenatchee National Forest, Lake Wenatchee Ranger District.
Activities: Hiking, fishing.
Finding the campground: From U.S. Highway 2, midway between Stevens Pass (20 miles) and Leavenworth (16 miles), turn north at Coles Corner onto Washington Highway 207 and drive toward Lake Wenatchee. From Coles Corner, drive 10.5 miles around the lake on North Shore Drive to Forest Road 6500. Turn left (west) onto FR 6500 and drive for 6.5 miles to the Riverside Campground and the intersection with FR 6701. Bear left (southwest) on FR 6701 (making sure in less than a half-mile to bear right and stay on FR 6701, not FR 6700) and stay on it for 4 miles to the campground.

About the campground: This primitive campground is within a few miles of the end of the road, so it is entirely remote and nicely situated on the Little Wenatchee River. This is a good spot for campers who bring their own entertainment. Wenatchee Ridge, to the north, is at the southern end of the Glacier Peak Wilderness. The campground is open from May to early November.

29 Lake Creek II

Location: 44 miles north of Wenatchee on the Entiat River, near Entiat.
Sites: 18 tent sites.
Facilities: Drinking water, picnic tables, fire grills, vault toilets.
Fee per night: $.
Elevation: 2,000 feet.
Management: Wenatchee National Forest, Entiat Ranger District.
Activities: Hiking, fishing.
Finding the campground: From Washington Highway 285, 2 miles north of Wenatchee, take U.S. Highway 97A north for 15 miles. Just before you reach the town of Entiat, turn left (northwest) onto County Road 371 (Entiat River Road). Continue 27 miles to the campground, making sure you stay on the paved road that becomes Forest Road 51.

About the campground: This is another easy-access campground on the Entiat River. This one is located where Lake Creek empties into the river after descending 4 miles from Pawn Lakes in the Chelan Mountains. Hiking trails here go in all directions. The campground is pretty basic but serviceable. It is open from May to mid-October.

30 Lakeshore RV Park

Location: 37 miles north of Wenatchee on Lake Chelan, in the town of Chelan.
Sites: 151 RV sites with full-service hookups, 9 tent sites.
Facilities: Drinking water, sewer, and electricity at RV sites, water and electricity at tent sites, restrooms, showers, telephones, cable TV, tennis courts, adjacent swimming area, 18-hole putting green, bumper boats, go carts, marina with boat ramp.
Fee per night: $$ to $$$.
Elevation: 1,099 feet.
Management: City of Chelan.
Activities: Swimming, boating, waterskiing, sailboarding, fishing.
Finding the campground: From Washington Highway 285, 2 miles north of Wenatchee, take U.S. Highway 97A and drive north for 35 miles to Chelan. The park is on the lake on the north side of town.

About the campground: Because of its in-town location, Lakeshore RV Park is for the social set, especially during the summer. It is within easy walking distance of shopping and restaurants, and Chelan is very busy during tourist season. It may even be the recreation center of eastern Washington. The attractions are the near-daily sun, water sports, and throngs of like-minded people. Quiet hours are enforced, however, between 11 P.M. and 7 A.M. No dogs are allowed from Memorial Day weekend through Labor Day. The campground is open from February through November. You can write to the city offices for reservations or visit in person (see contact information on page 235).

31 Lake Wenatchee State Park

Location: 21 miles northwest of Leavenworth on Lake Wenatchee.
Sites: 197 sites for tents or self-contained RVs no longer than 60 feet.
Facilities: Drinking water, fire grills, flush toilets, showers, 2 dump stations, bathhouse, amphitheater, playground, boat ramp, dock, boat rentals, horse rentals, food concession.
Fee per night: $ to $$.
Elevation: 1,900 feet.
Management: Washington State Parks and Recreation Commission.
Activities: Hiking, fishing, boating, canoeing, swimming, waterskiing, horseback riding, mountain biking, snowmobiling, cross-country skiing, snowshoeing.
Finding the campground: From U.S. Highway 2, midway between Stevens Pass (20 miles) and Leavenworth (16 miles), turn north at Coles Corner onto Washington Highway 207 toward Lake Wenatchee. Drive for 5 miles to the campground.

About the campground: The park covers 490 acres and has more than 2 miles of waterfront on Lake Wenatchee. There are campsites on both sides of the Wenatchee River at the point where it flows out of the lake. Nason Creek skirts the campground. The sites are spacious and pleasant and all are reasonably close to the lakeshore. Indian tribes traveling west used to stop at Lake Wenatchee during the sockeye salmon migration, and today's campers happily carry on the tradition of fishing, playing, and relaxing here. This is a very popular family campground, and with good reason. The recreation possibilities—including 3.5 miles of equestrian trail and 7.5 miles of trail for hiking, cross-country skiing, and snowmobiling— could keep you active and happy for a week or two. The campground is open year-round. For reservations, call Reservations Northwest (see contact information on page 236).

32 Leader Lake

Location: 9 miles west of Okanogan on Leader Lake.
Sites: 16 sites for tents or self-contained RVs of any length.
Facilities: Picnic tables, fire grills, tent pads, pit toilets, boat ramp; no drinking water.
Fee per night: None.
Elevation: 2,525 feet.
Management: Washington Department of Natural Resources, Northeast Region.
Activities: Hiking, fishing.
Finding the campground: From U.S. Highway 97 in Okanogan, take Washington Highway 20 West and drive south and then northwest for 9 miles to Leader Lake Road. Turn right to enter the campground.

About the campground: This is a nice little lakeshore campground on the dry side of the Cascade Mountains. It is a bit primitive, but the setting is lovely. The campground is open year-round.

33 Lone Fir

Location: 27 miles northwest of Winthrop on Early Winters Creek.
Sites: 27 sites for tents or self-contained RVs no longer than 21 feet.
Facilities: Drinking water, picnic tables, fire grills, vault toilets.
Fee per night: $.
Elevation: 3,640 feet.
Management: Okanogan National Forest, Methow Valley Visitor Center.
Activities: Hiking, fishing.
Finding the campground: From Winthrop, drive northwest on Washington Highway 20 West (North Cascades Highway) for 27 miles to the campground.

About the campground: Lone Fir is about 6 miles north of the Washington Pass Overlook on the North Cascades Highway, right beside Early Winters Creek. The sites are small, but the setting cannot be beat for its woodsy comfort and easy access to hiking trails in the area. The campground is open from June to late September.

34 Loup Loup

Location: 23 miles southeast of Winthrop.
Sites: 25 sites for tents or self-contained RVs no longer than 21 feet.
Facilities: Drinking water, picnic tables, vault toilets.
Fee per night: $.
Elevation: 4,200 feet.
Management: Okanogan National Forest, Methow Valley Visitor Center.
Activities: Hiking, fishing, mountain biking, cross-country skiing, snowmobiling.
Finding the campground: From Winthrop, drive south and then east on Washington Highway 20 East for 22 miles. Turn left (north) onto West Fork Road (Forest Road 42) and drive 1 mile to the campground.

About the campground: Right next to the Loup Loup Ski Area, this campground is quiet and removed from the highway. The western larch trees are beautiful here. While not spacious, the sites are certainly comfortable. The campground is open from May through September, depending on the weather.

35 Meadows

Location: About 34 miles northwest of Winthrop.
Sites: 14 tent sites.
Facilities: Picnic tables, fire grills, vault toilets; no drinking water.
Fee per night: $.
Elevation: 6,130 feet.

This lookout tower on Slate Peak is within hiking distance of Meadows Campground via the Pacific Crest National Scenic Trail.

Management: Okanogan National Forest, Methow Valley Visitor Center.
Activities: Hiking.
Finding the campground: From Winthrop, take Washington Highway 20 northwest for 13 miles to the Mazama turnoff on your right. At Mazama, a half-mile from the turnoff, turn left (northwest) onto Mazama Road toward Harts Pass and drive northwest for about 20 miles to Forest Road 500. At Harts Pass, turn left (south) onto FR 500 and drive 1 mile to the campground.

About the campground: This campground's one-lane dirt access road is considered treacherous by some, but regular cars do make the trip. The Pacific Crest National Scenic Trail runs right by camp, so most campers are hikers. Be prepared for seasonal biting flies. The campground is primitive, but the location cannot be beat. Meadows is open from mid-July to late September.

36 Mineral Springs

Location: About 102 miles southeast of Seattle on Medicine Creek, near Cle Elum.
Sites: 5 tent sites, 7 sites for tents or self-contained RVs no longer than 21 feet, 1 group site.
Facilities: Drinking water, picnic tables, vault toilets.
Fee per night: $.
Elevation: 2,500 feet.
Management: Wenatchee National Forest, Cle Elum Ranger District.
Activities: Hiking, fishing, hunting, snow sports.
Finding the campground: From Interstate 5 in Seattle, take exit 164 and head east on I-90 for 85 miles. Take exit 85 and cross the freeway to Cle Elum and Washington Highway 970. Turn right (east) onto WA 970 and continue 11 miles to U.S. Highway 97. Go north on US 97 for 6 miles to the campground.

About the campground: The campground is on the Blewett Pass Highway in mountainous terrain dotted with pines and mixed conifers. The 6-acre camp is nicely situated where Medicine Creek joins Swauk Creek, and the fishing is good. The camp is rather dusty in the dry season, but it makes a great base camp for winter sports activities. There is a snack bar on site. Mineral Springs Resort, a full-service restaurant and lounge, is just across the highway within walking distance of the campground, which is open from late May to early September.

37 Napeequa Crossing

Location: 33 miles northwest of Leavenworth on the White River.
Sites: 5 sites for tents or self-contained RVs no longer than 30 feet.
Facilities: Picnic tables, fire grills, pit toilets; no drinking water.
Fee per night: None.
Elevation: 1,800 feet.
Management: Wenatchee National Forest, Lake Wenatchee Ranger District.
Activities: Hiking, fishing.
Finding the campground: From U.S. Highway 2, midway between Stevens

Pass (20 miles) and Leavenworth (16 miles), turn north at Coles Corner onto Washington Highway 207 and drive 17 miles via WA 207, North Shore Drive, White River Road, and Forest Road 6400 to the campground.

About the campground: This rustic Forest Service campground is small and isolated. It serves as a good base camp for hiking into the Glacier Peak Wilderness. The campground is open from mid-May to late October.

38 Nason Creek

Location: About 20 miles northwest of Leavenworth on Nason Creek, near Lake Wenatchee.
Sites: 29 tent sites, 41 sites for tents or self-contained RVs no longer than 31 feet.
Facilities: Drinking water, fire grills, picnic tables, flush toilets.
Fee per night: $$.
Elevation: 1,470 feet.
Management: Wenatchee National Forest, Lake Wenatchee Ranger District.
Activities: Hiking, fishing, swimming, boating, waterskiing.
Finding the campground: From U.S. Highway 2, midway between Stevens Pass (20 miles) and Leavenworth (16 miles), turn north at Coles Corner onto Washington Highway 207 toward Lake Wenatchee. Drive for 3.5 miles and then turn left (west) onto Cedar Brae Road (County Road 413) into the campground.

About the campground: While not actually on Lake Wenatchee, this campground is less than a mile away, and the setting is quite nice for such a large campground. It is very popular with boaters and anglers. It is open from May to late October.

39 Nice

Location: About 13 miles north of Winthrop on Eightmile Creek.
Sites: 4 tent sites.
Facilities: Picnic tables, fire grills, vault toilets; no drinking water.
Fee per night: $.
Elevation: 2,728 feet.
Management: Okanogan National Forest, Methow Valley Visitor Center.
Activities: Hiking, fishing.
Finding the campground: From Winthrop, head north on Eastside Chewuch Road for 6 miles. At the junction with West Chewuch Road (Forest Road 51), turn right (north) and drive 2.5 miles to the intersection with Eightmile Creek Road (FR 5130). Turn left (northwest) and drive 4 miles to the campground. The road is paved all the way.

About the campground: This is a good site for group camping. There are only four tent sites, all of them situated nicely at the creek's edge. The campground is open from June to late September.

40 North Fork

Location: 51 miles north of Wenatchee on the Entiat River, near Entiat.
Sites: 8 tent sites, 1 small RV site, 1 group site.
Facilities: Drinking water, fire grills, picnic tables, pit toilets.
Fee per night: $.
Elevation: 2,600 feet.
Management: Wenatchee National Forest, Entiat Ranger District.
Activities: Hiking, fishing.
Finding the campground: From Washington Highway 285, 2 miles north of Wenatchee, take U.S. Highway 97A north for 15 miles. Just before the town of Entiat, turn left onto County Road 371 (Entiat River Road). Drive 34 miles west and north to the campground, making sure you stay on the paved road that becomes Forest Road 51 and then FR 317.

About the campground: This rustic camp is located at the point where the North Fork Entiat River meets the Entiat itself. Entiat Falls are less than a half-mile from camp. There are lots of creeks in the area to explore, so be sure to get a Forest Service map. The campground is open from mid-May to late-September.

41 Pearrygin Lake State Park

Location: About 4 miles northeast of Winthrop on Pearrygin Lake.
Sites: 53 tent sites, 30 sites with full hookups for RVs no longer than 60 feet, 2 primitive walk-in sites.
Facilities: Drinking water, picnic tables, fire grills, flush toilets, dump station, showers, firewood, boat ramp, floats.
Fee per night: $$ to $$$.
Elevation: 2,100 feet.
Management: Washington State Parks and Recreation Commission.
Activities: Fishing, boating, swimming, hiking, picnicking, cross-country skiing, snowmobiling, wildlife viewing.
Finding the campground: From Winthrop, head north on Eastside Chewuch Road for 1.5 miles. Turn right (east) onto Bear Creek Road and drive 2 miles to the park.

About the campground: This easy-to-reach state park bustles with water-skiers on summer weekends. It is just 4 miles away from the fun little western town of Winthrop, which still allows cattle drives down Main Street in the late summer. In the 1970s, "Old West" facades were added to many of Winthrop's buildings in a successful attempt to attract tourists. Pearrygin State Park covers 580 acres in the rolling, sagebrush-covered foothills of the eastern Cascades. It features 8,200 feet of shoreline on spring-fed/trout-filled Pearrygin Lake. It has a sandy beach. Mountain lions and bears are spotted here from time to time, but deer, groundhogs, and ospreys are the usual wildlife enjoyed by campers. The campground is open from April through October. For a fee, you can make reservations by calling Reservations Northwest (see contact information on page 236).

42 Phelps Creek

Location: 44 miles northwest of Leavenworth on the Chiwawa River.
Sites: 7 tent sites.
Facilities: Picnic tables, fire grills, pit toilets, horse facilities; no drinking water.
Fee per night: None.
Elevation: 2,788 feet.
Management: Wenatchee National Forest, Lake Wenatchee Ranger District.
Activities: Hiking, fishing, horse packing.
Finding the campground: From U.S. Highway 2, midway between Stevens Pass (20 miles) and Leavenworth (16 miles), turn north at Coles Corner onto Washington Highway 207 toward Lake Wenatchee. Drive for 4 miles. Just before Lake Wenatchee State Park, turn right (east) onto Chiwawa Loop Road and drive 1.5 miles. Turn left (north) onto Forest Road 62 (Meadow Creek Road). Stay on FR 62 (which joins Chiwawa River Road in about 3.5 miles) all the way to the campground. The distance from Lake Wenatchee to Phelps Creek Campground is about 24 miles.

About the campground: This camp is way out there, nestled between Chiwawa Ridge and the Entiat Mountains, just outside the Glacier Peak Wilderness boundary. The camp is very basic but nicely situated at the confluence of Phelps Creek and the Chiwawa River, with good trail access to the Glacier Peak Wilderness. The campground is open from mid-June to mid-October.

43 Red Mountain

Location: 97 miles southeast of Seattle on the Cle Elum River, near Cle Elum.
Sites: 15 tent sites.
Facilities: Picnic tables, fire grills, pit toilets, firewood; no drinking water.
Fee per night: $.
Elevation: 2,220 feet.
Management: Wenatchee National Forest, Cle Elum Ranger District.
Activities: Hiking, fishing, cross-country skiing, snowshoeing.
Finding the campground: From Interstate 5 in Seattle, take exit 164 and drive 80 miles east on I-90. Take exit 80 (4 miles west of Cle Elum) and go north on Bullfrog Road, which intersects with Washington Highway 903 in about 3 miles. Take WA 903 north through Roslyn and Ronald, driving about 5 miles to Salmon la Sac Road (Forest Road 4330) near the southern end of Cle Elum Lake. Take Salmon la Sac Road north along the east side of the lake for 9 miles to the campground.

About the campground: This rustic 2-acre campground is just about a mile above Cle Elum Lake, at the point where Thorp Creek empties into the Cle Elum River. The other camps in the area are better, but this will serve the purpose if the others are full. The campground is open from mid-May to mid-November, but it is not gated in the winter. It is quite popular with snow-sport enthusiasts, who are welcome to stay here (no fee, no services) until snow blocks the access road.

44 River Bend

Location: 22 miles northwest of Winthrop on the Methow River.
Sites: 5 sites for tents or self-contained RVs no longer than 16 feet.
Facilities: Picnic tables, fire grills, vault toilets; no drinking water.
Fee per night: $.
Elevation: 2,760 feet.
Management: Okanogan National Forest, Methow Valley Visitor Center.
Activities: Hiking, fishing, horse packing.
Finding the campground: From Winthrop, drive northwest on Washington Highway 20 for 13 miles to the Mazama turnoff on your right. At Mazama, a half-mile from the turnoff, turn left (northwest) onto Mazama Road toward Harts Pass and drive another 8.5 miles northwest to Forest Road 54060. Turn left (south) and drive a half-mile over rough road to the campground.

About the campground: This is quite a primitive campground, but camping on the river makes up for a lot. It is popular with horse packers because of the good trails in the area. The Pasayten Wilderness is within 2 miles. The campground is open from June to late September.

45 Roads End

Location: 35 miles southwest of Winthrop on the Twisp River.
Sites: 4 sites for tents or self-contained RVs.
Facilities: Picnic tables, fire grills, vault toilets; no drinking water.
Fee per night: $.
Elevation: 3,600 feet.
Management: Okanogan National Forest, Methow Valley Visitor Center.
Activities: Hiking, fishing.
Finding the campground: From Winthrop, drive south on Washington Highway 20 East for 9 miles to the town of Twisp. Turn right (west) onto Twisp River Road (County Road 9114), which becomes Forest Road 44 and then FR 4440, and drive 26 miles to the campground.

About the campground: You would have to hike to get any farther from civilization than this primitive campground. And since it sits a quarter-mile from the Lake Chelan-Sawtooth Wilderness boundary, that would be no problem. The campground nestles on the Twisp River near Gilbert Mountain. Good trails head north and west from camp. The campground is open from late May to early September.

46 Rock Creek

Location: 33 miles east of Winthrop on Rock and Loup Loup Creeks.
Sites: 6 sites for tents or self-contained RVs.
Facilities: Drinking water, picnic tables, fire grills, vault toilets, boat launch.
Fee per night: None.

Elevation: 2,650 feet.
Management: Washington Department of Natural Resources, Northeast Region.
Activities: Hiking, fishing.
Finding the campground: From Winthrop, drive south and then east on Washington Highway 20 East for 29 miles. Turn left (north) onto Loup Loup Canyon Road and drive 4 miles to the camp on the left.

About the campground: This rustic campground set at the confluence of Rock and Loup Loup Creeks is pleasant. There are plenty of hiking trails in the area. The campground is open year-round.

47 Rock Island

Location: 17 miles west of Leavenworth on Icicle Creek.
Sites: 12 tent sites, 10 sites for tents or self-contained RVs no longer than 21 feet.
Facilities: Drinking water, fire grills, picnic tables, vault toilets.
Fee per night: $.
Elevation: 2,900 feet.
Management: Wenatchee National Forest, Leavenworth Ranger District.
Activities: Hiking, fishing.
Finding the campground: From U.S. Highway 2 at the west end of Leavenworth, turn south onto Icicle Road and drive 17 miles south and west to the campground.

About the campground: This is the next to last Wenatchee National Forest campground as you head up Icicle Creek from Leavenworth. It is located on the south side of the creek below Blackjack Ridge. The trail leading to the Alpine Lakes Wilderness is about a mile farther downstream at Chatter Creek. The campground is open from May to late October.

48 Rock Lakes

Location: About 40 miles east of Winthrop on Rock Lakes.
Sites: 8 sites for tents or self-contained RVs.
Facilities: Picnic tables, fire grills, vault toilets; no drinking water.
Fee per night: None.
Elevation: 3,510 feet.
Management: Washington Department of Natural Resources, Northeast Region.
Activities: Hiking, fishing.
Finding the campground: From Winthrop, drive south and then east on Washington Highway 20 East for 29 miles. Turn left (north) onto Loup Loup Canyon Road and drive 5 miles to Rock Lakes Road. Turn left (west) and drive 6 miles, then turn left and go 0.3 mile to the site.

About the campground: This site is favored by anglers for the trout fishing in

Rock Lakes. The camp is primitive, but nicely situated on the lakeshore. It is open year-round.

49 Salmon la Sac

Location: About 100 miles southeast of Seattle on the Cle Elum River, near Cle Elum.
Sites: 30 tent sites, 96 sites for tents or self-contained RVs no longer than 21 feet.
Facilities: Drinking water, fire grills, picnic tables, flush toilets, horse camp.
Fee per night: $$.
Elevation: 2,400 feet.
Management: Wenatchee National Forest, Cle Elum Ranger District.
Activities: Hiking, fishing, horse packing.
Finding the campground: From Interstate 5 in Seattle, take exit 164 and drive east on I-90 for 80 miles. Four miles before you reach Cle Elum, take exit 80 and go north on Bullfrog Road. It intersects with Washington Highway 903 in about 3 miles. Take WA 903 northwest through Roslyn and Ronald, driving about 5 miles to Salmon la Sac Road (Forest Road 4330) near the southern end of Cle Elum Lake. Take Salmon la Sac Road north along the east side of the lake for 12 miles to the campground.

About the campground: Hiking trails head north and east from this 63-acre camp snuggled on the Cle Elum River about 3 miles north of Cle Elum Lake. This is a large and well-developed campground considering how remote it is. There is even a campground host in residence during the summer months. It is a good base camp for hikers and horse packers. The campground is open from late May to late September. For a fee, you can make reservations by calling the National Recreation Reservation Service (see contact information on page 236).

50 Silver Falls

Location: 47 miles north of Wenatchee on the Entiat River, near Entiat.
Sites: 30 sites for tents or self-contained RVs no longer than 21 feet.
Facilities: Drinking water, fire grills, picnic tables, vault toilets.
Fee per night: $.
Elevation: 2,300 feet.
Management: Wenatchee National Forest, Entiat Ranger District.
Activities: Hiking, fishing.
Finding the campground: From Washington Highway 285, 2 miles north of Wenatchee, take U.S. Highway 97A north for 15 miles. Just before you reach the town of Entiat, turn left (northwest) onto County Road 371 (Entiat River Road). Continue 30 miles to the campground, making sure you stay on the paved road that becomes Forest Road 51.

About the campground: The camp is on the east side of the Entiat River. It is named for Silver Falls, which are an easy half-mile hike up Silver Creek. Forest Road 5900 (Shady Pass Road) heads from here northeast to Shady Pass in the

Chelan Mountains and eventually ends at Twenty-five Mile Creek State Park on Lake Chelan, a distance of about 24 miles. The campground is open from Memorial Day through September.

51 Soda Springs

Location: 35 miles northwest of Leavenworth on the Little Wenatchee River.
Sites: 5 tent sites.
Facilities: Picnic tables, fire grills, pit toilets; no drinking water.
Fee per night: None.
Elevation: 2,033 feet.
Management: Wenatchee National Forest, Lake Wenatchee Ranger District.
Activities: Hiking, fishing.
Finding the campground: From U.S. Highway 2, midway between Stevens Pass (20 miles) and Leavenworth (16 miles), turn north at Coles Corner onto Washington Highway 207 toward Lake Wenatchee. Drive for 10.5 miles along the north shore of Lake Wenatchee via North Shore Drive to its intersection with Forest Road 6500. Turn left (west) onto FR 6500 and drive 8 miles to the campground.

About the campground: This is a rustic camp, bordering on primitive, but it is popular as a base camp for backpackers. The riverside setting is nice. The campground is open from May to late October.

52 South Creek

Location: 32 miles southwest of Winthrop on the Twisp River.
Sites: 6 sites for tents or self-contained RVs no longer than 30 feet.
Facilities: Picnic tables, fire grills, vault toilets, horse facilities; no drinking water.
Fee per night: $.
Elevation: 3,020 feet.
Management: Okanogan National Forest, Methow Valley Visitor Center.
Activities: Hiking, fishing, horse packing.
Finding the campground: From Winthrop, drive south on Washington Highway 20 East for 9 miles to the town of Twisp. Turn right (west) onto Twisp River Road (County Road 9114), which becomes Forest Road 44 and then FR 4440, and drive 23 miles to the campground.

About the campground: South Creek flows into the Twisp River at this campground site. The camp is popular with horse packers, who do not seem to care about the primitive conditions. There are several trails near camp that follow creeks into the mountains. The campground is open from late May to early September.

53 Sugarloaf

Location: 23 miles northwest of Okanogan on Sugarloaf Lake.
Sites: 4 tent sites, 1 site for tents or self-contained RVs no longer than 21 feet.
Facilities: Picnic tables, vault toilets, boat ramp; no drinking water.
Fee per night: None.
Elevation: 2,400 feet.
Management: Okanogan National Forest, Tonasket Ranger District.
Activities: Fishing, boating.
Finding the campground: From Okanogan, drive north on County Road 9229, which becomes Conconully Road. Drive about 18 miles to Conconully, turn northeast onto CR 4015 (Sinlahekin Road), and drive nearly 5 miles along the lake to the campground.

About the campground: This is a mighty small and primitive campground, but it is rarely busy and offers good access to Sugarloaf Lake. It is a good place for a private vacation. The campground is open from mid-May to mid-September.

54 Swauk

Location: 107 miles southeast of Seattle on Swauk Creek, near Cle Elum.
Sites: 23 sites for tents or self-contained RVs no longer than 21 feet.
Facilities: Fire grills, picnic tables, pit toilets, firewood; no drinking water.
Fee per night: $.
Elevation: 3,200 feet.
Management: Wenatchee National Forest, Cle Elum Ranger District.
Activities: Hiking, fishing, rockhounding, snowmobiling, snow sports.
Finding the campground: From Interstate 5 in Seattle, take exit 164 and head east on I-90 for 85 miles. Take exit 85 and cross the freeway to Cle Elum and Washington Highway 970. Turn right (east) onto WA 970 and continue 11 miles to U.S. Highway 97. Go north on US 97 for 11 miles to the campground.

About the campground: The campground, on Swauk Creek, is across the highway from a rockhounding area, and a good hiking trail leads west to Teanaway Ridge. This 130-acre camp is pretty basic, but it is one of the few still open on this stretch of highway between I-90 and US 2. The fishing is rumored to be good, and the camp is a popular day use area in the winter for snow play. The campground is open from mid-April to late September.

55 Tumwater

Location: 10 miles northwest of Leavenworth.
Sites: 84 sites for tents or self-contained RVs no longer than 30 feet, 1 group site.
Facilities: Drinking water, picnic tables, fire grills, flush toilets.
Fee per night: $.
Elevation: 2,050 feet.
Management: Wenatchee National Forest, Leavenworth Ranger District.

Activities: Hiking, fishing.
Finding the campground: From Leavenworth, drive west and then north on U.S. Highway 2 West for 10 miles to the campground.

About the campground: Hikers heading to the Alpine Lakes Wilderness set their base camp here, but it also makes a good layover for travelers on US 2. The surrounding countryside is stunning. The campground is near the head of Tumwater Canyon, which is steep enough to turn the Wenatchee River into a broiling waterslide. Do not go near the water—just look. The campground is open from May to mid-October. You can make group reservations only by calling the USDA National Reservation Line (see contact information on page 236).

56 Twenty-five Mile Creek State Park

Location: 49 miles north of Wenatchee on Lake Chelan, near Chelan.
Sites: 63 tent sites, 23 sites with electrical and water hookups (including 13 with sewer) for RVs no longer than 45 feet, 1 group site.
Facilities: Drinking water; picnic tables; restrooms; showers; grocery store; dump station; boat marina with docks, piers, ramp, marine gas pump.
Fee per night: $$ to $$$.
Management: Washington State Parks and Recreation Commission.
Activities: Hiking, fishing, swimming, sailboarding, boating, mountain biking.
Finding the campground: From Washington Highway 285, 2 miles north of Wenatchee, take U.S. Highway 97A north for 31 miles to South Lakeshore Road on Lake Chelan. Turn left (northwest) and drive 16 miles to the campground.

About the campground: Creeks flowing into 55-mile-long Lake Chelan were named for their distance up the lake from the town of Chelan. Thus, Twenty-five Mile Creek's name. The 235-acre park includes 1,500 feet of lakeshore. The camp is used as a base for long backpacking trips into the Chelan Mountains. There are several trailheads in the vicinity. This was originally a lakeside resort, used by early Chelan Valley residents as a place to camp at the end of the road before heading up the lake by boat or horseback. The campground is open from early April to late October. For a fee, you can make reservations by calling Reservations Northwest (see contact information on page 236).

57 War Creek

Location: 24 miles southwest of Winthrop on the Twisp River.
Sites: 11 sites for tents or self-contained RVs no longer than 21 feet.
Facilities: Drinking water, picnic tables, fire grills, vault toilets.
Fee per night: $.
Elevation: 2,460 feet.
Management: Okanogan National Forest, Methow Valley Visitor Center.
Activities: Hiking, fishing.
Finding the campground: From Winthrop, drive south on Washington Highway 20 East for 9 miles to the town of Twisp. Turn right (west) onto Twisp River

Road (County Road 9114), which becomes Forest Road 44 and then FR 4440, and drive 15 miles to the campground.

About the campground: Located just 2 trail miles from the boundary of the Lake Chelan-Sawtooth Wilderness, this forested camp is popular with hikers and backpackers. The setting is very pleasant. The campground is open from May to September.

58 Wenatchee River County Park

Location: About 7 miles northwest of Wenatchee on the Wenatchee River, in Monitor.
Sites: 15 tent sites, 64 sites with full hookups for RVs.
Facilities: Drinking water, picnic tables, flush toilets, showers, dump station, playground.
Fee per night: $$ to $$$.
Elevation: 853 feet.
Management: Wenatchee River County Park.
Activities: Fishing.
Finding the campground: From Washington Highway 285, 2 miles north of Wenatchee, take U.S. Highway 97/2 west for 4.5 miles to Monitor. The campground is close to the highway on the left.

About the campground: This is a nice layover park on the Wenatchee River, with all the amenities. It is open year-round.

59 White River Falls

Location: About 37 miles northwest of Leavenworth on the White River.
Sites: 5 tent sites.
Facilities: Picnic tables, fire grills, pit toilets; no drinking water.
Fee per night: None.
Elevation: 2,230 feet.
Management: Wenatchee National Forest, Lake Wenatchee Ranger District.
Activities: Hiking, fishing.
Finding the campground: From U.S. Highway 2, midway between Stevens Pass (20 miles) and Leavenworth (16 miles), turn north at Coles Corner onto Washington Highway 207 toward Lake Wenatchee. The campground is about 20.5 miles from this turnoff. WA 207 becomes North Shore Drive, then White River Road, and finally Forest Road 6400 as you make your way around the lake to the campground.

About the campground: This isolated campground is just about at the end of the road that runs alongside the White River. It sits below the steep White Mountains in the Glacier Peak Wilderness. There is a good trail from the nearby falls that leads west to Mount David (elevation 7,420 feet). From the end of the road, trails lead northwest into the wilderness area. The campground is open from June to mid-October.

60 Wish Poosh

Location: About 91 miles southeast of Seattle on Cle Elum Lake, near Cle Elum.
Sites: 17 tent sites, 22 sites for tents or self-contained RVs no longer than 21 feet.
Facilities: Drinking water, fire grills, picnic tables, flush toilets, firewood, restaurant, grocery store, ice, boat ramp, docks.
Fee per night: $$.
Elevation: 2,224 feet.
Management: Wenatchee National Forest, Cle Elum Ranger District.
Activities: Hiking, fishing, swimming, boating, sailing, waterskiing, cross-country skiing, snowshoeing.
Finding the campground: From Interstate 5 in Seattle, take exit 164 and head east on I-90 for 80 miles. Four miles before you reach Cle Elum, take exit 80 and go north on Bullfrog Road, which intersects with Washington Highway 903 in about 3 miles. Take WA 903 northwest through Roslyn and Ronald, driving about 5 miles to Salmon la Sac Road (Forest Road 4330) near the southern end of Cle Elum Lake. Take Salmon la Sac Road north along the east side of the lake for 2.5 miles to the campground.

About the campground: Cle Elum Lake is about 7.5 miles long, and this 100-acre camp is on the east shore, about 2 miles up the lake from the Cle Elum Dam. It is the only campground currently open on the lake. There are several access points to the lake from Salmon la Sac Road, which runs the length of the east shore and into the Wenatchee Mountains beyond. This campground has most of the amenities and is popular with families. The campground is open from mid-May to mid-September.

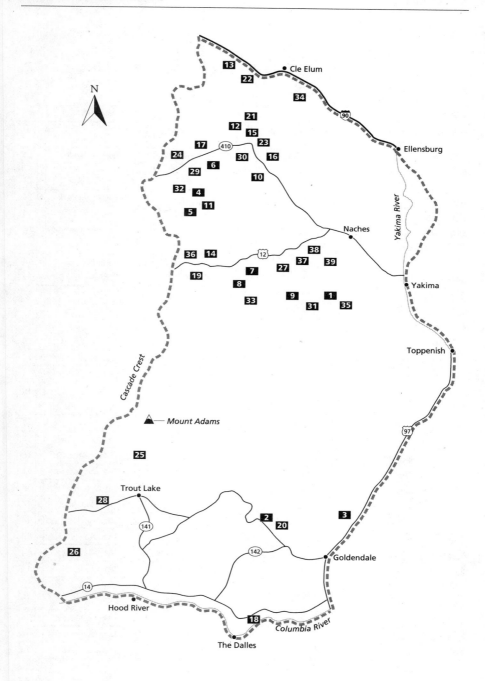

SOUTH CASCADES

	Group sites	RV sites	Total # of sites	Max. RV length	Hookups	Toilets	Showers	Drinking water	Dump station	Pets	Wheelchair	Recreation	Fee	Season	Can reserve	Stay limit
1 Ahtanum Camp and Ahtanum Meadows		•	18			P	•			•		F				7
2 Bird Creek		•	8			P				•		H		May–mid Oct		7
3 Brooks Memorial State Park		•	47	30	WES	F	•	•	•	•		HFR	$–$$$			10
4 Bumping Crossing		•	12	15		V				•		HFBSORC		May–late Nov		14
5 Bumping Lake and Boat Landing		•	45	30		V	•			•		HFBSROC	$$	mid May–late Nov	*	14
6 Cedar Springs		•	15	22		P	•	•		•		HF	$	late May–late Nov		14
7 Clear Lake North		•	34	22		V		•		•	•	HFB	$	mid Apr–late Nov		14
8 Clear Lake South		•	23	22		V	•	•		•		HFB	$	mid Apr–late Nov		14
9 Clover Flats		•	9	21		P	•			•		H				7
10 Cottonwood		•	18	22		P	•	•		•		HF	$	Apr–Nov	•	14
11 Cougar Flat		•	12	20		V	•	•		•		HF	$	late May–mid Sep	•	14
12 Crow Creek		•	15	30		P	•	•		•		HFO	$	mid Apr–Nov		14
13 Crystal Springs		•	26	21		P	•			•		HF	$$	mid May–mid Sep		14
14 Dog Lake		•	11	20		P		•		•		HF	$	late May–late Nov		14
15 Halfway Flat		•	8	27		P		•		•		HFO	$	Apr–late Nov		14
16 Hause Creek		•	42	30		F	•	•		•	•	HFB	$–$$$	late May–late Nov	•	14
17 Hells Crossing		•	18	16		P	•	•		•		HF	$	late May–late Nov	•	14
18 Horsethief Lake State Park		•	14	30		F	•	•		•		HFB	$–$$	Apr–Oct		10
19 Indian Creek		•	39	32		V	•	•		•		HFSB	$–$$	late May–mid Sep	•	14
20 Island Camp		•	6			P		•		•		H				7
21 Kaner Flat		•	41	30		F	•	•		•		HFO	$–$$$	mid Apr–Nov		14
22 Lake Easton State Park	•	•	140	60		F	•	•	•	•	•	HFBSC	$–$$$	late Apr–mid Oct	•	10
23 Little Naches		•	21	20		V	•	•		•		HF	$	late May–late Nov	•	14
24 Lodge Pole		•	35	20		V	•	•		•		HF	$	mid June–mid Sep	•	14
25 Morrison Creek			12			V				•		HF		July–late Sep		14
26 Moss Creek		•	18	32		V	•	•		•	•	HF	$	mid May–early Sep	•	14
27 Peninsula		•	19	20		V						HFSB		mid Apr–late Nov		14
28 Peterson Prairie	•	•	24	32		P	•		•	•		H	$	May–late Sep	•	14
29 Pleasant Valley		•	16	32		P	•	•		•		HF	$	mid Jun–Nov	•	14
30 Sawmill Flat	•	•	25	24		V	•	•		•	•	HF	$	Apr–Nov		14
31 Snow Cabin		•	8			P		•		•		HFRC				7
32 Soda Springs		•	26	30		V	•	•		•	•	HF	$	May–late Nov	•	14
33 South Fork		•	15	20		V		•		•		HF	$	late May–mid Sep		14
34 Taneum		•	15	21		V	•			•	•	HFO	$	May–late Sep		14

continued on following page

	Group sites	RV sites	Total # of sites	Max. RV length	Hookups	Toilets	Showers	Drinking water	Dump station	Pets	Wheelchair	Recreation	Fee	Season	Can reserve	Stay limit
35 Tree Phones		•	14			P				•		RC				7
36 White Pass Lake		•	16	20		V		•		•	•	HFB	$	Jun–late Nov		14
37 Wildrose		•	8	22		V		•		•	•	HF	$	Apr–late Nov		14
38 Willows		•	16	20		V	•	•	•	•		HF	$	Apr–late Nov	•	14
39 Windy Point		•	15	22		V		•	•	•		HF	$	Apr–late Nov	•	14

Hookups: W = Water   E = Electric   S = Sewer
Toilets: F = Flush   V = Vault   P = Pit
Recreation: C = Bicycling/Mountain Biking   H = Hiking   S = Swimming   F = Fishing   B = Boating
O = Off-highway driving   R = Horseback Riding
Maximum Trailer/RV Length given in feet.   **Stay Limit** given in days.
Fee $ = less than $10; $$ = $10-$15; $$$ = $16–20; $$$$ = more than $20.
If no entry under **Season,** campground is open all year. If no entry under **Fee,** camping is free.

1 Ahtanum Camp and Ahtanum Meadows

Location: 34 miles west of Yakima on Ahtanum Creek.
Sites: 18 sites for tents or self-contained RVs.
Facilities: Drinking water, picnic tables, fire grills, tent pads, pit toilets.
Fee per night: None.
Elevation: 3,280 feet.
Management: Washington Department of Natural Resources, Southeast Region.
Activities: Fishing, snowmobiling.
Finding the campground: From Yakima, drive 3 miles south to Union Gap via Interstate 82. Turn west onto Ahtanum Road and drive for 21 miles to Tampico. Continue west on North Fork Ahtanum Road for 9.5 miles to Ahtanum Meadows on the left and Ahtanum Camp on the right.

About the campground: Snowmobiling in the winter is one of the main attractions of these primitive campgrounds on Ahtanum Creek in the Ahtanum Multiple Use Area. There are 60 miles of groomed trails in the area. Winter users are required to have a SnoPark permit (available at sporting goods stores and ranger stations). The campground is open year-round, except during heavy snows.

2 Bird Creek

Location: About 110 miles southwest of Yakima on Bird Creek, near Goldendale.
Sites: 8 sites for tents or self-contained RVs.
Facilities: Picnic tables, fire grills, tent pads, pit toilets; no drinking water.
Fee per night: None.
Elevation: 2,200 feet.

Management: Washington Department of Natural Resources, Southeast Region.
Activities: Hiking, snowmobiling.
Finding the campground: From Yakima, drive 5 miles south on Interstate 82/
U.S. Highway 97 through the town of Union Gap. Stay on US 97 as it leaves I-82
and continue 64 miles southwest to Goldendale. Turn west onto Washington
Highway 142 and drive about 12 miles. Then turn right (north) onto Glenwood-
Goldendale Road and drive about 24 miles to Glenwood. From the post office in
Glenwood, continue 0.3 mile west out of town. Then turn right onto Bird Creek
Road and drive 0.9 mile. Turn left onto Road K-3000, cross over the cattleguard,
and drive 1.2 miles. Turn right onto gravel Road S-4000 and drive 1.3 miles. Turn
left onto Road K-4000 and stay left for the next 2 miles. Turn left into the camp-
ground.

About the campground: This small, rustic campground is in a forested area
beside Bird Creek. It is a nice place to relax, or you can use it as a base camp
from which to explore the Mount Adams Wilderness. The campground is open
from May to mid-October.

3 Brooks Memorial State Park

Location: 48 miles south of Yakima, near Goldendale.
Sites: 23 RV sites with water, sewer and electrical hookups, 22 sites for tents or
self-contained RVs no longer than 30 feet, 2 walk-in sites.
Facilities: Drinking water, picnic tables, fire grills, flush toilets, playground,
coin-operated showers, dump station, environmental learning center, 7 cabins, 4
tepees.
Fee per night: $ to $$$.
Elevation: 3,000 feet.
Management: Washington State Parks and Recreation Commission.
Activities: Hiking, fishing, horseback riding, cross-country skiing.
Finding the campground: From Yakima, drive south on U.S. Highway 97 for
48 miles to the park, which is just south of Satus Pass.

About the campground: This forested, 700-acre park memorializes an area
citizen, Nelson R. Brooks, who became a local celebrity for his efforts to help
build an excellent local road system. The East Prong Klickitat River is just across
the highway, and the trout fishing is reputed to be great. The hiking is good, too;
there are 3 miles of foot trail in camp. The campground is open year-round, with
limited services in winter.

4 Bumping Crossing

Location: 55 miles northwest of Yakima on the Bumping River.
Sites: 12 sites for tents or self-contained RVs no longer than 15 feet.
Facilities: Picnic tables, fire grills, tent pads, vault toilets; no drinking water.
Fee per night: None.
Elevation: 3,440 feet.

Management: Wenatchee National Forest, Naches Ranger District.
Activities: Hiking, bicycling, fishing, horseback riding, educational programs, boating, climbing, hunting, off-highway driving, winter sports, wildlife viewing, waterskiing, swimming.
Finding the campground: From Interstate 82 in Yakima, take U.S. Highway 12 northwest for 17 miles, passing through Naches to the junction with Washington Highway 410. Take WA 410 northwest for 28 miles to Bumping Lake Road (Forest Road 18). Turn left (southwest) onto Bumping Lake Road and drive 10 miles to the campground on the right.

About the campground: Set close to the Bumping River, between two sections of the William O. Douglas Wilderness, this campground is just a mile downstream from Bumping Lake. The 4-mile-long lake has plenty of room for boating and fishing for kokanee salmon and rainbow trout. The campground is a bit basic, but it is pleasant enough, not to mention free, and quieter than the campgrounds on the lake. It is open from late May to late November.

5 Bumping Lake and Boat Landing

Location: 56 miles northwest of Yakima on Bumping Lake.
Sites: 45 sites for tents or self-contained RVs no longer than 30 feet.
Facilities: Drinking water, picnic tables, vault toilets, firewood, boat ramp.
Fee per night: $$.
Elevation: 3,400 feet.
Management: Wenatchee National Forest, Naches Ranger District.
Activities: Hiking, bicycling, fishing, horseback riding, educational programs, boating, climbing, hunting, off-highway driving, winter sports, wildlife viewing, waterskiing, swimming.
Finding the campground: From Interstate 82 in Yakima, take U.S. Highway 12 northwest and drive 17 miles, passing through Naches to the junction with Washington Highway 410. Take WA 410 northwest and continue 28 miles to Bumping Lake Road (Forest Road 18). Turn left (southwest) onto Bumping Lake Road and drive 11 miles to the campground on the right.

About the campground: This is a very popular campground because of its proximity to the 1,300-acre lake, which holds kokanee salmon and rainbow trout. Some campsites are right at the water's edge. There are also some backpacking routes and day trails in the area that lead into the William O. Douglas Wilderness. The campground is open from mid-May to late November. For reservations, call the National Recreation Reservation Service (see contact information on page 236).

6 Cedar Springs

Location: About 45 miles northwest of Yakima on the Bumping River.
Sites: 15 sites for tents or self-contained RVs no longer than 22 feet.
Facilities: Drinking water, picnic tables, pit toilets, dump station, firewood.

Fee per night: $.
Elevation: 2,800 feet.
Management: Wenatchee National Forest, Naches Ranger District.
Activities: Hiking, trout fishing.
Finding the campground: From Interstate 82 in Yakima, take U.S. Highway 12 northwest for 17 miles, passing through Naches to the junction with Washington Highway 410. Take WA 410 northwest for 28 miles to Bumping Lake Road (Forest Road 18). Turn left (southwest) onto Bumping Lake Road and drive a half-mile to the campground.

About the campground: Set nicely on the Bumping River, this small campground is close to good hiking trails and is 11 miles downstream from Bumping Lake. It is also popular with picnickers. The campground is open from late May to late November. For reservations, call the National Recreation Reservation Service (see contact information on page 236).

7 Clear Lake North

Location: About 50 miles west of Yakima on Clear Lake.
Sites: 34 sites for tents or self-contained RVs no longer than 22 feet.
Facilities: Picnic tables, vault toilets, dump station, firewood, boat ramp, docks; no drinking water.
Fee per night: $.
Elevation: 3,100 feet.
Management: Wenatchee National Forest, Naches Ranger District.
Activities: Hiking, fishing.
Finding the campground: From Interstate 82 in Yakima, take U.S. Highway 12 northwest for 17 miles, passing through Naches to the junction with Washington Highway 410. Stay on US 12 for another 31 miles to County Road 1200 (Tieton Reservoir Road) at the west end of Rimrock Lake. Turn left (south) onto CR 1200 and follow it for 1 mile. Continue on Forest Road 1200-840 for a half-mile to the campground.

About the campground: This campground is quite primitive but lovely in the spring and early summer when Rimrock and Clear Lakes, created by a dam on the Tieton River, are full. It is not so lovely in the fall when the reservoir is drawn down and much of the lakebed turns to mud. That is when the dirt bikers take over. Swimming is not allowed anytime. The campground is about 5 miles east of the Pacific Crest National Scenic Trail, and it is open from mid-April to late November.

8 Clear Lake South

Location: 49 miles west of Yakima on Clear Lake.
Sites: 23 sites for tents or self-contained RVs no longer than 22 feet.
Facilities: Drinking water, picnic tables, vault toilets, dump station, boat ramp, docks.

Fee per night: $.
Elevation: 3,100 feet.
Management: Wenatchee National Forest, Naches Ranger District.
Activities: Hiking, fishing.
Finding the campground: From Interstate 82 in Yakima, take U.S. Highway 12 northwest for 17 miles, passing through Naches to the junction with Washington Highway 410. Stay on US 12 for another 31 miles to County Road 1200 (Tieton Reservoir Road) at the west end of Rimrock Lake. Turn left onto CR 1200 and follow it for 1 mile to the campground.

About the campground: This campground is a bit nicer than Clear Lake North. The lake is very beautiful when it is full in the spring and early summer. The kokanee fishing is pretty good, and nearby hiking trails lead into the Goat Rocks Wilderness. The campground is open from mid-April to late November.

9 Clover Flats

Location: 43 miles southwest of Yakima.
Sites: 9 sites for tents or self-contained RVs no longer than 21 feet.
Facilities: Drinking water, picnic tables, fire grills, tent pads, pit toilets.
Fee per night: None.
Elevation: 6,230 feet.
Management: Washington Department of Natural Resources, Southeast Region.
Activities: Hiking, snowmobiling.
Finding the campground: From Yakima, drive 3 miles south on Interstate 82 to Union Gap. Turn west onto Ahtanum Road and drive for 21 miles to Tampico. Then continue west on North Fork Ahtanum Road for 9.5 miles to Ahtanum Camp. Turn left (south) onto Middle Fork Ahtanum Road and drive for 9.2 miles to the Clover Flats Campground. All of this last stretch of road is one-lane gravel. It becomes very steep, a 12 to 13 percent grade, about 6 miles beyond Ahtanum Camp. The road beyond Clover Flats is impassable.

About the campground: Clover Flats is way out there, and therefore it is pretty quiet. It is a good base camp for hikers. Nearby trails head west into the Goat Rocks Wilderness. For winter users, there are 60 miles of groomed snowmobiling trails in the area. The campground is open year-round, except during heavy snows.

10 Cottonwood

Location: 35 miles northwest of Yakima on the Naches River.
Sites: 18 sites for tents or self-contained RVs no longer than 22 feet.
Facilities: Drinking water, picnic tables, fire grills, tent pads, pit toilets, dump station.
Fee per night: $.
Elevation: 2,300 feet.
Management: Wenatchee National Forest, Naches Ranger District.

Activities: Hiking, fishing.

Finding the campground: From Interstate 82 in Yakima, take U.S. Highway 12 northwest and drive 17 miles, through Naches, to the junction with Washington Highway 410. Take WA 410 northwest and continue 18 miles to the campground on the left.

About the campground: Set on the banks of the Naches River, this wooded campground is just right for sitting around with or without a fishing rod and maybe taking a hike or two. The campground is open from April through November. For reservations, call the National Recreation Reservation Service (see contact information on page 236).

11 Cougar Flat

Location: 51 miles west of Yakima on the Bumping River.

Sites: 12 sites for tents or self-contained RVs no longer than 20 feet.

Facilities: Drinking water, picnic tables, fire grills, tent pads, vault toilets, dump station.

Fee per night: $.

Elevation: 3,100 feet.

Management: Wenatchee National Forest, Naches Ranger District.

Activities: Hiking, fishing.

Finding the campground: From Interstate 82 in Yakima, take U.S. Highway 12 northwest for 17 miles, passing through Naches to the junction with Washington Highway 410. Take WA 410 northwest for 28 miles to Bumping Lake Road (Forest Road 18). Turn left (southwest) onto Bumping Lake Road and drive 6 miles to the campground.

About the campground: This is a nice riverside campground with good access to fishing and hiking. Some trails lead from camp into the William O. Douglas Wilderness. The campground is open from late May to mid-September. For reservations, call the National Recreation Reservation Service (see contact information on page 236).

12 Crow Creek

Location: About 45 miles northwest of Yakima on the Naches River.

Sites: 15 sites for tents or self-contained RVs no longer than 30 feet.

Facilities: Drinking water, picnic tables, fire grills, tent pads, pit toilets, dump station.

Fee per night: $.

Elevation: 2,900 feet.

Management: Wenatchee National Forest, Naches Ranger District.

Activities: Hiking, fishing, off-road driving.

Finding the campground: From Interstate 82 in Yakima, take U.S. Highway 12 northwest for 17 miles, passing through Naches to the junction with Washington Highway 410. Take WA 410 northwest for 24.5 miles to Forest Road 1900.

Turn right (northwest) onto FR 1900 and drive for 2.5 miles. Then turn left (west) onto FR 1904. The campground is a half-mile farther on the right.

About the campground: Located just 3 miles off the highway, this riverside campground is most popular with off-road driving enthusiasts. The main trail out of camp divides into several others that lead to other rivers and creeks in the area and on to the Norse Peak Wilderness. The campground is open from mid-April to November.

13 Crystal Springs

Location: About 62 miles east of Seattle, near the town of Cle Elum and Kachess and Keechelus Lakes.
Sites: 20 tent sites, 6 sites for tents or self-contained RVs no longer than 21 feet.
Facilities: Drinking water, picnic tables, fire grills, tent pads, pit toilets, boat ramps and docks at nearby lakes.
Fee per night: $$.
Elevation: 2,400 feet.
Management: Wenatchee National Forest, Cle Elum Ranger District.
Activities: Hiking, fishing, cross-country skiing, snowmobiling.
Finding the campground: From Interstate 5 in Seattle, head east on Interstate 90 for about 62 miles to exit 62. Take the exit, turn southwest onto Forest Road 54, and drive a half-mile to the campground.

About the campground: This 8-acre site is a SnoPark trailhead in winter, for which a parking permit is required. Permits are available from sporting goods stores and ranger stations. The campground is close to I-90, just 2 miles southeast of Keechelus Dam. It is nice and roomy, and there are plenty of hiking trails in the area. The camp is open from mid-May to mid-September.

14 Dog Lake

Location: 53 miles west of Yakima on Dog Lake.
Sites: 11 sites for tents or self-contained RVs no longer than 20 feet.
Facilities: Picnic tables, fire grills, tent pads, pit toilets, dump station, boat ramp, docks; no drinking water.
Fee per night: $.
Elevation: 3,400 feet.
Management: Wenatchee National Forest, Naches Ranger District.
Activities: Hiking, fishing.
Finding the campground: From Interstate 82 in Yakima, go northwest on U.S. Highway 12 for 17 miles, passing through Naches to the junction with Washington Highway 410. Stay on US 12 for another 36 miles to reach the campground on the right.

About the campground: Dog Lake is favored as a base camp by h¹ may be a bit too rustic for everyone else. It is squeezed into a f between the lakeshore and rugged mountains. The campground is open from late May to late November.

15 Halfway Flat

Location: 41 miles northwest of Yakima on the Naches River.
Sites: 8 sites for tents or self-contained RVs no longer than 27 feet.
Facilities: Picnic tables, fire grills, tent pads, pit toilets, dump station; no drinking water.
Fee per night: $.
Elevation: 2,050 feet.
Management: Wenatchee National Forest, Naches Ranger District.
Activities: Hiking, fishing, off-road driving.
Finding the campground: From Interstate 82 in Yakima, take U.S. Highway 12 and drive northwest for 17 miles, passing through Naches to the junction with Washington Highway 410. Take WA 410 northwest for 21 miles. Turn left (northwest) onto Forest Road 1704 and drive 3 miles to the campground on the left.

About the campground: This is a pleasant, though primitive, campground on the bank of the Naches River. The fishing is pretty good, and there are plenty of trails in the area to explore. The campground is open from April to late November.

16 Hause Creek

Location: 35 miles west of Yakima on the Tieton River.
Sites: 42 sites for tents or self-contained RVs no longer than 30 feet.
Facilities: Drinking water, picnic tables, flush toilets, dump station, boat ramp, docks.
Fee per night: $ to $$$.
Elevation: 2,500 feet.
Management: Wenatchee National Forest, Naches Ranger District.
Activities: Hiking, fishing, boating on nearby Rimrock Lake.
Finding the campground: From Interstate 82 in Yakima, take U.S. Highway 12 and drive northwest for 17 miles, passing through Naches to the junction with Washington Highway 410. Stay on US 12 for another 18 miles to reach the campground on the right.

About the campground: This is one of the nicest campgrounds in the vicinity. Located downstream from Tieton Dam and Rimrock Lake, it is bigger than most and so are the sites. It is open from late May to late November. For reservations, call the National Recreation Reservation Service (see contact information on page 236).

17 Hells Crossing

Location: 51 miles northwest of Yakima on the American River.
Sites: 18 sites for tents or self-contained RVs no longer than 16 feet.
Facilities: Drinking water, picnic tables, fire grills, pit toilets, dump station.
Fee per night: $.
Elevation: 3,250 feet.
Management: Wenatchee National Forest, Naches Ranger District.
Activities: Hiking, fishing.
Finding the campground: From Interstate 82 in Yakima, take U.S. Highway 12 and drive northwest for 17 miles, passing through Naches to the junction with Washington Highway 410. Take WA 410 northwest for 34 miles to the campground.

About the campground: This campground is a favorite of tent campers, but small RVs fit in some of the sites. Especially appealing are the nearby hiking trails that connect with higher-elevation streams and lakes in the William O. Douglas Wilderness. The campground is open from late May to late November. For reservations, call the National Recreation Reservation Service (see contact information on page 236).

18 Horsethief Lake State Park

Location: 90 miles east of Vancouver on the Columbia River, near The Dalles.
Sites: 12 sites for tents or self-contained RVs no longer than 30 feet, 2 walk-in sites.
Facilities: Drinking water, fire grills, picnic tables, flush toilets, firewood, 2 boat ramps, dump station.
Fee per night: $ to $$.
Management: Washington State Parks and Recreation Commission.
Activities: Hiking, fishing, boating (non-motorized on Horsethief Lake), rock climbing, sailboarding.
Finding the campground: From Interstate 5 in Vancouver, take exit 1 and head east on Washington Highway 14 for 90 miles to the campground.

About the campground: The campground is on the shore of 90-acre Horsethief Lake, which is actually a backwater created by a railroad jetty on the Columbia River. Sun-worshippers will appreciate the campground's lack of shade. This park covers 340 acres and is large for the number of sites. Access to the Columbia River is easy, but beginning sailboarders would be safer starting out on the lake. Some of the oldest petroglyphs in the Northwest are upriver, but you can view them only as part of a guided tour with a park ranger. You can make arrangements in advance by calling the park at 509-767-1159. The campground, which is open from April through October, was once an Indian campground and burial site, one of the biggest along the river. A small graveyard is just a short walk away.

19 Indian Creek

Location: 44 miles west of Yakima on Rimrock Lake.
Sites: 39 sites for tents or self-contained RVs no longer than 32 feet.
Facilities: Drinking water, picnic tables, fire grills, vault toilets, dump station, boat ramp, docks.
Fee per night: $ to $$.
Elevation: 3,000 feet.
Management: Wenatchee National Forest, Naches Ranger District.
Activities: Hiking, fishing, swimming, boating, waterskiing.
Finding the campground: From Interstate 82 in Yakima, take U.S. Highway 12 and drive northwest for 17 miles, passing through Naches to the junction with Washington Highway 410. Stay on US 12 for another 27 miles to the campground.

About the campground: Located next to the Rimrock Lake Marina, this comfy campground offers plenty of water recreation, and nearby trails head into the William O. Douglas Wilderness. The campground is open from late May to mid-September. For reservations, call the National Recreation Reservation Service (see contact information on page 236).

20 Island Camp

Location: About 113 miles southwest of Yakima on Bird Creek.
Sites: 6 sites for tents or self-contained RVs.
Facilities: Picnic tables, fire grills, tent pads, pit toilets, dump station; no drinking water.
Fee per night: None.
Elevation: 2,950 feet.
Management: Washington Department of Natural Resources, Southeast Region.
Activities: Hiking, snowmobiling.
Finding the campground: From Yakima, drive 5 miles south on Interstate 82/U.S. Highway 97, through the town of Union Gap. Stay on US 97 as it leaves I-82 and continue southwest for about 64 miles to Goldendale. Turn west onto Washington Highway 142 and drive about 12 miles. Turn right onto Glenwood-Goldendale Road and drive about 24 miles to Glenwood. From the post office in Glenwood, go 0.3 mile west, turn right onto Bird Creek Road, and drive 0.9 mile. Turn left onto Road K-3000, cross over the cattleguard, and drive 1.2 miles. Turn right onto Road S-4000 (gravel) and drive 1.3 miles. Turn left onto Road K-4000 and stay left for the next 3.4 miles. Turn left onto K-4200 Road and go 1.1 mile. Turn left into the campground.

About the campground: This forested, creekside campground appeals mainly to winter snowmobilers and to summer backpackers who appreciate its proximity to the Mount Adams Wilderness. The campground is open year-round.

21 Kaner Flat

Location: 45 miles northwest of Yakima on the Naches River.
Sites: 41 sites for tents or self-contained RVs no longer than 30 feet.
Facilities: Drinking water, picnic tables, vault, composting, and flush toilets, dump station.
Fee per night: $ to $$$.
Elevation: 3,250 feet.
Management: Wenatchee National Forest, Naches Ranger District.
Activities: Hiking, fishing, off-road driving.
Finding the campground: From Interstate 82 in Yakima, take U.S. Highway 12 and drive northwest for 17 miles, passing through Naches to the junction with Washington Highway 410. Take WA 410 northwest for 24.5 miles to Forest Road 1900. Turn right (northwest) onto FR 1900 and drive for 2.5 miles to the campground on the right.

About the campground: Located just 2.5 miles off the highway, this riverside campground is on the Old Naches Trail, a 19th-century wagon trail. Dirt bikers and off-roaders are the main trail users now. The campground is large and has spacious campsites. It is open from mid-April to November.

22 Lake Easton State Park

Location: 71 miles southeast of Seattle on Lake Easton.
Sites: 92 developed tent sites, 2 primitive tent sites, 45 sites for tents or self-contained RVs no longer than 60 feet, 1 group site (capacity 50).
Facilities: Drinking water, picnic tables, fire grills, flush toilets, showers, dump station, playground, boat ramp, boat dock, beach, roped-off swimming section.
Fee per night: $ to $$$.
Elevation: 2,130 feet.
Management: Washington State Parks and Recreation Commission.
Activities: Hiking, bicycling, fishing, boating, swimming, snowshoeing, snow-mobiling, cross-country skiing, mushroom hunting.
Finding the campground: From Interstate 5 in Seattle, take exit 164 and drive east on Interstate 90 for 70 miles to exit 70 (signed as the Lake Easton State Park exit). Follow the signs for 1 mile to the park.

About the campground: The 516-acre park lies in a glacial valley 16 miles southeast of Snoqualmie Pass in the Cascades. It features 24,000 feet of shoreline on manmade Lake Easton and 2,000 feet on the Yakima River. Kachess, Keechelus, and Cle Elum Lakes are nearby. This large, wooded campground offers fun for the whole family. There is a golf course nearby, but the boating is what attracts most campers. The trout fishing is good to excellent. In the winter, there are 37 miles of cross-country ski trails to explore. Local wildlife includes marmots, pikas, red-tailed hawks, Steller's jays, whiskey jacks, and black-tailed deer. The campground is open from late April through mid-October. For a fee, you can make reservations by calling Reservations Northwest (see contact information on page 236).

23 Little Naches

Location: 42 miles northwest of Yakima on the Little Naches River.
Sites: 21 sites for tents or self-contained RVs no longer than 20 feet.
Facilities: Drinking water, picnic tables, fire grills, vault toilets, dump station.
Fee per night: $.
Elevation: 2,560 feet.
Management: Wenatchee National Forest, Naches Ranger District.
Activities: Hiking, fishing.
Finding the campground: From Interstate 82 in Yakima, take U.S. Highway 12 and drive northwest for 17 miles, passing through Naches to the junction with Washington Highway 410. Take WA 410 northwest for 24.5 miles to Forest Road 1900. Turn north onto FR 1900, and the campground is right there on the left.

About the campground: This is a nice family campground near the confluence of the Little Naches and American Rivers. Some of the campsites are wide enough for two vehicles. The campground is open from late May to late November. For reservations, call the National Recreation Reservation Service (see contact information on page 236).

24 Lodge Pole

Location: 58 miles northwest of Yakima on the American River.
Sites: 35 sites for tents or self-contained RVs no longer than 20 feet.
Facilities: Drinking water, picnic tables, vault toilets, dump station.
Fee per night: $.
Elevation: 3,500 feet.
Management: Wenatchee National Forest, Naches Ranger District.
Activities: Hiking, fishing.
Finding the campground: From Interstate 82 in Yakima, head northwest on U.S. Highway 12 and drive 17 miles, passing through Naches to the junction with Washington Highway 410. Take WA 410 northwest for 41 miles to the campground.

About the campground: This is the first campground you pass along the American River while driving toward Mount Rainier from the east. The campsites are nestled in the pines. As in most campgrounds in the vicinity, the primary activity is hiking. The Norse Peak Wilderness lies just to the north, while the William O. Douglas Wilderness is to the south. The campground is open from mid-June to mid-September. For reservations, call the National Recreation Reservation Service (see contact information on page 236).

25 Morrison Creek

Location: About 105 miles northeast of Vancouver on Morrison Creek, near the town of Trout Lake.
Sites: 12 tent sites.

Facilities: Picnic tables, fire rings, vault toilets; no drinking water.
Fee per night: None.
Elevation: 4,600 feet.
Management: Gifford Pinchot National Forest, Mount Adams Ranger District.
Activities: Hiking, fishing.
Finding the campground: From Interstate 5 in Vancouver, take exit 1 and drive east on Washington Highway 14 for 66 miles. At Bingen, turn north onto Washington Highway 141 and drive 27 miles to the town of Trout Lake. From there, head north on County Road 17 (Mount Adams Recreation Area Road) for 2 miles. Turn left (north) onto Forest Road 80, drive for 3.5 miles, and then turn right (north) onto FR 8040. Continue 6 miles to the campground. The access roads can be rough if they have not recently been graded.

About the campground: This wooded camp on the banks of Morrison Creek is used mainly by hikers heading into the Mount Adams Wilderness. There are not many amenities or much comfort, but the setting is beautiful. The campground is open from July to late September.

26 Moss Creek

Location: 58 miles east of Vancouver on the Little White Salmon River.
Sites: 18 sites for tents or self-contained RVs no longer than 32 feet.
Facilities: Drinking water, picnic tables, fire rings, vault toilets, dump station.
Fee per night: $.
Elevation: 1,400 feet.
Management: Gifford Pinchot National Forest, Mount Adams Ranger District.
Activities: Hiking, fishing.
Finding the campground: From Interstate 5 in Vancouver, take exit 1 and head east on Washington Highway 14 for 50 miles to the town of Cook. Turn north onto County Road 1800 and drive 8 miles to the campground. The name of the route will change from Cook-Underwood Road to Willard Road to Oklahoma Road, but it is still CR 1800 the whole way.

About the campground: This wooded, creekside campground provides plenty of privacy, and the fishing is good. It is open from mid-May to early September. For reservations, call the National Recreation Reservation Service (see contact information on page 236).

27 Peninsula

Location: 39 miles west of Yakima on Rimrock Lake.
Sites: 19 sites for tents or self-contained RVs no longer than 20 feet.
Facilities: Picnic tables, fire grills, tent pads, vault toilets, boat ramp, docks; no drinking water.
Fee per night: None.
Elevation: 3,000 feet.
Management: Wenatchee National Forest, Naches Ranger District.

Activities: Hiking, fishing, swimming, waterskiing, cross-country skiing, snow-mobiling.

Finding the campground: From Interstate 82 in Yakima, head northwest on U.S. Highway 12 for 17 miles, passing through Naches to the junction with Washington Highway 410. Stay on US 12 for another 18 miles, turn left (south) onto County Road 1200/Forest Road 12 (Tieton Reservoir Road), and drive 3 miles. Turn right (west) onto Forest Road 1382 and drive 1 mile to the campground.

About the campground: Set on the southeastern shore of Rimrock Lake, this campground offers stunning views of the region's mountain peaks. The amenities are not much, but easy access to the lake counts for a lot. The campground is open from mid-April to late November.

28 Peterson Prairie

Location: About 100 miles northeast of Vancouver, near the town of Trout Lake.
Sites: 23 sites for tents or self-contained RVs no longer than 32 feet, 1 group site.
Facilities: Drinking water, picnic tables, fire rings, pit toilets.
Fee per night: $.
Elevation: 2,800 feet.
Management: Gifford Pinchot National Forest, Mount Adams Ranger District.
Activities: Hiking, berry picking, cross-country skiing, snowmobiling.
Finding the campground: From Interstate 5 in Vancouver, take exit 1 and head east on Washington Highway 14 for 66 miles to Bingen. Turn north onto WA 141 and drive 27 miles to the town of Trout Lake. Continue west and then southwest on WA 141 for 5 miles to the Skamania County line. The road becomes Forest Road 24 at this point. Stay on it for 2.5 miles to the campground on the right.

About the campground: This is huckleberry central for the state of Washington. Late August through mid-September is prime time. The campground feels like it is way out on the flats, but it is close to mild adventure—the nearby Ice Cave and Big Lava Bed. The campground is nicely shaded and has spacious sites, but the amenities are primitive. It is open from May to late September. For reservations, call the National Recreation Reservation Service (see contact information on page 236).

29 Pleasant Valley

Location: 50 miles northwest of Yakima on the American River.
Sites: 16 sites for tents or self-contained RVs no longer than 32 feet.
Facilities: Drinking water, pit toilets, dump station.
Fee per night: $.
Elevation: 3,300 feet.
Management: Wenatchee National Forest, Naches Ranger District.
Activities: Hiking, fishing, cross-country skiing.

Finding the campground: From Interstate 82 in Yakima, head northwest on U.S. Highway 12 for 17 miles, passing through Naches to the junction with Washington Highway 410. Take WA 410 northwest for 33 miles to the campground on the left.

About the campground: Popular with RVers, this riverside campground is often used as a base camp for hiking into the nearby Norse Peak and William O. Douglas Wildernesses. It is pretty basic, but the sites are big. The campground is open from mid-June to November. For reservations, call the National Recreation Reservation Service (see contact information on page 236).

30 Sawmill Flat

Location: 38 miles west of Yakima on the Naches River.
Sites: 25 sites for tents or self-contained RVs no longer than 24 feet.
Facilities: Drinking water, picnic tables, vault toilets, dump station, Adirondack group shelter.
Fee per night: $.
Elevation: 2,500 feet.
Management: Wenatchee National Forest, Naches Ranger District.
Activities: Hiking, fishing.
Finding the campground: From Interstate 82 in Yakima, head northwest on U.S. Highway 12 for 17 miles, passing through Naches to the junction with Washington Highway 410. Take WA 410 northwest for 21 miles to the campground on the left.

About the campground: Popular with families, this campground sits in a pine forest on the Naches River, where the fishing is good. Some campsites are double-wide family sites. Backcountry trails, as well as Horsetail and Devils Creek Falls and the popular Boulder Cave, are nearby. The campground is open from April through November.

31 Snow Cabin

Location: About 40 miles southwest of Yakima on the North Fork Ahtanum Creek.
Sites: 8 sites for tents or self-contained RVs.
Facilities: Picnic tables, fire grills, pit toilets, dump station, horse facilities; no drinking water.
Fee per night: None.
Elevation: 2,950 feet.
Management: Washington Department of Natural Resources, Southeast Region.
Activities: Hiking, fishing, horseback riding, mountain biking.
Finding the campground: From Interstate 82 in Yakima, drive 3 miles south to Union Gap. Turn west onto Ahtanum Road and drive for 21 miles to Tampico. Then continue west on North Fork Ahtanum Road for 9.5 miles to Ahtanum Camp. From there, continue on North Fork Ahtanum Road for 4.5 miles. Keep

left for 1.1 miles to the Gray Rock Trailhead. Continue 1.5 miles to the campground on the left.

About the campground: Oddly, Snow Cabin Campground does not have a snow shelter, though nearby Tree Phones Campground does. Still, there are plenty of old logging roads for horseback riding and mountain biking, and the campground is equipped for horses. It is open year-round, except during heavy snows.

32 Soda Springs

Location: 50 miles northwest of Yakima on the Bumping River.
Sites: 26 sites for tents or self-contained RVs no longer than 30 feet.
Facilities: Drinking water, picnic tables, vault toilets, dump station.
Fee per night: $.
Elevation: 3,100 feet.
Management: Wenatchee National Forest, Naches Ranger District.
Activities: Hiking, fishing.
Finding the campground: From Interstate 82 in Yakima, head northwest on U.S. Highway 12 for 17 miles, passing through Naches to the junction with Washington Highway 410. Take WA 410 northwest for 28 miles to Bumping Lake Road (Forest Road 18). Turn left (southwest) onto Bumping Lake Road and drive 5 miles to the campground on the left.

About the campground: RVers consider Soda Springs one of the best campgrounds in the vicinity. It is farther from the road than most and closer to the Bumping River. There is actually a Soda Springs, which burbles up minerals due to the forces that created nearby Mount Rainier and the Cascades. Bumping Lake is just 6 miles upriver. Nearby trails lead into the William O. Douglas Wilderness. The campground is open from May to late November. For reservations, call the National Recreation Reservation Service (see contact information on page 236).

33 South Fork

Location: About 40 miles west of Yakima on the South Fork Tieton River.
Sites: 15 sites for tents or self-contained RVs no longer than 20 feet.
Facilities: Picnic tables, vault toilets, dump station; no drinking water.
Fee per night: $.
Elevation: 3,000 feet.
Management: Wenatchee National Forest, Naches Ranger District.
Activities: Hiking, fishing.
Finding the campground: From Interstate 82 in Yakima, head northwest on U.S. Highway 12 for 17 miles, passing through Naches to the junction with Washington Highway 410. Stay on US 12 for another 18 miles, turn left (south) onto County Road 1200 (Tieton Reservoir Road), and drive 4 miles to Forest Road 1203. Turn left (south) onto FR 1203 and drive a half-mile to the campground.

About the campground: More of a parking lot than a campground, South Fork is used mainly by RVers. The attractions here are the nearby natural phenomena, like the Blue Slide, Goose Egg Mountain, and numerous land masses and waterfalls of giant proportions. The campground is open from late May to mid-September.

34 Taneum

Location: 103 miles southeast of Seattle on Taneum Creek, near Cle Elum.
Sites: 15 sites for tents or self-contained RVs no longer than 21 feet.
Facilities: Drinking water, picnic tables, vault toilets.
Fee per night: $.
Elevation: 2,558 feet.
Management: Wenatchee National Forest, Cle Elum Ranger District.
Activities: Hiking, fishing, off-road driving, cross-country skiing.
Finding the campground: From Interstate 5 in Seattle, head southeast on Interstate 90 and drive 93 miles to Exit 93 just beyond Cle Elum. Take the exit, drive over the freeway, and turn south onto Thorp Prairie Road. Drive for 4 miles and cross back over I-90 to Taneum Road. Turn west (right) onto Taneum Road, which becomes Forest Road 33, and drive 6 miles to the campground.

About the campground: For a rustic camping experience, this 8-acre campground is just the place. Conditions are basic, but it is still popular because there is so much to do in the area. There are plenty of hiking trails nearby in the L.T. Murray Wildlife Area below the South Cle Elum Ridge, as well as numerous cross-country ski trails for winter recreation. The campground is open from May to late September.

35 Tree Phones

Location: About 39 miles southwest of Yakima on Middle Fork Ahtanum Creek.
Sites: 14 sites for tents or small, self-contained RVs.
Facilities: Picnic tables, fire grills, tent pads, pit toilets, horse facilities, snow shelter with wood stove; no drinking water.
Fee per night: None.
Elevation: 4,165 feet.
Management: Washington Department of Natural Resources, Southeast Region.
Activities: Horseback riding, mountain biking, trail biking, snowmobiling.
Finding the campground: From Interstate 82 in Yakima, drive 3 miles south to Union Gap. Turn west onto Ahtanum Road and drive 21 miles to Tampico. Then continue west on Road A-2000 for 15 miles. Turn left and drive 0.1 mile to the campground.

About the campground: Winter and summer trail riders of all stripes are attracted to this campground, with its abundance of trails that crisscross through the Ahtanum Multiple Use Area. The primitive campground sits on the bank of a forest stream. It is open year-round.

36 White Pass Lake

Location: About 55 miles west of Yakima on Leech Lake.
Sites: 16 sites for tents or self-contained RVs no longer than 20 feet.
Facilities: Picnic tables, vault toilets, dump station, boat ramp, docks; no drinking water.
Fee per night: $.
Elevation: 4,500 feet.
Management: Wenatchee National Forest, Naches Ranger District.
Activities: Hiking, fly fishing.
Finding the campground: From Interstate 82 in Yakima, head northwest on U.S. Highway 12 for 17 miles, passing through Naches to the junction with Washington Highway 410. Stay west on US 12 for another 37.7 miles to the campground entrance road on the right.

About the campground: White Pass Lake Campground is at the White Pass Summit, across the highway from the White Pass Ski Area. Fly fishing is good when the water warms a bit, but that is also when the mosquitoes swarm at this altitude. The Pacific Crest National Scenic Trail runs right by Leech Lake, and other trails lead into the William O. Douglas Wilderness. The campground is open from June to late November.

37 Wildrose

Location: 34 miles west of Yakima on the Tieton River.
Sites: 8 sites for tents or self-contained RVs no longer than 22 feet.
Facilities: Picnic tables, vault toilets, dump station; no drinking water.
Fee per night: $.
Elevation: 2,400 feet.
Management: Wenatchee National Forest, Naches Ranger District.
Activities: Hiking, fishing.
Finding the campground: From Interstate 82 in Yakima, head northwest on U.S. Highway 12 for 17 miles, passing through Naches to the junction with Washington Highway 410. Stay west on US 12 for another 17 miles to the campground.

About the campground: Wildrose sits on the banks of the Tieton River about 5 miles downstream from Rimrock Lake. The river is not very big, except in the fall when the dam is opened to draw down the lake. The campground is small and rudimentary, but the setting is very nice and the camp is usually not crowded. It is open from April to late November.

38 Willows

Location: 33 miles west of Yakima on the Tieton River.
Sites: 16 sites for tents or self-contained RVs no longer than 20 feet.
Facilities: Drinking water, picnic tables, vault toilets, dump station.

Fee per night: $.
Elevation: 2,400 feet.
Management: Wenatchee National Forest, Naches Ranger District.
Activities: Hiking, fishing.
Finding the campground: From Interstate 82 in Yakima, head northwest on U.S. Highway 12 for 17 miles, passing through Naches to the junction with Washington Highway 410. Stay west on US 12 for another 16 miles to the campground.

About the campground: Willows occupies a nicer setting than some of the other campgrounds in this area. It is on the banks of the Tieton River, just over 5 miles downstream from Rimrock Lake. Washington is not known for its fall foliage because there are so many evergreens, but this valley is one place where they shine. Local trees include larch, alder, and aspen. The campground is open from April to late November. For reservations, call the National Recreation Reservation Service (see contact information on page 236).

39 Windy Point

Location: 26 miles west of Yakima on the Tieton River.
Sites: 15 sites for tents or self-contained RVs no longer than 22 feet.
Facilities: Drinking water, picnic tables, vault toilets, dump station.
Fee per night: $.
Elevation: 2,000 feet.
Management: Wenatchee National Forest, Naches Ranger District.
Activities: Hiking, fishing.
Finding the campground: From Interstate 82 in Yakima, head northwest on U.S. Highway 12 for 17 miles, passing through Naches to the junction with Washington Highway 410. Stay west on US 12 for another 9 miles to the campground.

About the campground: Drinking water is a bonus for campgrounds in the Tieton Valley. Windy Point also feels more isolated than the other camps along the river. The Oak Creek Wildlife Area is just across the road, and trails lead to and through other canyons to the south. The campground is open from April to late November. For reservations, call the National Recreation Reservation Service (see contact information on page 236).

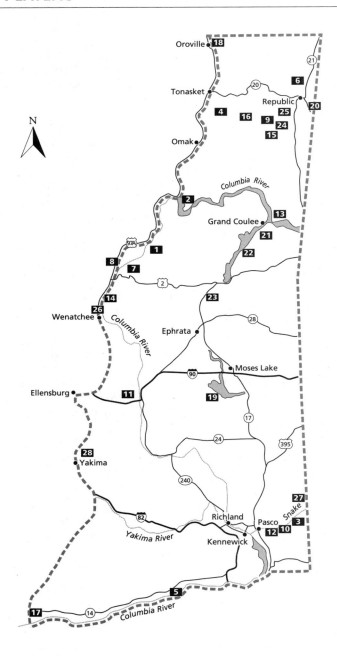

COLUMBIA PLATEAU

		Group sites	RV sites	Total # of sites	Max. RV length	Hookups	Toilets	Showers	Drinking water	Dump station	Pets	Wheelchair	Recreation	Fee	Season	Can reserve	Stay limit
1	Beebe Bridge Park		•	46		WE	F	•		•	•		HFBS	$$	Apr–Oct		10
2	Bridgeport State Park		•	34	45	WE	F	•	•	•	•	•	FBS	$$–$$$	Apr–late Oct		10
3	Charbonneau Park		•	55		WES	F	•	•	•	•	•	HFBS	$$–$$$	Apr–Nov		
4	Crawfish Lake		•	19	31		V				•		HFBS		mid May–mid Sep		14
5	Crow Butte State Park	•	•	52	60	WES	F	•	•	•	•		HFBS	$–$$$			10
6	Curlew Lake State Park		•	87	30	WES	F	•	•	•	•		HFBS	$$–$$$	Apr–late Oct	•	10
7	Daroga State Park	•	•	42	45	WE	V		•	•	•		HFBSC	$$–$$$	mid Mar–mid Oct	•	10
8	Entiat City Park		•	81		WES	F	•	•	•			FSB	$$–$$$	Apr–mid Sep	•	
9	Ferrry Lake		•	9	20		V				•		HFSC		May–Sep		14
10	Fishhook Park		•	61		WE	F	•	•	•	•		HFSB	$$–$$$	mid May–mid Sep		
11	Ginko-Wanapum State Park		•	50	60	WES	F	•	•		•	•	HFBS	$$$	Apr–Oct	•	10
12	Hood Park		•	68		E	F	•	•	•	•	•	FB	$–$$	mid May–mid Sep		
13	Keller Ferry		•	50	16		F		•	•	•		FBS	$–$$			
14	Lincoln Rock State Park		•	94	65	WES	F	•	•	•	•	•	HFBSC	$–$$		•	10
15	Long Lake		•	12	21		V	•		•	•		HFSC		May–Sep		
16	Lyman Lake		•	4	31		V				•		F		mid May–mid Sep		
17	Maryhill State Park	•	•	73	50	WES	F	•	•	•	•	•	HFBS	$$–$$$		•	10
18	Osoyoos Lake State Veteran's Memorial Park		•	85	45		F	•	•	•	•	•	FBS	$$–$$$		•	10
19	Potholes State Park	•	•	128	50	WES	F	•	•	•	•	•	HFBS	$–$$$	Apr–Oct	•	10
20	Sherman Pass Overlook		•	9	30		V	•		•			HR		mid May–late Sep		10
21	Spring Canyon		•	87	26		F		•	•	•	•	HFBS	$–$$			14
22	Steamboat Rock State Park	•	•	139	60	WES	F	•	•		•	•	HFBSR	$–$$$		•	10
23	Sun Lakes State Park	•	•	192	50	WES	F	•	•	•	•	•	HFBSR	$$–$$$		•	10
24	Swan Lake		•	25	31		V		•		•		HFSC	$	May–Sep		14
25	Tenmile		•	9	21		V				•		HFC		mid May–mid Oct		14
26	Wenatchee Confluence State Park	•	•	59	65	WES	F	•	•	•	•	•	HFBS	$$–$$$		•	10
27	Windust		•	24			F		•	•	•	•	FBS	$	Apr–Oct		
28	Yakima Sportsman State Park		•	67	60	WES	F	•	•	•	•		HF	$–$$$			10

Hookups: W = Water   E = Electric   S = Sewer
Toilets: F = Flush   V = Vault   P = Pit
Recreation: C = Bicycling/Mountain Biking   H = Hiking   S = Swimming   F = Fishing   B = Boating
O = Off-highway driving   R = Horseback Riding
Maximum Trailer/RV Length given in feet. **Stay Limit** given in days.
Fee $ = less than $10; $$ = $10-$15; $$$ = $16-20; $$$$ = more than $20.
If no entry under **Season,** campground is open all year. If no entry under **Fee,** camping is free.

1 Beebe Bridge Park

Location: 41 miles northwest of Wenatchee on the Columbia River.
Sites: 46 sites with electricity and water for tents or RVs.
Facilities: Drinking water, restrooms, showers, 2-lane boat ramp, docks, short-term boat moorage, swimming beach, tennis courts, horseshoe pits, playground, dump station.
Fee per night: $$.
Elevation: 750 feet.
Management: Chelan County Public Utility District.
Activities: Boating, fishing, swimming, hiking, tennis, volleyball, horseshoes.
Finding the campground: From Washington Highway 285, 2 miles north of Wenatchee, head north on U.S. Highway 97 for 39 miles to the campground.

About the campground: This 56-acre park is great for families who want to spend some quiet time along the mighty Columbia. It is clean, roomy, and only a few miles from Chelan. Chelan Falls and the Chelan Butte Wildlife Area are just across the river. There is plenty to do here, including hiking the trails that run along the riverbank. The campground is open from early April to the end of October.

2 Bridgeport State Park

Location: About 80 miles north of Wenatchee on Rufus Woods Lake, near Brewster.
Sites: 10 tent sites, 20 sites with water and electrical hookups for RVs no longer than 45 feet, 4 walk-in sites.
Facilities: Drinking water, restrooms, showers, dump station, boat ramp, boat docks.
Fee per night: $$ to $$$.
Elevation: 885 feet.
Management: Washington State Parks and Recreation.
Activities: Swimming, play area, boating, fishing, waterskiing.
Finding the campground: From Washington Highway 285, 2 miles north of Wenatchee, head north on U.S. Highway 97 (or use US 97A—the two routes converge after following opposite banks of the Columbia River) for 65 miles to Brewster. From there, take WA 173 southeast and drive 12 miles across the Columbia River to Bridgeport and Chief Joseph Dam. Drive over the dam via WA 17 and immediately turn right. Follow the signs for about 2 miles to Bridgeport State Park.

About the campground: Ralph Van Slyke, a retired employee of the U.S. Army Corps of Engineers, took it upon himself to create this park in the valley above Chief Joseph Dam in the early 1960s. He used common garden tools to build roads, plant trees and lawn, and install many of the park's amenities. The 800-acre park features 7,500 feet of waterfront and a sandy swimming beach on Rufus Woods Lake, which is actually a section of the Columbia River. The campground is grassy, shady, and very relaxing. There is an adjacent 18-hole golf course, clubhouse, and snack bar. A quarter-mile trail leads to an observation point from which to look down on the water. Keep an eye out for rattlesnakes. Other local wildlife includes bull snakes, rabbits, mule deer, coyotes, quail, chukars, owls, and songbirds. Chief Joseph Dam is southwest of the park. The campground is open from April to late October.

3 Charbonneau Park

Location: 15 miles northeast of Pasco on Lake Sacajawea.
Sites: 40 sites with electricity for tents or RVs, 15 RV sites with full hookups, primitive overflow camping area.
Facilities: Drinking water, picnic tables, fire grills, flush toilets, showers, pay phone, dump station, playground, marina, boat docks, boat ramp, marine dump station.
Fee per night: $$ to $$$.
Elevation: 440 feet.
Management: U.S. Army Corps of Engineers.
Activities: Hiking, fishing, boating, swimming, waterskiing.
Finding the campground: From Pasco, drive southeast on U.S. Highway 12 for 5 miles. Just after crossing the Snake River, turn east onto Washington Highway 124 at Burbank Heights. Continue east for 8 miles to Sun Harbor Road. Turn left (north) onto Sun Harbor Road and drive 2 miles to the park.

About the campground: Located along the historic route of Lewis and Clark, this park is 1.5 miles upriver from Ice Harbor Dam, which turns this stretch of the Snake River into Lake Sacajawea. The 31-mile long reservoir sits amid eastern Washington's channeled scablands and black-rock canyons. The campground is on the eastern shore. At the Ice Harbor Lock and Dam Visitor Center, you can visit the fish viewing room to see salmon migrating upriver. Outside, you can watch barges negotiate the 100-foot-tall locks. The campground is open from April to November. The day-use area is open year-round.

4 Crawfish Lake

Location: 29 miles northeast of Okanogan on Crawfish Lake.
Sites: 19 sites for tents or self-contained RVs no longer than 31 feet.
Facilities: Picnic tables, fire grills, vault toilets, firewood; no drinking water.
Fee per night: None.
Elevation: 4,500 feet.
Management: Okanogan National Forest, Tonasket Ranger District.
Activities: Swimming, boating, fishing, hiking.
Finding the campground: From Okanogan, drive north on U.S. Highway 97 for 8 miles to Riverside. From there, turn northeast across the Okanogan River onto County Road 9320, which joins Tunk Creek Road, (which in turn becomes Haden Road) and drive 21 miles to the campground.

About the campground: If you like isolated and primitive camping with your fishing and hiking, Crawfish Lake Campground is for you. There are plenty of crawfish to catch, too. The lake is half in the Okanogan National Forest and half in the Colville Indian Reservation. The campground is open from mid-May to mid-September.

5 Crow Butte State Park

Location: 155 miles east of Vancouver on the Columbia River, near Paterson.
Sites: 50 sites with full hookups for RVs no longer than 60 feet, 2 primitive tent sites.
Facilities: Drinking water, fire grills, picnic tables, flush toilets, showers, dump station, 3 boat ramps, boat moorage, bathhouse.
Fee per night: $ to $$$.
Elevation: 266 feet.
Management: Washington State Parks and Recreation.
Activities: Hiking, fishing, boating (no gas motors), swimming, waterskiing, sailboarding, bird watching.
Finding the campground: From the Tri-Cities (Richland, Pasco, and Kennewick), drive southwest on U.S. Highway 395 for 24 miles. Turn east onto Washington Highway 14 and drive 27 miles to the campground on the left.

About the campground: Crow Butte is called the "Maui of the Columbia" by campers who return year after year. The winds for sailboarding on the Columbia River are just as reliable as those on Maui, and it is usually as sunny here during the summer months. Like Maui, Crow Butte is even on an island, accessible by bridge from Washington. The park is on the historic Lewis and Clark Trail, adjacent to the McNary (Umatilla) National Wildlife Refuge. Hundreds of thousands of migratory waterfowl spend the winter here each year. Lake Umatilla was created when John Day Dam was built to hold back the Columbia River. The dam flooded some of the original 19th-century homesteads, but descendants of the early pioneers still live in the area. The park covers 1,300 acres and features 6.5 miles of shoreline, including 750 feet of unguarded swimming beach. The campground is open year-round, with limited services in winter.

6 Curlew Lake State Park

Location: 10 miles northeast of Republic on Curlew Lake.
Sites: 57 tent sites, 18 sites with full hookups for RVs no longer than 30 feet, 7 RV sites with water and electricity, 5 primitive sites with tie-downs for people who fly in to Ferry County Airport.
Facilities: Drinking water, picnic tables, flush toilets, showers, dump station, firewood, 2-lane boat ramp.
Fee per night: $$ to $$$.
Management: Washington State Parks and Recreation Commission.
Activities: Hiking, fishing, boating, waterskiing, swimming, cross-country skiing.
Finding the campground: From Republic, drive 3 miles east on Washington Highway 20, turn north onto WA 21, and drive 7 miles to the campground.

About the campground: This 123-acre state park has nearly a mile of waterfront on Curlew Lake, including a good swimming beach. This was apparently the site of an early Indian settlement. Relics that include flint chips, construction tools, and household implements have been found here and on other parts of the lakeshore. Flint does not exist here naturally, so it was either packed in or acquired through trade with people from another area. The trout and bass fishing are reputed to be excellent here. There is also a 1-mile hiking trail. The campground is open from April to late October. It is open for day-use only the rest of the year. For a fee, you can make reservations by calling Reservations Northwest. (See contact information on page 236).

7 Daroga State Park

Location: 20 miles north of Wenatchee on the Columbia River, near Entiat.
Sites: 25 sites with water and electrical hookups for RVs no longer than 45 feet, 17 sites for campers who boat, bicycle, or walk in.
Facilities: Drinking water, picnic tables, vault toilets, moorage space, 2-lane boat ramp, 3 boat docks, restrooms, bathhouse, trailer dump station, boat dump station, basketball and tennis courts, ball field, volleyball area.
Fee per night: $$ to $$$.
Elevation: 708 feet.
Management: Washington State Parks and Recreation Commission.
Activities: Hiking, fishing, boating, waterskiing, sailing, sailboarding, swimming, tennis, basketball, volleyball, baseball, soccer, bicycling, bird watching, jet skiing.
Finding the campground: From Washington Highway 285, 2 miles north of Wenatchee, head north on U.S. Highway 97 for 18 miles to the campground.

About the campground: This is a very pleasant campground, with just about everything an active camper would want. It encompasses 90 acres, including 1.5 miles of shoreline on the east side of the Columbia River and a 295-foot swim beach. Access to the river is easy. Just over 2 miles of trail follow the shoreline. The campground is open from mid-March to mid-October. For a fee, you can make reservations by calling Reservations Northwest (see contact information on page 236).

8 Entiat City Park

Location: 18 miles north of Wenatchee on Lake Entiat, in the town of Entiat.
Sites: 50 tent sites, 31 RV sites with full hookups.
Facilities: Drinking water, restrooms, showers, boat ramp, docks, playground, swimming area, dump station.
Fee per night: $$ to $$$.
Elevation: 708 feet.
Management: City of Entiat.
Activities: Fishing, swimming, boating.
Finding the campground: From Washington Highway 285, 2 miles north of

The campground in Entiat City Park hugs the shore of Lake Entiat, which is actually a dammed segment of the Columbia River.

Wenatchee, take U.S. Highway 97A north for 16 miles to Entiat. Follow the sign for a right turn to the park.

About the campground: This 40-acre park sits on the shore of Lake Entiat, which is actually a portion of the Columbia River that has been dammed. The fish ladders at Rocky Reach Dam, 10 miles farther south, make a fun excursion, plus a lot of people enjoy leaving food for the rabbits that live among the shrubbery there. Since the campground is essentially in town, grocery shopping is easy, and it is a good place to mingle with the locals. No dogs are allowed in the campground, but motorcycles are permitted. The campground is open from April to mid-September. To make reservations, contact Entiat City Park (see contact information on page 235).

---

9 Ferry Lake

Location: About 128 miles northwest of Spokane on Ferry Lake, near Republic.
Sites: 9 sites for tents or self-contained RVs no longer than 20 feet.
Facilities: Picnic tables, fire grills, vault toilets; no drinking water.
Fee per night: None.
Elevation: 3,700 feet.
Management: Colville National Forest, Republic Ranger District.
Activities: Hiking, fishing, swimming, mountain biking.
Finding the campground: From Interstate 90 in Spokane, take exit 287 and drive 61 miles west on U.S. Highway 2 to Wilbur. Turn right (north) onto Washington Highway 21 and drive 60 miles toward Republic. About 7 miles before Republic, turn left (west) onto Forest Road 53 (Scatter Creek Road) and drive 6

miles to FR 5330. Then turn right (north) and continue a bit over 1 mile to the campground.

About the campground: This far into the boonies, campers are thankful for an available campsite no matter what the amenities. This one is on the rustic side; the main appeal is the small lake amidst the forest of lodgepole pines. No gas motors are permitted on the lake. The campground is open from May through September.

10 Fishhook Park

Location: 25 miles northeast of Pasco on Lake Sacajawea.
Sites: 41 sites with water and electricity for tents or RVs, 20 sites for tents only.
Facilities: Drinking water, picnic tables, fire grills, flush toilets, dump station, showers, public phone, playground, boat ramp, docks.
Fee per night: $$ to $$$.
Elevation: 440 feet.
Management: U.S. Army Corps of Engineers.
Activities: Hiking, fishing, swimming, boating, waterskiing.
Finding the campground: From Pasco, drive southeast on U.S. Highway 12 for 5 miles. Just after crossing the Snake River, at Burbank Heights, turn east onto Washington Highway 124 and continue for 16 miles east and then northeast on some of the straightest road you will ever see. When WA 124 makes an oblique right turn, take an oblique left onto Fish Hook Road and continue north for 4 miles to the park.

About the campground: This park is truly in the middle of the proverbial nowhere on the eastern shore of the Snake River, where it has been dammed to create Lake Sacajawea. Ice Harbor Dam is 10 miles downriver, Eureka Flat is to the east, and the Juniper Dunes Wilderness is to the west across the river. Any towns nearby are on the other side of the river, so a boat would be good transportation. The campground is wooded and water access is easy. It sits on the historic Lewis and Clark Trail. Tents on the lawns must be moved every 2 days. The park gates are locked from 10 P.M. to 6 A.M. The campground is open from mid-May to mid-September.

11 Ginkgo-Wanapum State Park

Location: 32 miles east of Ellensburg on Wanapum Lake, near Vantage.
Sites: 50 sites with full hookups for RVs no longer than 60 feet, 1 wheelchair-accessible site.
Facilities: Drinking water, picnic tables, fire grills, flush toilets, showers, firewood, 2-lane boat ramp, bathhouse, concession stand, binocular rentals, interpretive center.
Fee per night: $$$.
Elevation: 571 feet.
Management: Washington State Parks and Recreation Commission.
Activities: Hiking, waterskiing, boating, swimming, fishing.

Finding the campground: From Ellensburg, drive east on Interstate 90 for 29 miles, take exit 136 at Vantage, and drive 3 miles south on Wanapum Road to the park.

About the campground: One of the primary attractions of this park is a petrified forest—the remains of trees that grew here as long as 25 million years ago. It was discovered in the early 1930s during highway construction and includes many samples of petrified ginkgo, a tree that no longer grows anywhere in the wild.

The site actually encompasses Wanapum State Recreation Area, where the campsites are located, and Ginkgo State Park, which is 7 miles to the north. The latter is a day-use area where you can view the petrified forest. Wanapum State Recreation Area, named for a now-extinct Indian tribe that once inhabited the area, covers 7,500 acres and features 5 miles of shoreline on manmade Wanapum Lake, a dammed segment of the Columbia River. Three miles of hiking trails and a 1-mile interpretive trail meander through the area. The campground is open from April through October. For reservations, call the National Recreation Reservation Service (see contact information on page 236).

12 Hood Park

Location: About 6 miles southeast of Pasco on the Snake River.
Sites: 68 sites with electric hookups for tents or self-contained RVs of any length, primitive overflow camping area.
Facilities: Drinking water, fire grills, picnic tables, showers, flush toilets, dump station, electricity, playground, boat ramp, docks.
Fee per night: $ to $$.
Elevation: 340 feet.
Management: U.S. Army Corps of Engineers.
Activities: Fishing, boating, basketball, horseshoes.
Finding the campground: From Pasco, drive southeast on U.S. Highway 12 for 5 miles. Just after crossing the Snake River, at Burbank Heights, turn east onto Washington Highway 124 and follow the signs for about 1 mile to the park.

About the campground: This easy-access campground on the Snake River has all the amenities and is just over a mile from the Snake's confluence with the Columbia. It is well-developed and offers good access to both rivers. This is a very pleasant vacation spot, yet close to civilization. The park gates are locked from 10 P.M. to 6 A.M. The campground is open from mid-May to mid-September.

13 Keller Ferry

Location: 110 miles northeast of Wenatchee on Franklin D. Roosevelt Lake, near Wilbur.
Sites: 50 sites for tents or self-contained RVs no longer than 16 feet.
Facilities: Drinking water, fire grills, picnic tables, flush toilets, dump station, ice, playground, boat ramp (fee), docks, fuel, marine dump station.
Fee per night: $ to $$.

The ferry ride across Franklin D. Roosevelt Lake offers about 15 minutes of free entertainment.

Elevation: 393 feet.
Management: Coulee Dam National Recreation Area.
Activities: Fishing, boating, swimming, waterskiing, wildlife viewing.
Finding the campground: From Wenatchee, take U.S. Highway 97 north for 16 miles and then head east on US 2 for 75 miles to Wilbur. From there, take Washington Highway 21 north for 14 miles to the campground. Alternatively, from Grand Coulee Dam, take WA 174 southeast for 19 miles to Wilbur and drive north via WA 21 from there.

About the campground: This campground is adjacent to the Keller Ferry, which is a main link between the Colville Indian Reservation and the south side of the Columbia River. The ferry is part of the Washington State Ferry system, and the ride is free. The campground is large, wooded, and right on the lake, which is actually a dammed segment of the Columbia River. The camp feels a bit busy in the summer, but it is still nice to spend a few days here. There is a lifeguard on duty from July through Labor Day weekend. The campground is open year-round, weather permitting.

14 Lincoln Rock State Park

Location: 9 miles north of Wenatchee on the Columbia River.
Sites: 94 sites for tents or RVs no longer than 65 feet, including 35 sites with electricity and water and 32 with electricity, water, and sewer.
Facilities: Drinking water, restrooms, showers, 3-lane boat ramp, boat trailer parking, short-term moorage, playground, volleyball area, tennis court, horse-

shoe pits, amphitheater, dump station.
Fee per night: $ to $$.
Elevation: 700 feet.
Management: Washington State Parks and Recreation Commission.
Activities: Hiking, fishing, swimming, jet skiing, sailboarding, bicycling, roller skating, tennis, basketball, volleyball, soccer, softball, horseshoes, cross-country skiing.
Finding the campground: From Washington Highway 285, 2 miles north of Wenatchee, take U.S. Highway 97 north for 7 miles to the campground, which is just north of Rocky Reach Dam.

About the campground: Tucked along the east bank of the Columbia, 80-acre Lincoln Rock State Park is a popular place for boaters, swimmers, and anglers to access the river. It has nearly a half-mile of waterfront. The park has plenty of roads and paved trails for walkers and bicyclists, and they offer views of Lincoln Rock across the river. This outcropping is said to resemble the profile of Abraham Lincoln. It reportedly got its name in 1889, after a photo of it was entered in a *Ladies Home Journal* contest and won first prize. The campground is open year-round. For a fee, you can make reservations by calling Reservations Northwest (see contact information on page 236).

15 Long Lake

Location: About 130 miles northwest of Spokane on Long Lake, near Republic.
Sites: 12 sites for tents or self-contained RVs no longer than 21 feet.
Facilities: Drinking water, fire grills, picnic tables, vault toilets, boat ramp.
Fee per night: None.
Elevation: 3,700 feet.
Management: Colville National Forest, Republic Ranger District.
Activities: Hiking, fly fishing, swimming, mountain biking.
Finding the campground: From Interstate 90 in Spokane, take exit 287 and drive 61 miles west on U.S. Highway 2 to Wilbur. Turn north onto Washington Highway 21 toward Republic and drive 60 miles. About 7 miles before you reach Republic, turn left (west) onto Forest Road 53 (Scatter Creek Road). Drive 8 miles, turn left (south) onto FR 400, and drive 1.5 miles to the campground.

About the campground: Despite its name, Long Lake is the smallest of the three lakes in this vicinity (Swan and Ferry Lakes are the others). An easy trail runs around the perimeter of this lake, which sits in a forest of lodgepole pines. Fly fishing is the main activity, but there some good trails in the area for hiking and mountain biking. Boats with gas motors are not allowed on the lake. The campground is open from May through September.

16 Lyman Lake

Location: 57 miles northeast of Okanogan on Lyman Lake.
Sites: 4 sites for tents or self-contained RVs no longer than 31 feet.
Facilities: Picnic tables, fire grills, vault toilets, firewood; no drinking water.

Fee per night: None.
Elevation: 2,900 feet.
Management: Okanogan National Forest, Tonasket Ranger District.
Activities: Fishing.
Finding the campground: From Okanogan, head north on U.S. Highway 97 for 29 miles to Tonasket. Turn east onto Washington Highway 20 and drive 12.5 miles. Then turn right (southeast) onto Aeneas Valley Road and go 13 miles. Turn right (south) onto Lyman Lake-Moses Meadow Road and drive 2.5 miles to the campground entrance.

About the campground: This campground is very small and very primitive, but for the self-reliant camper it offers a rewarding experience. Plan on being alone, because few people venture this far into the Okanogan National Forest. The lake appears too small for fish, but they are reputed to be there. The campground is open from mid-May to mid-September.

17 Maryhill State Park

Location: 79 miles south of Yakima on the Columbia River, near Goldendale.
Sites: 20 tent sites, 50 sites with full hookups for RVs no longer than 50 feet, 3 walk-in sites.
Facilities: Drinking water, picnic tables, flush toilets, showers, firewood, dump station, boat ramp, docks, unguarded swimming beach, bathhouse.
Fee per night: $$ to $$$.
Elevation: 161 feet.
Management: Washington State Parks and Recreation Commission.
Activities: Hiking, boating, fishing, swimming, waterskiing, sailboarding.
Finding the campground: From Yakima, drive south on U.S. Highway 97 for 79 miles to the park on the Columbia River. To get there from Vancouver, take exit 1 off Interstate 5 onto Washington Highway 14 and drive 108 miles east to the campground. The campground is 1 mile south of WA 14 on US 97.

About the campground: The park covers nearly 100 acres and features a mile of waterfront on the Columbia River, which has been slowed here by breakwaters to make access easier. There is a 10-day limit on camping here during the summer because this is such a nice place to take a vacation. Most of the sites are shaded and grassy, and the campground offers more amenities than most in the state. Fishing for salmon and sturgeon is perhaps the most popular activity. Gas stations and restaurants are right across the river at Biggs Junction. The campground is open year-round. For a fee, you can make reservations by calling Reservations Northwest (see contact information on page 236).

Three miles to the east, the Maryhill Museum of Art sits well above the river, offering great vistas. Its tree-shaded grounds are a welcome respite on a hot summer day. The museum and its grounds have been designated a national historic place. The museum was built in 1926 by Sam Hill as a home for his wife Mary. She did not take to its location, and Hill's friends convinced him to convert the home to a museum. One of those friends was Queen Marie of Romania,

The Maryhill Museum, built in 1926 to be a family home, now houses an impressive collection of French, Russian, and Native American art.

granddaughter of Queen Victoria, and some of her belongings are exhibited in the museum. There are also many authentic sketches and replicas of sculptures by the French artist Auguste Rodin, as well as Native American artifacts. Hill, who owned 7,000 acres here, also tried to establish a colony of Belgian Quakers before World War II. The plan did not work, but one of his successes is a full-scale model of Stonehenge, which he built between 1918 and 1929. It sits adjacent to the park overlooking the Columbia. Hill was a Quaker who was appalled by the carnage of World War I. He had visited England's Stonehenge and built this replica to honor the fallen WWI soldiers of Klickitat County.

18 Osoyoos Lake State Park

Location: 48 miles north of Okanogan on Osoyoos Lake, near Oroville.
Sites: 78 sites for tents or self-contained RVs no longer than 45 feet (including 2 that are wheelchair-accessible), 1 RV site with full hookups, 6 primitive walk-in sites.
Facilities: Drinking water, picnic tables, fire grills, flush toilets, showers, firewood, dump station, store, cafe, playground, bathhouse, concession, boat ramp.
Fee per night: $$ to $$$.
Elevation: 912 feet.
Management: Washington State Parks and Recreation Commission.
Activities: Swimming, boating, fishing, waterskiing, ice skating, sledding, ice fishing.

Finding the campground: From Okanogan, head north on U.S. Highway 97 for 47 miles to Oroville. Continue north for 1 mile to the campground.

About the campground: Osoyoos Lake stretches across the U.S./Canadian border and is advertised in Canada as that country's warmest freshwater lake. The 47-acre park has nearly 1.5 miles of shoreline and 300 feet of swimming beach. This site has been a gathering place for as long as people have known about it. Native American tribes from all over the Northwest rendezvoused at this part of the lake. Later, much later, it became the site of the Okanogan County and International Fair, which featured an Indian encampment, a grandstand show with local talent, horse races, a rodeo, and an exhibition hall. Migrant orchard workers were housed here during World War II to alleviate labor shortages. Until the 1950s, when the site became a state park, travelers and Oroville residents flocked here to relax and be rejuvenated. The campground is open year-round. For a fee, you can make reservations by calling Reservations Northwest (see contact information on page 236).

19 Potholes State Park

Location: 24 miles south of Moses Lake on Potholes Reservoir.
Sites: 60 sites with full hookups for RVs no longer than 50 feet, 66 primitive sites, 2 hike-in/bike-in sites.
Facilities: Drinking water, picnic tables, fire grills, flush toilets, coin-operated showers, dump station, store, playground, firewood (fee), boat ramp.
Fee per night: $ to $$$.
Elevation: 1,040 feet.
Management: Washington State Parks and Recreation Commission.
Activities: Hiking, boating, swimming, waterskiing, fishing.
Finding the campground: From Moses Lake, drive 3 miles east on Interstate 90. Take exit 179 and head southeast onto Washington Highway 17. Drive 10 miles, turn right (west) onto WA 262, and drive 11 miles to the park entrance on the right.

About the campground: Potholes State Park covers 640 acres and features over a mile of shoreline that includes a good swimming beach. Potholes is named for, well, the potholes—great big ones. They are actually depressions in the sand dunes that were created by glaciers during the ice age and subsequently flooded. Some of them are large enough to be called lakes. This desert park is near the center of the Columbia Basin, a terrain consisting of sand dunes, lakes, and rocky canyons. A good hiking trail follows the Frenchman Hills Wasteway. Local bird life includes white pelicans, sandhill cranes, and great blue herons. Fish include largemouth and smallmouth bass, rainbow trout, crappie, bluegill, and perch. The campground is open from April through October. For a fee, you can make reservations by calling Reservations Northwest (see contact information on page 236).

20 Sherman Pass Overlook

Location: About 100 miles northwest of Spokane, near Republic.
Sites: 9 sites for tents or self-contained RVs no longer than 30 feet.
Facilities: Drinking water, fire grills, picnic tables, vault toilets.
Fee per night: None.
Elevation: 5,400 feet.
Management: Colville National Forest, Kettle Falls Ranger District.
Activities: Hiking, trail riding.
Finding the campground: From Interstate 90 in Spokane, take exit 281 and head north and then northwest on U.S. Highway 395 for 81 miles to Kettle Falls. Continue west on Washington Highway 20 for about 20 miles to the campground.

About the campground: This is a very basic campground, but it is an excellent stopover if you come to enjoy the views from the highest elevation highway open year-round in the state. From 5,575-foot Sherman Pass, trails lead along both sides of the highway and out to some of the high peaks. The campground is open from mid-May to late September.

21 Spring Canyon

Location: 3 miles east of Grand Coulee Dam on Franklin D. Roosevelt Lake.
Sites: 87 sites for tents or self-contained RVs no longer than 26 feet.
Facilities: Drinking water, fire grills, picnic tables, flush toilets, dump station, playground, boat ramp (fee), docks, cafe.
Fee per night: $ to $$.
Elevation: 393 feet.
Management: Lake Roosevelt National Recreation Area.
Activities: Hiking, fishing, boating, swimming, waterskiing, wildlife viewing, free ranger-guided canoe trips, historical tours, campfire talks.
Finding the campground: From the town of Grand Coulee, drive east on Washington Highway 174 for 3 miles to the campground entrance.

About the campground: You cannot go wrong camping on Franklin D. Roosevelt Lake in the Lake Roosevelt National Recreation Area. The "lake" is actually a segment of the Columbia River, held back by Grand Coulee Dam 2.5 miles downriver. This is a great campground, with lots of ranger support services. It is very popular with families, and there are plenty of things to do in the nearby towns of Grand Coulee, Coulee Dam, and Electric City. Coulee City is 34 miles south of the campground, at the south end of Banks Lake. The campground is open year-round.

22 Steamboat Rock State Park

Location: 15 miles southwest of Grand Coulee Dam on Banks Lake.
Sites: 100 sites with full hookups for RVs no longer than 60 feet, 22 tent sites, 2 wheelchair-accessible sites, 2 primitive tent sites, 13 boat-in sites.

Facilities: Drinking water, picnic tables, fire grills, flush toilets, cafe, playground, coin-operated showers, swimming beach, 4 boat ramps, handling docks, 6 mooring buoys, 2 fish cleaning stations, public phones, bathhouse, concession.
Fee per night: $ to $$$.
Elevation: 1,571 feet.
Management: Washington State Parks and Recreation Commission.
Activities: Hiking, boating, fishing, swimming, climbing, horseback riding, waterskiing, scuba diving, sailboarding, cross-country skiing, snowshoeing, ice fishing, kite flying, metal detecting. Hunting with shotguns is allowed on adjacent lands administered jointly by the Washington Department of Fish and Wildlife and the parks commission. A permit, available at most sporting goods stores, is required.
Finding the campground: From the town of Grand Coulee, drive southwest on Washington Highway 155 for 8 miles along Banks Lake to the park entrance on your right. Follow the signs to the camping area 2 miles ahead.

About the campground: This park covers 3,520 acres, including 9.5 miles of shoreline on Banks Lake, a 26-mile-long, 27,000-acre reservoir of irrigation water. The campground is located on a large peninsula that juts into the lake, and prominent on this peninsula is 800-foot Steamboat Rock, a flat-topped butte made of columnar basalt. Banks Lake is a wildlife preserve, and there are two bald eagle roosts on the butte. The park also attracts American white pelicans, one of the largest and most spectacular birds, according to John James Audubon. Keep an eye out for bobcats, cougars, and rattlesnakes. Fish in the lake include largemouth and smallmouth bass, yellow perch, rainbow trout, walleye, kokanee, black crappie, bullhead, and whitefish. Thirty-four miles of hiking trails crisscross the park, and equestrian trails can be found in nearby Northrup Canyon State Park. Winter here at Steamboat attracts snowmobilers, cross-country skiers, snowshoers, and ice fishers.

Steamboat requires advance reservations. You can make these, for a fee, by calling Reservations Northwest (see contact information on page 236). There are no drop-in sites except for a boat-in tent area that is inaccessible by car. There is a large day-use area. The campground is open year-round, with limited services in winter.

23 Sun Lakes State Park

Location: 38 miles north of the town of Moses Lake, near Coulee City.
Sites: 174 tent sites, 18 sites (with full hookups) for RVs no longer than 50 feet.
Facilities: Drinking water, picnic tables, flush toilets, showers, dump station, laundry room, ice, swimming pool, firewood, stables, visitor center, boat ramp, environmental learning center, golf course, cafe, general store, boat rentals.
Fee per night: $$ to $$$.
Elevation: 918 feet.
Management: Washington State Parks and Recreation Commission.
Activities: Hiking, mountain biking, rock climbing, swimming, boating, fishing, golf, canoeing, horseback riding,

Finding the campground: From Interstate 90 in the town of Moses Lake, head north on Washington Highway 17 for 35.5 miles. Turn right (east) onto Park Lake Road and drive 2.5 miles along the east shore of Park Lake to the park.

About the campground: Sun Lakes State Park is located in the Lower Grand Coulee, below and including Dry Falls. Four of the seven lakes in the park were originally plunge pools formed by the falls. The campground is on Park Lake, which has a paved boat ramp and is the most popular with boaters, personal watercraft users, and water-skiers. There is also a 300-foot beach. Motorized watercraft are prohibited on Dry Falls Lake. In all, the park covers 4,000 acres and offers 14 miles of freshwater shoreline. The lakes are stocked with rainbow and German brown trout and are popular fly-fishing destinations. For hikers, the park has about 15 miles of trails through the rocky desert and canyons. More than 5 miles of trails are open to mountain bikers. Local wildlife includes deer, yellow-bellied marmots, pheasants, and quail. The canyons, called channeled scablands, were carved by the Columbia River during the ice age. Rock climbing is permitted, but rattlesnakes are common in the area. Sun Lakes State Park also includes the Lake Lenore Caves, where visitors may view petroglyphs, ancient Native American cave drawings. The campground is open year-round. For a fee, you can make reservations by calling Reservations Northwest (see contact information on page 236).

A separate park within Sun Lakes State Park is Sun Lakes State Park Resort. It is operated by a concessionaire, and the facilities are more developed. Cabins and trailers are available for rent, and there are 110 sites for RVs of any length. The concessionaire also runs the golf course and marina, which rents boats. The 9-hole golf course, built on a dredged lakebed, is the only one located within a Washington state park.

24 Swan Lake

Location: 129 miles northwest of Spokane on Swan Lake, near Republic.
Sites: 25 sites for tents or self-contained RVs no longer than 31 feet.
Facilities: Drinking water, picnic tables fire grills, vault toilets, firewood, boat docks, boat ramp.
Fee per night: $.
Elevation: 3,700 feet.
Management: Colville National Forest, Republic Ranger District.
Activities: Hiking, fishing, swimming, mountain biking.
Finding the campground: From Interstate 90 in Spokane, take exit 287 and drive west for 61 miles to Wilbur. Turn north onto Washington Highway 21 toward Republic and drive 60 miles. About 7 miles before you reach Republic, turn left (west) onto Forest Road 53 (Scatter Creek Road) and drive 8 miles west and south to the campground.

About the campground: There are some lakefront campsites at Swan Lake, a bonus for anglers. This camp is more comfortable than others in the area (Ferry Lake and Long Lake) and so it is more popular. It is nestled in a lodgepole pine

A wide variety of recreational opportunities makes Wenatchee Confluence State Park a great family camping destination.

forest in the Sanpoil River drainage. Boats with gas motors are not permitted on the lake. The campground is open from May through September.

25 | Tenmile

Location: 118 miles northwest of Spokane on the Sanpoil River, near Republic.
Sites: 9 sites for tents or self-contained RVs no longer than 21 feet.
Facilities: Picnic tables, vault toilets, dump station; no drinking water.
Fee per night: None.
Elevation: 2,230 feet.
Management: Colville National Forest, Republic Ranger District.
Activities: Hiking, fishing, mountain biking.
Finding the campground: From Interstate 90 in Spokane, take exit 287 and drive west for 61 miles to Wilbur. Turn north onto Washington Highway 21 toward Republic and drive 57 miles to the campground entrance.

About the campground: Situated where Tenmile Creek enters the Sanpoil River, this campground makes a good overnight stop between Wilbur and Republic. It is rustic, but you cannot beat camping along the river. The campground is open from mid-May to mid-October.

26 Wenatchee Confluence State Park

Location: 2 miles north of Wenatchee on the Wenatchee River.
Sites: 8 tent sites, 51 sites with full hookups for tents or RVs no longer than 65 feet.
Facilities: Drinking water, restrooms, showers, dump station, 2-lane boat ramp, ball field, picnic shelter, playground, sport courts.
Fee per night: $$ to $$$.
Elevation: 630 feet.
Management: Washington State Parks and Recreation Commission.
Activities: Hiking, fishing, boating, waterskiing, sailing, sailboarding, swimming, tennis, basketball, volleyball, baseball, soccer, bicycling, bird watching, interpretive walks, cross-country skiing.
Finding the campground: Simply take the main road (Washington Highway 285/Wenatchee Avenue) north out of Wenatchee for 2 miles to the Wenatchee River. Follow signs to the park at the end of Olds Station Road.

About the campground: This 200-acre park has a 2-mile shoreline trail and a 97-acre natural area and wetland wildlife habitat. The campground is on one side of the Wenatchee River, and the preserve is on the other. They are connected by a pedestrian bridge near the Wenatchee's confluence with the Columbia. The nature trail has 16 viewing stations. This is a park with a lot of variety. It is relatively peaceful, yet all kinds of activities are right at hand. The campground is open year-round. For a fee, you can make reservations by calling Reservations Northwest (see contact information on page 236).

27 Windust

Location: About 40 miles northeast of Pasco on Lake Sacajawea.
Sites: 24 primitive sites for tents or self-contained RVs.
Facilities: Drinking water, picnic tables, fire grills, flush toilets, dump station, pay phone, playground, boat ramp, docks.
Fee per night: $.
Elevation: 540 feet.
Management: U.S. Army Corps of Engineers.
Activities: Swimming, boating, fishing.
Finding the campground: From the interchange of U.S. Highway 12 and US 395 in Pasco, drive southeast on US 12 for 2 miles. Turn left (east) onto the Pasco-Kahlotus Road. Drive 30 miles to Burr Canyon Road, turn right, and drive 6 miles to the park.

About the campground: They do not call this campground in the coulees of southeastern Washington Windust for nothing. The lake, actually a dammed segment of the Snake River, provides great relief from the hot weather, and the park is right at the water's edge, 3 miles downriver from Lower Monumental Dam. There is a 3-day minimum stay on holiday weekends, and tents set up on lawns must be moved every two days. The campground is open from April to October.

28 Yakima Sportsman State Park

Location: 1 mile east of Yakima on the Yakima River.

Sites: 28 tent sites, 37 sites (with full hookups) for RVs no longer than 60 feet, 2 primitive tent sites.

Facilities: Drinking water, picnic tables, fire grills, flush toilets, coin-operated showers (fee), dump station, playground.

Fee per night: $ to $$$.

Elevation: 1,100 feet.

Management: Washington State Parks and Recreation Commission.

Activities: Hiking, fishing, bird watching.

Finding the campground: From Interstate 82 in Yakima, take exit 34 and drive less than a mile east on Washington Highway 24 to the park.

About the campground: This 50-acre park has 3.6 miles of waterfront on the east side of the Yakima River, just across the water from the city of Yakima. Swimming is not allowed in the river, but kayaking and rafting are popular. There is a variety of ponds and vegetation in the park, nurtured first by the Yakima Sportsman Association, then by Yakima County, and now by the state. Fishing ponds in the park are for children under 16. The river is open seasonally to adult anglers. The Yakima Canyon, through which the river passes on its way toward Yakima, is a shrubby steppe that hosts rare Washington birds like the sage thrasher, long-billed curlew, and sage sparrow. The Bureau of Land Management considers this a vanishing habitat. The campground is open year-round.

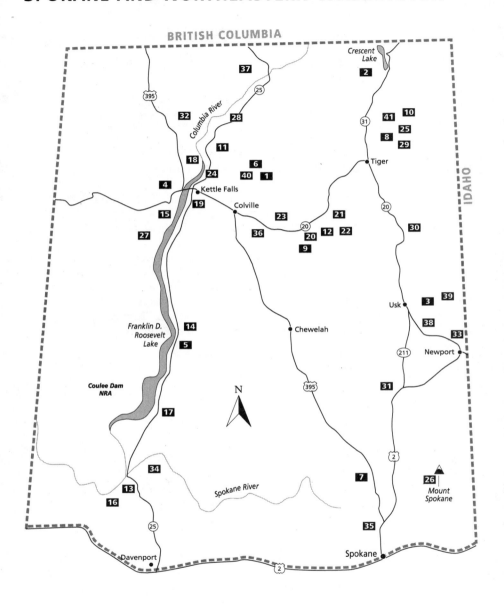

		Group sites	RV sites	Total # of sites	Max. RV length	Hookups	Toilets	Showers	Drinking water	Dump station	Pets	Wheelchair	Recreation	Fee	Season	Can reserve	Stay limit
1	Big Meadow Lake		•	16	32		V				•	•	HF		May–Sep		14
2	Boundary Dam		•	4			V				•		HFBRC				14
3	Browns Lake		•	18	21		V	•			•	•	HFB	$	late May–late Sep		14
4	Canyon Creek		•	12	30		V	•			•	•	HF		mid Apr–late Oct		14
5	Clover Leaf			8			V	•			•		FBS	$–$$			14
6	Douglas Falls Grange Park		•	8			F	•	•	•	•		H		Apr–Nov		7
7	Dragoon Creek		•	22			V	•			•		F		Apr–Sep		3
8	Edgewater		•	23	20		V	•			•		FB	$$	late May–early Sep		14
9	East Lake Gillette		•	30	31		V	•	•	•	•	•	HFBS	$–$$	mid May–late Sep		14
10	East Sullivan		•	38	50		V	•	•	•	•	•	HFBS	$$	mid May–Sep	•	14
11	Evans		•	46	26		F	•	•	•			FBS	$–$$			14
12	Flodelle Creek		•	8	20		V	•			•		HFC				7
13	Fort Spokane		•	67	26		F	•	•	•	•	•	FBS	$–$$			14
14	Gifford		•	47	20		P	•			•		FBS	$–$$			14
15	Haag Cove		•	18	26		P	•			•		FBS	$–$$			14
16	Hawk Creek		•	25	16		P	•			•		HFBS	$–$$			14
17	Hunters		•	42	26		F	•			•		FBS	$–$$			14
18	Kamloops Island			14			P				•		HFSB	$–$$			14
19	Kettle Falls		•	77	26		F	•	•	•	•	•	FSB	$–$$			14
20	Lake Gillette		•	14	31		V	•	•	•	•	•	HFBS	$–$$	mid May–late Sep		14
21	Lake Leo		•	8	15		P	•			•		HFS	$	mid May–mid Sep		14
22	Lake Thomas			15			V	•	•	•	•		HFBCO	$	mid May–late Sep		14
23	Little Twin Lakes		•	20	16		P				•		FBO		mid May–late Sep		14
24	Marcus Island		•	20	20		P	•			•		FSB	$–$$			14
25	Mill Pond		•	10	21		V	•			•		HFB	$$	late May–early Sep		14
26	Mount Spokane State Park	•	•	15	30		F	•			•		HRC	$–$$	Snowmelt–early Oct		10
27	North East Lake Ellen		•	11	22		V	•			•	•	FS		mid Apr–mid Oct		14
28	North Gorge		•	10	26		P	•			•		FBS	$–$$			14
29	Noisy Creek		•	19	35		V	•			•		HFB	$$	late May–early Sep	•	14
30	Panhandle		•	11	30		V	•			•		HFSBCO	$	late May–late Sep		14
31	Pend Oreille County Park		•	36			F	•	•		•		H	$	Mem Day–Lab Day	•	
32	Pierre Lake		•	15	24		V	•			•		HFBS		mid Apr–mid Oct		14
33	Pioneer Park		•	14	24		V	•			•	•	FBS	$	late May–late Sep		14
34	Porcupine Bay		•	31	20		F	•			•	•	HFBS	$–$$			14
35	Riverside State Park		•	101	45		F	•	•		•		HFBROC	$–$$			10
36	Rocky Lake		•	7			V	•			•		FB				7
37	Sheep Creek		•	11	20		V	•			•		HFO				7

continued on following page

	Group sites	RV sites	Total # of sites	Max. RV length	Hookups	Toilets	Showers	Drinking water	Dump station	Pets	Wheelchair	Recreation	Fee	Season	Can reserve	Stay limit
38 Skookum Creek		•	10			V	•			•		HFB				7
39 South Skookum Lake		•	24	30		V	•			•	•	HFB	$	late May–late Sep		14
40 Williams Lake		•	8			V	•	•	•			HFBC				7
41 West Sullivan		•	6	30		V	•				•	HFB	$$	mid May–Sep	•	14

Hookups: W = Water E = Electric S = Sewer
Toilets: F = Flush V = Vault P = Pit
Recreation: C = Bicycling/Mountain Biking H = Hiking S = Swimming F = Fishing B = Boating
O = Off-highway driving R = Horseback Riding
Maximum Trailer/RV Length given in feet. **Stay Limit** given in days.
Fee $ = less than $10; $$ = $10-$15; $$$ = $16-20; $$$$ = more than $20.
If no entry under **Season,** campground is open all year. If no entry under **Fee,** camping is free.

1 Big Meadow Lake

Location: 99 miles north of Spokane on Big Meadow Lake, near Colville.
Sites: 16 sites for tents or self-contained RVs no longer than 32 feet.
Facilities: Fire grills, picnic tables, vault toilets, boat ramp, fishing pier, wheelchair-accessible nature trail, wildlife viewing platform, environmental education lab; no drinking water.
Fee per night: None.
Elevation: 3,400 feet.
Management: Colville National Forest, Colville Ranger District.
Activities: Hiking, fishing, wildlife viewing.
Finding the campground: From Interstate 90 in Spokane, take exit 281 and head north on U.S. Highway 395. Drive 71 miles to Colville and turn east onto Washington Highway 20. Drive for 1 mile and turn left (north) onto Colville-Aladdin-Northport Road. Drive 20 miles to Meadow Creek Road, which is 1 mile past Aladdin. Turn right (east) onto rough and rocky Meadow Creek Road and drive 7 miles to the campground.

About the campground: The amenities are not much at this campground, and the road may give your passengers fits, but the location is idyllic. The campground sits at the edge of 70-acre Big Meadow Lake and is quiet and pristine. It is rarely full. It is open from May through September.

2 Boundary Dam

Location: About 105 miles north of Spokane on the Pend Oreille River, near Metaline Falls.
Sites: 4 primitive sites for tents or self-contained RVs.

Facilities: Picnic tables, vault toilet; no drinking water.
Fee per night: None.
Elevation: 2,130 feet.
Management: Bureau of Land Management.
Activities: Hiking, fishing, boating, bicycling, climbing, horseback riding, berry picking.
Finding the campground: From Spokane, take U.S. Highway 2 north for 32 miles to Washington Highway 211. Turn left (north) onto WA 211 and follow it for 15 miles to Usk and its junction with WA 20. Continue north, now on WA 20, for 31 miles to Tiger. From Tiger, drive north for another 13 miles on what is now WA 31. A half-mile past Metaline, turn left onto Boundary Road (County Road 62). There should be signs for Gardner Cave and Crawford State Park (day use only). Drive 11.5 miles to reach the access road to the dam.

About the campground: The Boundary Dam area covers about 1,000 acres of wilderness terrain in northeastern Washington. The campground is in a beautiful forested setting on the west bank of the Pend Oreille River, which is hemmed in by precipitous rock walls that rise 100 to 200 feet. The Salmo Priest Wilderness is on the east side of the river. Local wildlife includes elk, bears, and deer. Rainbow trout are not too hard to catch. Huckleberries are ready to pick beginning in early July. The campground is open year-round.

Boundary Dam holds back the waters of the Pend Oreille River in the far northeastern corner of the state.

3 Browns Lake

Location: About 57 miles north of Spokane on Browns Lake, near Newport.
Sites: 18 sites for tents or self-contained RVs no longer than 21 feet.
Facilities: Drinking water, picnic tables, vault toilets, boat ramp.
Fee per night: $.
Elevation: 3,150 feet.
Management: Colville National Forest, Newport Ranger District.
Activities: Hiking, fly fishing, canoeing.
Finding the campground: Drive north from Spokane on U.S. Highway 2 for 32 miles to Washington Highway 211. Turn left (north) onto WA 211 and continue for 15 miles to Usk. Cross the Pend Oreille River via Kings Lake Road (which eventually becomes Forest Road 5030) and stay on it all the way to Browns Lake, a distance of about 10 miles.

About the campground: You pass both South and North Skookum Lakes on the way to Browns Lake, but this campground is worth the extra few miles. It is basic but peaceful, and the lake is very nice. No motorized boats are permitted on the water. There are myriad Forest Service roads and trails in the area to explore if the fish are not biting. There is also a barrier-free interpretive trail nearby. The campground is open from late May to late September.

4 Canyon Creek

Location: 91 miles northwest of Spokane on Canyon Creek, near Colville.
Sites: 12 sites for tents or self-contained RVs no longer than 30 feet.
Facilities: Drinking water, fire grills, picnic tables, vault toilets.
Fee per night: None.
Elevation: 2,050 feet.
Management: Colville National Forest, Kettle Falls Ranger District.
Activities: Hiking, fishing.
Finding the campground: From Interstate 90 in Spokane, take exit 281 and head northwest on U.S. Highway 395. Drive 81 miles to Kettle Falls, which is 10 miles past Colville. Continue west on WA 20 for 10 miles, crossing the Columbia River, to reach the campground.

About the campground: Situated where Canyon Creek flows into Sherman Creek, this campground offers some good fishing opportunities. The highway here is the Sherman Pass Scenic Byway, and the region is upholstered in forest and meadows. A nice mile-long, barrier-free trail runs along Canyon Creek. Forest Road 136 runs along the other side. The campground is open from mid-April to late October.

5 Clover Leaf

Location: 91 miles northwest of Spokane on Franklin D. Roosevelt Lake, near Gifford.
Sites: 8 tent sites.

Facilities: Drinking water, fire grills, picnic tables, vault toilets, boat ramp (fee), dock.
Fee per night: $ to $$.
Elevation: 1,289 feet.
Management: Lake Roosevelt National Recreation Area.
Activities: Fishing, boating, swimming.
Finding the campground: From Interstate 90 in Spokane, take exit 277 and head west on U.S. Highway 2 for 32 miles to Davenport. Turn north onto Washington Highway 25 and drive 59 miles to the campground, just south of Gifford.

About the campground: There is not much to do at this small and rustic campground except fish and enjoy the water. The Gifford-Inchelium Ferry is just 2 miles south of camp. It offers free passage across the Columbia River to the Colville Indian Reservation every half hour. The campground is open year-round, with limited winter services.

6 | Douglas Falls Grange Park

Location: About 77 miles northwest of Spokane on Mill Creek, near Colville.
Sites: 8 sites for tents or self-contained RVs.
Facilities: Drinking water, tent pads, picnic tables, fire grills, restrooms, dump station, baseball field.
Fee per night: None.
Elevation: 1,870 feet.
Management: Washington Department of Natural Resources, Northeast Region.
Activities: Hiking.
Finding the campground: From Interstate 90 in Spokane, take exit 281 and head northwest on U.S. Highway 395. Drive 71 miles to Colville and turn east onto Washington Highway 20. Drive for 1 mile and turn left (north) onto Colville-Aladdin Road (which becomes Douglas Falls Road). Drive just over 5 miles to the campground on the left.

About the campground: Set on the edge of Douglas Falls Grange County Park, this wooded campground is a delight. There are hiking trails nearby, but the main activity seems to be sitting in camp and enjoying the company of the other campers. And somebody always seems to be getting a baseball game together. Douglas Falls presents a fine photo opportunity. The campground is open from April through November.

7 | Dragoon Creek

Location: About 16 miles north of Spokane on Dragoon Creek.
Sites: 22 sites for tents or self-contained RVs.
Facilities: Drinking water, picnic tables, fire grills, tent pads, vault toilets.
Fee per night: None.
Elevation: 2,100 feet.

Management: Washington Department of Natural Resources, Northeast Region.
Activities: Fishing.
Finding the campground: From Interstate 90 in Spokane, take exit 281 and head north on U.S. Highway 395. Drive 16 miles, turn left onto Dragoon Creek Road, and drive a half-mile to the campground entrance.

About the campground: This is a nice little forested campground on the Half Mile Prairie. It sits next to Dragoon Creek about 4 miles from its confluence with the Little Spokane River. Camp conditions are on the rustic side, but the place is relaxing. The campground is open from April through September.

---

8 Edgewater

Location: About 86 miles north of Spokane on the Pend Oreille River, near Ione.
Sites: 23 sites for tents or self-contained RVs no longer than 20 feet.
Facilities: Drinking water, fire grills, picnic tables, vault toilets, boat ramp.
Fee per night: $$.
Elevation: 2,030 feet.
Management: Colville National Forest, Sullivan Lake Ranger District.
Activities: Fishing, boating, waterskiing.
Finding the campground: From Interstate 90 in Spokane, take exit 281 and head north on U.S. Highways 2/395. Drive 6 miles to where the two highways split, bear right with US 2, and stay on it for 28 miles to its junction with Washington Highway 211. Turn left (north) onto WA 211 and continue for 15 miles to Usk. There, you join WA 20 and drive north for 31 miles to Tiger. From there, go north on WA 31 for 3 miles and then turn right onto Sullivan Lake Road. You cross the Pend Oreille River within a half-mile. Immediately turn left (north) onto Box Canyon-LeClerc Road and drive 2 miles to the campground entrance on the left.

About the campground: This 10-acre campground lies 2 miles upstream from Box Canyon Dam on the Pend Oreille River, at its confluence with Exposure Creek. It is a nice setting, and the camp faces west across the river toward Cement Mountain. Access to the river is easy. The campground is open from late May to early September.

---

9 East Lake Gillette

Location: About 92 miles north of Spokane on Lake Gillette, near Colville.
Sites: 30 sites for tents or self-contained RVs no longer than 31 feet.
Facilities: Drinking water, picnic tables, fire grills, vault toilets, dump station, boat ramp, moorage, docks, boat rentals.
Fee per night: $ to $$.
Elevation: 3,200 feet.
Management: Colville National Forest, Colville Ranger District.

Activities: Hiking, fishing, boating, swimming.
Finding the campground: From Interstate 90 in Spokane, take exit 281 and head north on U.S. Highway 395. Drive 71 miles to Colville and turn east onto Washington Highway 20. Drive for 20 miles, turn right (east) onto Forest Road 200, and drive a half-mile to the campground.

About the campground: Located on 7-acre, glacier-formed Lake Gillette, this campground is very popular and often full. It is right across the road from the Lake Gillette Campground. The lake offers wonderful recreational opportunities, and the nearby forest roads and trails are heavily used by off-road vehicle enthusiasts—so it can get noisy here. Trout fishing is good, and an interpretive trail meanders through the area. The campground is open from mid-May to late September.

10 East Sullivan

Location: 95 miles north of Spokane on Sullivan Lake, near the town of Metaline Falls.
Sites: 38 sites for tents or self-contained RVs no longer than 50 feet.
Facilities: Drinking water, fire grills, picnic tables, vault toilets, dump station, boat ramp, dock.
Fee per night: $$.
Elevation: 2,600 feet.
Management: Colville National Forest, Sullivan Lake Ranger District.
Activities: Hiking, fishing, boating, swimming, waterskiing.
Finding the campground: From Interstate 90 in Spokane, take exit 281 and head north on U.S. Highways 2/395. The two highways split in 6 miles. Branch right with US 2 and stay on it for 28 miles to the junction with Washington Highway 211. Turn left (north) onto WA 211 and continue for 15 miles to Usk. There, join WA 20 and drive north for 31 miles to Tiger. From Tiger, go north on WA 31 for 3 miles and then turn right onto Sullivan Lake Road. Cross the Pend Oreille River and drive 12 miles to the campground at the north end of Sullivan Lake. Or you can simply fly in, landing at Sullivan Lake Airport next to the campground. It has a grass airstrip.

About the campground: The East Sullivan Campground is separated from the West Sullivan Campground by an airstrip. Four-mile-long Sullivan Lake is surrounded by the mountains of the Colville National Forest, and the Salmo Priest Wilderness is just to the north and east. It offers some good hiking trails. A foot trail also runs down the east side of the lake, which is very popular with anglers and water-skiers. The campground is quite nice and clean. It is a good family campground and is open from mid-May through September. For a fee, you can make reservations by calling the National Recreation Reservation Service (see contact information on page 236).

11 Evans

Location: About 90 miles northwest of Spokane on Franklin D. Roosevelt Lake, near Colville.
Sites: 46 sites for tents or self-contained RVs no longer than 26 feet.
Facilities: Drinking water, fire grills, picnic tables, flush toilets, dump station, store, boat ramp (fee), dock, playground.
Fee per night: $ to $$.
Elevation: 1,290 feet.
Management: Lake Roosevelt National Recreation Area.
Activities: Fishing, boating, swimming, waterskiing.
Finding the campground: From Interstate 90 in Spokane, take exit 281 and head north on U.S. Highway 395 for 81 miles to Kettle Falls. A half-mile beyond Kettle Falls, turn right (north) onto Washington Highway 25 and drive 8 miles to the campground.

About the campground: This 16-acre campground is in a wonderful setting, on a small promontory that juts into Franklin D. Roosevelt Lake. It is a pretty comfortable camp and is roomy without being too big. The campground is open year-round.

12 Flodelle Creek

Location: About 92 miles north of Spokane on Flodelle Creek, near Colville.
Sites: 8 sites for tents or self-contained RVs no longer than 20 feet.
Facilities: Drinking water, picnic tables, fire grills, tent pads, vault toilets.
Fee per night: None.
Elevation: 3,100 feet.
Management: Washington Department of Natural Resources, Northeast Region.
Activities: Hiking, fishing, mountain biking, trail biking, snowmobiling.
Finding the campground: From Interstate 90 in Spokane, take exit 281 and head north on U.S. Highway 395. Drive 71 miles to Colville and turn east onto Washington Highway 20. Drive for 20.4 miles and turn right (south) onto a 2-lane gravel road. Go 0.3 mile, stay left at a junction, and continue 0.1 mile to the campground.

About the campground: This small rustic campground is not far off the highway, but it is not well known by the camping public. It sits right along forested Flodelle Creek, and there are plenty of trails to explore nearby. Trail biking on motorcycles is popular here, so be prepared for the noise. The campground is open year-round.

13 Fort Spokane

Location: About 54 miles northwest of Spokane on Franklin D. Roosevelt Lake.
Sites: 67 sites for tents or self-contained RVs no longer than 26 feet.

In the late 1800s, soldiers were stationed at Fort Spokane to keep the peace between white settlers and local Indians.

Facilities: Drinking water, picnic tables, fire grills, flush toilets, playground, dump station, boat docks, boat ramps (fee), marine dump station.
Fee per night: $ to $$.
Elevation: 1,289 feet.
Management: Lake Roosevelt National Recreation Area.
Activities: Fishing, boating, swimming, waterskiing.
Finding the campground: From Interstate 90 in Spokane, take exit 277 and head west on U.S. Highway 2 for 32 miles to Davenport. Turn right (north) onto Washington Highway 25 and drive 21 miles to the intersection with Miles-Creston Road. Turn left (south) onto Miles-Creston Road; the campground is within a half-mile. The actual Fort Spokane is a little farther west on WA 25, near the bridge over the Spokane River.

About the campground: This modern, 22-acre campground sits at the confluence of the Spokane and Columbia Rivers, along a segment of the Columbia that has been dammed to create Franklin D. Roosevelt Lake. The camp offers ranger-guided daytime activities and evening campfire programs. The campground is open year-round, with limited winter services.

Fort Spokane was completed in 1894; the post comprised 45 buildings. At the height of army occupation, over 300 soldiers lived there, but it was emptied at the outbreak of the Spanish-American War in 1898. In subsequent years, the Bureau of Indian Affairs used the post as a boarding school, tuberculosis sanatorium, and general hospital for local Indians. Now operated by the National Park Service, four of the fort's buildings remain. The guardhouse serving as the visitor center.

14 Gifford

Location: 90 miles northwest of Spokane on Franklin D. Roosevelt Lake, near Gifford.
Sites: 47 sites for tents or self-contained RVs no longer than 20 feet.
Facilities: Drinking water, fire grills, picnic tables, pit toilets, boat docks, boat ramp (fee), moorage.
Fee per night: $ to $$.
Elevation: 1,289 feet.
Management: Lake Roosevelt National Recreation Area.
Activities: Fishing, boating, swimming, waterskiing.
Finding the campground: From Interstate 90 in Spokane, take exit 277 and drive west on U.S. Highway 2 for 32 miles to Davenport. Turn right (north) onto Washington Highway 25 and drive 58 miles to the campground.

About the campground: This large, nice campground sometimes seems like a waterski camp for children. It is an excellent facility for boaters, and the fishing is rumored to be good on this stretch of the Columbia, where it has been dammed to form Franklin D. Roosevelt Lake. The Gifford-Inchelium Ferry is just 1 mile south of camp. It offers free passage across the Columbia to the Colville Indian Reservation every half hour. The campground is open year-round, with limited winter services.

15 Haag Cove

Location: 91 miles northwest of Spokane on Franklin D. Roosevelt Lake, near Kettle Falls.
Sites: 18 sites for tents or self-contained RVs no longer than 26 feet.
Facilities: Drinking water, fire grills, picnic tables, pit toilets, boat dock.
Fee per night: $ to $$.
Elevation: 1,285 feet.
Management: Lake Roosevelt National Recreation Area.
Activities: Fishing, boating, swimming, waterskiing.
Finding the campground: From Interstate 90 in Spokane, take exit 281 and head north on U.S. Highway 395 for 81 miles to Kettle Falls. Continue west through town for 3 miles, cross the bridge over the Columbia, and immediately turn left (south) with Washington Highway 20. Continue for 4 miles, turn left (south) onto Kettle Falls Road, and drive 3 miles to the campground.

About the campground: This campground, located on the segment of the Columbia River dammed to create Franklin D. Roosevelt Lake, is farther off the beaten track than others in the area. It is pleasantly situated near a long, narrow cove that is fun to explore, and the campground is quite comfortable. It is open year-round.

16 Hawk Creek

Location: 61 miles northwest of Spokane on Franklin D. Roosevelt Lake.
Sites: 25 sites for tents or self-contained RVs no longer than 16 feet.
Facilities: Drinking water, picnic tables, fire grills, pit toilets, boat docks, boat ramp (fee).
Fee per night: $ to $$.
Elevation: 1,289 feet.
Management: Lake Roosevelt National Recreation Area.
Activities: Hiking, fishing, swimming, boating, waterskiing.
Finding the campground: From Interstate 90 in Spokane, take exit 277 and drive west on U.S. Highway 2 for 32 miles to Davenport. Turn right (north) onto Washington Highway 25 and drive 21 miles to the intersection with Miles-Creston Road. Turn left (south) onto Miles-Creston Road and drive 8 miles to the campground at the mouth of Hawk Creek.

About the campground: This campground is on the north side of a 2.5-mile-long bay of Franklin D. Roosevelt Lake, which was created by damming a segment of the Columbia River. The bay is fed by Hawk Creek, and Hawk Creek Falls is about a half-mile to the east, at the head of the bay. This is a nice camp, away from the hubbub on the Columbia River. The campground is open year-round, with limited winter services.

17 Hunters

Location: 79 miles northwest of Spokane on Franklin D. Roosevelt Lake.
Sites: 42 sites for tents or self-contained RVs no longer than 26 feet.
Facilities: Drinking water, picnic tables, fire grills, flush toilets, store, ice, boat docks, boat ramp (fee).
Fee per night: $ to $$.
Elevation: 1,289 feet.
Management: Lake Roosevelt National Recreation Area.
Activities: Fishing, boating, swimming, waterskiing.
Finding the campground: From Interstate 90 in Spokane, take exit 277 and drive west on U.S. Highway 2 for 32 miles to Davenport. Turn right (north) onto Washington Highway 25 and drive 47 miles to Hunters. Hunters Park is 1.5 miles west of Hunters via a signed access road.

About the campground: This is a good family camp near an estuary formed by Hunters Creek as it flows into Franklin D. Roosevelt Lake, which is actually a dammed segment of the Columbia River. The camp is comfortable and offers a bit of shopping and fine access to the water. The campground is open year-round, with limited services in winter.

18 Kamloops Island

Location: About 88 miles northwest of Spokane on Franklin D. Roosevelt Lake, near Colville.
Sites: 14 tent sites.
Facilities: Picnic tables, pit toilets, boat docks; no drinking water.
Fee per night: $ to $$.
Elevation: 1,289 feet.
Management: Lake Roosevelt National Recreation Area.
Activities: Hiking, fishing, swimming, boating, waterskiing.
Finding the campground: From Interstate 90 in Spokane, take exit 281 and head north on U.S. Highway 395 for 81 miles to Kettle Falls. Continue west through town for 4 miles, crossing the bridge over the Columbia, and immediately turn right (north) with US 395. Continue 3.5 miles to the campground entrance on the right and cross the bridge to Kamloops Island.

About the campground: This island camp is perfect for tenters who can appreciate the primitive conditions. Kamloops Island is at the mouth of the Kettle River Arm of this segment of the Columbia River, which has been dammed to form Franklin D. Roosevelt Lake. The campground is open year-round.

19 Kettle Falls

Location: About 86 miles northwest of Spokane on Franklin D. Roosevelt Lake, near Colville.
Sites: 77 sites for tents or self-contained RVs no longer than 26 feet.

Facilities: Drinking water, picnic tables, fire grills, restrooms, dump station, boat ramp (fee), docks, playground, cafe.
Fee per night: $ to $$.
Elevation: 1,200 feet.
Management: Lake Roosevelt National Recreation Area.
Activities: Fishing, swimming, boating, waterskiing, campfire programs.
Finding the campground: From Interstate 90 in Spokane, take exit 281 and head north on U.S. Highway 395 for 81 miles to Kettle Falls. Continue through town, still on US 395, for 3 miles. The campground access road branches off to the left just before you cross the bridge over the Columbia River, and the campground itself is 1.5 miles south on this road.

About the campground: This 22-acre park sits right on the shore of Franklin D. Roosevelt Lake, which was created with the damming of the Columbia River. It is a popular park with local residents. The layout and amenities are good, and so is the water access. Lions Island, directly south of the campground, is fun to explore. The campground is open year-round, with limited services in the winter.

20 Lake Gillette

Location: About 92 miles north of Spokane on Lake Gillette, near Colville.
Sites: 14 sites for tents or self-contained RVs no longer than 31 feet.
Facilities: Drinking water, picnic tables, fire grills, vault toilets, dump station, boat ramp, moorage, docks, boat rentals.
Fee per night: $ to $$.
Elevation: 3,200 feet.
Management: Colville National Forest, Colville Ranger District.
Activities: Hiking, fishing, boating, swimming.
Finding the campground: From Interstate 90 in Spokane, take exit 281 and head north on U.S. Highway 395. Drive 71 miles to Colville and turn east onto Washington Highway 20. Drive for 20 miles to Forest Road 200, turn right (east), and drive a half-mile to the campground.

About the campground: This campground sits on the shore of 7-acre, glacier-formed Lake Gillette, right across the road from the East Lake Gillette Campground. It is very popular and is often full. The lake offers wonderful recreational opportunities, and the nearby forest roads and trails are heavily used by off-road vehicle enthusiasts—so it can get noisy here. The trout fishing is good, and an interpretive trail meanders through the area. The campground is open from mid-May to late September.

21 Lake Leo

Location: 95 miles north of Spokane on Lake Leo, near Colville.
Sites: 8 sites for tents or self-contained RVs no longer than 15 feet.
Facilities: Drinking water, picnic tables, fire grills, pit toilets, firewood, boat ramp.

Fee per night: $.
Elevation: 3,200 feet.
Management: Colville National Forest, Colville Ranger District.
Activities: Hiking, fishing, swimming, cross-country skiing.
Finding the campground: From Interstate 90 in Spokane, take exit 281 and head north on U.S. Highway 395 for 71 miles to Colville. Turn right (east) onto Washington Highway 20 and drive 24 miles to the campground.

About the campground: This is a small, quiet campground on one of the glacially carved Little Pend Oreille Lakes. It is pretty basic, but its lakeside location counts for a lot. The campground is open from mid-May to mid-September.

22 Lake Thomas

Location: 92 miles north of Spokane on Lake Thomas, near Colville.
Sites: 15 tent sites.
Facilities: Drinking water, picnic tables, fire grills, vault toilets, dump station, boat ramp, docks, boat rentals, groceries.
Fee per night: $.
Elevation: 3,200 feet.
Management: Colville National Forest, Colville Ranger District.
Activities: Hiking, fishing, boating, waterskiing, mountain biking.
Finding the campground: From Interstate 90 in Spokane, take exit 281 and head north on U.S. Highway 395 for 71 miles to Colville. Turn right (east) onto Washington Highway 20. Drive for 20 miles, turn right (east) onto Forest Road 200, and drive 1 mile to the campground.

About the campground: This 2-mile-long glacial lake sits in the midst of a thick forest. The campground amenities are pretty good, and the recreational opportunities are impressive. There are even some places nearby to drive off-road vehicles, especially the Radar Dome ORV Trail, which is open summer and winter. It is located across WA 20 from the campground, a half-mile toward Colville. There are camping and fishing spots all along the Little Pend Oreille River, but nothing beats camping on a lake. The campground is open from mid-May to late September.

23 Little Twin Lakes

Location: 89 miles north of Spokane on Little Twin Lakes, near Colville.
Sites: 20 sites for tents or self-contained RVs no longer than 16 feet.
Facilities: Picnic tables, fire grills, pit toilets, boat docks, boat ramp; no drinking water.
Fee per night: None.
Elevation: 3,800 feet.
Management: Colville National Forest, Colville Ranger District.
Activities: Fishing, boating, off-road driving.
Finding the campground: From Interstate 90 in Spokane, take exit 281 and

head north on U.S. Highway 395. Drive 71 miles to Colville and turn right (east) onto Washington Highway 20. Drive for 12.5 miles to Black Lake-Squaw Creek Road, turn left (north), and go 4.5 miles to the junction with Forest Road 150. Go straight onto FR 150 and drive 1 mile to the campground.

About the campground: The road to this remote, 20-acre site is rough, but the campground is worth the effort. A four-wheel-drive vehicle is a good idea, but not always necessary, depending on recent weather conditions. If the access road is not enough of a challenge, there are miles and miles of old logging roads in the area for you to try. The wooded camp is rustic, but the setting is beautiful. It is open mid-May through September.

24 Marcus Island

Location: About 85 miles northwest of Spokane on Franklin D. Roosevelt Lake, near Colville.
Sites: 20 sites for tents or self-contained RVs no longer than 20 feet.
Facilities: Drinking water, fire grills, picnic tables, pit toilets, dock.
Fee per night: $ to $$.
Elevation: 1,290 feet.
Management: Lake Roosevelt National Recreation Area.
Activities: Fishing, boating, swimming, waterskiing.
Finding the campground: From Interstate 90 in Spokane, take exit 281 and head northwest on U.S. Highway 395 for 81 miles to the town of Kettle Falls. A half-mile beyond town, turn right (north) onto Washington Highway 25 and drive 4 miles to the campground on Marcus Island.

About the campground: This is a fair-sized campground on a segment of the Columbia River that has been dammed to form Franklin D. Roosevelt Lake. Because of its close proximity to the water, the campground offers plenty of recreational opportunities. It is a bit less comfortable and more rustic than Evans Campground, 4 miles to the north. Marcus Island Campground is open year-round.

25 Mill Pond

Location: 96 miles north of Spokane on Mill Pond, near Ione.
Sites: 10 sites for tents or self-contained RVs no longer than 21 feet.
Facilities: Drinking water, picnic tables, fire grills, vault toilets, boat ramp.
Fee per night: $$.
Elevation: 2,500 feet.
Management: Colville National Forest, Sullivan Lake Ranger District.
Activities: Hiking, fishing, boating, waterskiing.
Finding the campground: From Interstate 90 in Spokane, take exit 281 and head north on U.S. Highways 2/395. In 6 miles, the two highways split. Branch right with US 2 and stay on it for 28 miles to the junction with Washington Highway 211. Turn left (north) onto WA 211 and continue for 15 miles to Usk.

There, you join WA 20 and continue north for another 31 miles to Tiger. From there, go north on WA 31 for 3 miles and turn right (east) onto Sullivan Lake Road. Cross the Pend Oreille River and drive 13 miles to the campground, just beyond Sullivan Lake.

About the campground: This sparse campground is favored by backpackers, who use it as a base camp. The pond is nice, but the real action is on Sullivan Lake, a mile to the south. The campground is open from late May to early September.

26 Mount Spokane State Park

Location: 30 miles northeast of Spokane on Mount Spokane.
Sites: 2 tent sites, 12 sites for tents or self contained RVs no longer than 30 feet, 1 group site (capacity 90). Skiers may park self-contained RVs in the day-use area during the winter.
Facilities: Drinking water, picnic tables, flush toilets, 2 horse feeding stations, ski resort, restaurant.
Fee per night: $ to $$.
Elevation: Mount Spokane is 5,880 feet. The campground is lower.
Management: Washington State Parks and Recreation Commission.
Activities: Hiking, horseback riding, huckleberry picking, picnicking, mountain biking, downhill and cross-country skiing, sledding, snowmobiling.
Finding the campground: From Interstate 90 in Spokane, take exit 281 and drive north on U.S. Highway 2 for 6 miles. Turn right (east) onto Washington Highway 206 and drive 24 miles to the campground.

About the campground: Encompassing 13,643 acres and providing parking for 1,588 vehicles, this park is obviously more than your ordinary campground. In fact, Mount Spokane is also a ski area with 32 runs, two rope tows, and a lodge. Built by the Civilian Conservation Corps in the 1930s, Mount Spokane was the first Washington state park east of the Cascades. By 1950, the mountain had become popular with skiers. It also offers 50 miles of hiking and equestrian trails and sweeping views of the Inland Empire. The park, the city, and the campground all derive their name from an Indian word that means "sun." This popular campground is open from snowmelt to early October.

27 North East Lake Ellen

Location: About 98 miles northwest of Spokane on Lake Ellen, near Colville.
Sites: 11 sites for tents or self-contained RVs no longer than 22 feet.
Facilities: Drinking water, picnic tables, fire grills, vault toilets, boat docks.
Fee per night: None.
Elevation: 2,500 feet.
Management: Colville National Forest, Kettle Falls Ranger District.
Activities: Fishing, swimming.
Finding the campground: From Interstate 90 in Spokane, take exit 281 and

head north and then northwest on U.S. Highway 395 for 81 miles to the town of Kettle Falls. Continue west through town for 3 miles, cross the bridge over the Columbia River, and immediately turn left (south) with Washington Highway 20. Drive 4 miles, turn left (south) onto Kettle Falls Road, and drive 4.5 miles. At Lake Ellen Road, turn right (west) and drive 5 miles to the campground.

About the campground: This is a small campground on a small lake, but the amenities are okay and this is a wonderful place to kick back and enjoy the water in forested surroundings. The campground is open from mid-April to mid-October.

28 North Gorge

Location: About 100 miles northwest of Spokane on Franklin D. Roosevelt Lake, near Colville.
Sites: 10 sites for tents or self-contained RVs no longer than 26 feet.
Facilities: Drinking water, fire grills, picnic tables, pit toilets, boat ramp (fee), dock, playground.
Fee per night: $ to $$.
Elevation: 1,290 feet.
Management: Lake Roosevelt National Recreation Area.
Activities: Fishing, boating, swimming, waterskiing.
Finding the campground: From Interstate 90 in Spokane, take exit 281 and head northwest on U.S. Highway 395 for 81 miles to the town of Kettle Falls. A half-mile beyond town, turn right (north) onto Washington Highway 25 and drive 20 miles to the campground.

About the campground: This is the best of three campgrounds along this section of the Columbia River, which has been dammed to form Franklin D. Roosevelt Lake. The amenities at North Gorge are serviceable, and the camp is relatively small and isolated. Bass, sunfish, trout, and walleye await anglers. The campground is open year-round.

29 Noisy Creek

Location: 90 miles north of Spokane on Sullivan Lake, near Ione.
Sites: 19 sites for tents or self-contained RVs no longer than 35 feet.
Facilities: Drinking water, picnic tables, fire grills, vault toilets, boat ramp.
Fee per night: $$.
Elevation: 2,546 feet.
Management: Colville National Forest, Sullivan Lake Ranger District.
Activities: Hiking, fishing, boating, waterskiing.
Finding the campground: From Interstate 90 in Spokane, take exit 281 and head north on U.S. Highways 2/395. In 6 miles, the two highways split. Branch right with US 2 and stay on it for 28 miles to the junction with Washington Highway 211. Turn left (north) onto WA 211 and continue for 15 miles to Usk. From there, join WA 20 and continue north for 31 miles to Tiger. From Tiger, go

north on WA 31 for 3 miles and then turn right (east) onto Sullivan Lake Road. The campground is in 7 miles on the south end of Sullivan Lake.

About the campground: Situated where Noisy Creek enters Lake Sullivan, this primitive campground has great access to the southern end of the 4-mile-long lake. Fishing and waterskiing are the most popular activities. The hiking is good, too. There is a trail that runs along the eastern shore of the lake to the campgrounds at the other end. The campground is open from late May to early September. For a fee, you can make reservations by calling the National Recreation Reservation Service (see contact information on page 236).

30 Panhandle

Location: About 64 miles north of Spokane on the Pend Oreille River, near Ione.
Sites: 11 sites for tents or self-contained RVs no longer than 30 feet.
Facilities: Drinking water, picnic tables, vault toilets.
Fee per night: $.
Elevation: 2,050 feet.
Management: Colville National Forest, Newport Ranger District.
Activities: Hiking, fishing, boating, swimming, waterskiing, mountain biking, off-road driving.
Finding the campground: From Interstate 90 in Spokane, take exit 281 and head north on U.S. Highways 2/395. In 6 miles, the two highways split. Branch right with US 2 and stay on it for 28 miles to the junction with Washington Highway 211. Turn left (north) onto WA 211 and continue for 15 miles to Usk. Continue through town and across the Pend Oreille River. Immediately after crossing the bridge, turn left onto LeClerc Creek Road and drive 15 miles north to the campground on the left.

About the campground: Adjacent to the LeClerc Creek Wildlife Area, this small rustic campground is a good place for water sports enthusiasts. Nearby are some good trails for hiking, mountain biking, and off-road driving. The campground is open from late May to late September.

31 Pend Oreille County Park

Location: 31 miles north of Spokane.
Sites: 34 standard tent sites, 2 sites for tents or self-contained RVs.
Facilities: Drinking water, picnic tables, fire grills, flush toilets, showers.
Fee per night: $.
Elevation: 2,200 feet.
Management: Pend Oreille County Department of Public Works.
Activities: Hiking.
Finding the campground: From Interstate 90 in Spokane, take exit 281 and head north on U.S. Highways 2/395. In 6 miles, the two highways split. Branch right with US 2 and stay on it for 25 miles to the campground on the left.

About the campground: This campground makes a better layover than a destination. It is perfectly nice, but there is not a lot to do. Trails in the nearby Fertile Valley are a good possibility. The campground is open from Memorial Day through Labor Day. For reservations, call the Pend Oreille County Department of Public Works (see contact information on page 235).

32 Pierre Lake

Location: 104 miles northwest of Spokane on Pierre Lake, near Kettle Falls.
Sites: 15 sites for tents or self-contained RVs no longer than 24 feet.
Facilities: Drinking water, picnic tables, fire grills, vault toilets, boat ramp, docks.
Fee per night: None.
Elevation: 2,150 feet.
Management: Colville National Forest, Kettle Falls Ranger District.
Activities: Hiking, fishing, boating, swimming.
Finding the campground: From Interstate 90 in Spokane, take exit 281 and head north on U.S. Highway 395 for 81 miles to the town of Kettle Falls. Continue another 14 miles north on US 395 to Barstow. Turn right (east) onto County Road 4013 (Barstow-Pierre Lake Road) and continue 9 miles to the campground.

About the campground: Located about 7 miles from the Canadian border, Pierre Lake is very nice indeed. The campground is used mostly by anglers, but it is fine for families, too. There is an easy hike along the west shore of the lake, as well as a bit tougher one up Hungry Hill. The campground is on the rustic side but perfectly adequate. It is open from mid-April to mid-October.

33 Pioneer Park

Location: About 50 miles northeast of Spokane on the Pend Oreille River, near Newport.
Sites: 14 sites for tents or self-contained RVs no longer than 24 feet.
Facilities: Drinking water, picnic tables, vault toilets, boat docks, boat ramps, nearby boat rentals.
Fee per night: $.
Elevation: 490 feet.
Management: Colville National Forest, Newport Ranger District.
Activities: Fishing, boating, swimming, waterskiing.
Finding the campground: From Interstate 90 in Spokane, take exit 281 and head north on U.S. Highways 2/395. In 6 miles, the two highways split. Branch right with US 2 and stay on it for 41 miles to Newport on the Idaho border. Stay on US 2 through town and over the bridge into Idaho, but take an immediate left onto LeClerc Creek Road and drive for 2 miles to the park. It is on the Washington side of the border.

About the campground: The Pend Oreille River flows smooth and wide here, a consequence of Box Canyon Dam 50 miles to the north. A barrier-free interpretive trail with a boardwalk allows campers to enjoy the beautiful waterway.

There is a protected inlet, and Cooks Island is just offshore. Native Americans lived along the river as long as 9,000 years ago, and an archaeological dig at the campground provides a glimpse of early life. The campground is open from late May to late September.

34 Porcupine Bay

Location: 54 miles northwest of Spokane on the Spokane River.
Sites: 31 sites for tents or self-contained RVs no longer than 20 feet.
Facilities: Drinking water, picnic tables, fire grills, flush toilets, playground, boat docks, boat ramp (fee).
Fee per night: $ to $$.
Elevation: 1,289 feet.
Management: Lake Roosevelt National Recreation Area.
Activities: Hiking, fishing, boating, swimming.
Finding the campground: From Interstate 90 in Spokane, take exit 277 onto U.S. Highway 2 West and drive 32 miles to Davenport. Turn north onto Washington Highway 25 and drive 13.5 miles. At Porcupine Bay Road and the sign for the Coulee Dam National Recreation Area, turn right (north) and drive 6.5 miles to the campground.

About the campground: This 7-acre riverside campground is popular with boaters. It is rather isolated in the small hills that border the Spokane River. The campground is open year-round, weather permitting.

35 Riverside State Park

Location: 6 miles northwest of downtown Spokane on the Spokane River.
Sites: 101 sites for tents or RVs no longer than 45 feet.
Facilities: Drinking water, picnic tables, fire grills, flush toilets, showers, boat ramp, riding stables, off-road vehicle park.
Fee per night: $ to $$.
Elevation: 1,640 feet.
Management: Washington State Parks and Recreation Commission.
Activities: Boating, fishing, hiking, bicycling, horseback riding, motorcycle and ATV riding, snowmobiling, cross-country skiing, bird watching.
Finding the campground: From downtown Spokane, take the Maple Street Bridge Route north to Northwest Boulevard. Turn left onto Northwest Boulevard and continue 2.5 miles to H Street. Turn left as the brown Riverside State Park sign directs, and follow park signs past Downriver Golf Course to the park entrance.

About the campground: This 7,600-acre park with 37 miles of freshwater shoreline feels like it is way out in the country, but it is easily accessible from Spokane. The ponderosa forest along the Spokane River extends to a ridge with great views of the city. A concession operates equestrian facilities in the Fort George Wright portion of the park, and there is a 600-acre motorcycle and off-road vehicle park. Horseback riding is a great way to see the park, and the park stables rents mounts by the hour or day. There are 37 miles of foot and horse trails to explore. A lava formation in the park, called the Bowl and Pitcher, attracts photography classes from local colleges. You can reach it via a 218-foot-high pedestrian suspension bridge over the Spokane River. The campground is open year-round.

36 Rocky Lake

Location: About 82 miles north of Spokane on Rocky Lake, near Colville.
Sites: 7 sites for tents or self-contained RVs.
Facilities: Drinking water, picnic tables, fire grills, tent pads, vault toilets, boat ramp.
Fee per night: None.
Elevation: 1,620 feet.
Management: Washington Department of Natural Resources, Northeast Region.
Activities: Fishing, canoeing.
Finding the campground: From Interstate 90 in Spokane, take exit 281 and head north and then northwest on U.S. Highway 395 for 71 miles to Colville. Turn east onto Washington Highway 20 and drive 5.9 miles. Then turn right (south) onto Artman-Gibson Road and continue 3.2 miles. Turn right (northwest) again onto a one-lane gravel road and drive 0.3 mile. Stay to the left at the junction and continue another 2 miles to the site.

About the campground: This small rustic campground is an ideal place to kick back and maybe do a bit of canoe fishing on a big pond. Just remember, it is named Rocky Lake for a reason. The campground, open year-round, is very close to the Little Pend Oreille Habitat Management Area, which offers good hiking and fishing.

37 Sheep Creek

Location: About 120 miles northwest of Spokane on Sheep Creek, near Northport.
Sites: 11 sites for tents or self-contained RVs no longer than 20 feet.
Facilities: Drinking water, picnic tables, fire grills, tent pads, vault toilets, group shelter.
Fee per night: None.
Elevation: 1,960 feet.
Management: Washington Department of Natural Resources, Northeast Region.
Activities: Hiking, fishing, off-road driving.
Finding the campground: From Interstate 90 in Spokane, take exit 281 and head north and then northwest on U.S. Highway 395 for 81 miles to the town of Kettle Falls. A half-mile beyond Kettle Falls, turn right (north) onto Washington Highway 25 and drive 33 miles to Northport. Continue 0.7 mile north on WA 25,

cross the Columbia River, turn left onto Sheep Creek Road and drive 4.3 miles. Turn right into the campground.

About the campground: This is a very basic campground but nicely positioned along forested Sheep Creek. There are plenty of nearby hiking trails and four-wheel-drive routes. The campground is open year-round.

38 Skookum Creek

Location: About 50 miles north of Spokane on Skookum Creek, near Newport.
Sites: 10 sites for tents or self-contained RVs.
Facilities: Drinking water, picnic tables, fire grills, tent pads, vault toilets.
Fee per night: None.
Elevation: 2,290 feet.
Management: Washington Department of Natural Resources, Northeast Region.
Activities: Hiking, fishing, boating.
Finding the campground: From Interstate 90 in Spokane, take exit 281 and head north and then northwest on U.S. Highway 2 for 32 miles to the intersection with Washington Highway 211. Turn left onto WA 211 and continue for 15 miles to Usk. Cross the Pend Oreille River via Kings Lake Road. In 0.9 mile, turn right onto LeClerc Creek Road and drive 2.2 miles. Turn left onto a one-lane gravel road, drive just 0.1 mile, and turn left for 0.3 mile to the campground.

About the campground: This is a nice place for canoeing or kayaking. The campsites are wooded and are close to the creek. The campground is open year-round.

39 South Skookum Lake

Location: About 55 miles north of Spokane on South Skookum Lake, near Newport.
Sites: 24 sites for tents or self-contained RVs no longer than 30 feet.
Facilities: Drinking water, picnic tables, vault toilets, small boat ramp, wheelchair-accessible fishing dock.
Fee per night: $.
Elevation: 2,224 feet.
Management: Colville National Forest, Newport Ranger District.
Activities: Hiking, fishing, boating.
Finding the campground: From Interstate 90 in Spokane, take exit 281 and head north and then northwest on U.S. Highway 2 for 32 miles to the intersection with Washington Highway 211. Turn left (north) onto WA 211 and continue for 15 miles to Usk. Cross the Pend Oreille River via Kings Lake Road and stay on it for 7 miles. Then turn right (northeast) onto Forest Road 50. It swings around the north end of King Lake for 1.5 miles. Turn right (south) onto the campground access road.

About the campground: This medium-sized campground is a very pleasant respite from the workaday world. There is an easy walking trail around the small lake and a more ambitious one up 4,383-foot Kings Mountain. The campground is open from late May to late September.

40 Williams Lake

Location: About 87 miles northwest of Spokane on Williams Lake, near Colville.
Sites: 8 sites for tents or small self-contained RVs.
Facilities: Drinking water, picnic tables, fire grills, vault toilets, dump station, boat ramp.
Fee per night: None.
Elevation: 2,160 feet.
Management: Washington Department of Natural Resources, Northeast Region.
Activities: Hiking, fishing, boating, mountain biking.
Finding the campground: From Interstate 90 in Spokane, take exit 281 and head north on U.S. Highway 395 for 71 miles to Colville. Continue on US 395 for another 2 miles to Williams Lake Road. Turn right (north) and stay on Williams Lake Road for 13.7 miles. Turn left and immediately right to reach the campground.

About the campground: This basic campground is set on the shore of Williams Lake in a mountainous region punctuated by old mining sites. The Columbia River is only about 4 miles farther north up Williams Lake Road. The campground is open year-round.

41 West Sullivan

Location: 95 miles north of Spokane on Sullivan Lake, near Ione.
Sites: 6 sites for tents or self-contained RVs no longer than 30 feet.
Facilities: Drinking water, picnic tables, fire grills, vault toilets.
Fee per night: $$.
Elevation: 2,546 feet.
Management: Colville National Forest, Sullivan Lake Ranger District.
Activities: Hiking, fishing, boating, waterskiing.
Finding the campground: From Interstate 90 in Spokane, take exit 281 and head north on U.S. Highways 2/395. In 6 miles, the two highways split. Branch right with US 2 and stay on it for 28 miles to the junction with Washington Highway 211. Turn left (north) onto WA 211 and continue for 15 miles to Usk. From there, join WA 20 and continue north for 31 miles to Tiger. From Tiger, go north on WA 31 for 3 miles and then turn right onto Sullivan Lake Road. The campground is in 12 miles, at the north end of Sullivan Lake. Or you can simply fly in, landing at Sullivan Lake Airport next to the campground. It has a grass airstrip.

About the campground: Four-mile-long Sullivan Lake is surrounded by the mountains of the Colville National Forest. The Salmo Priest Wilderness is just to the north and east. It offers some good hiking trails. A foot trail also runs down the east side of the lake, which is very popular with anglers and water-skiers. The campground is nice and clean. It is a good family campground and is open from mid-May through September. For a fee, you can make reservations by calling the National Recreation Reservation Service (see contact information on page 236).

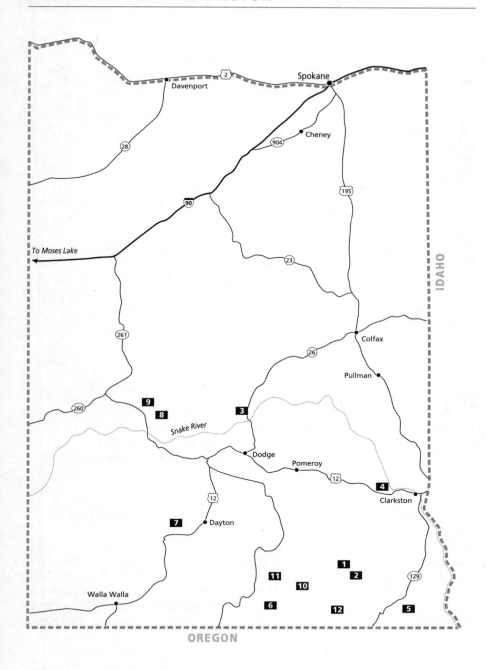

	Group sites	RV sites	Total # of sites	Max. RV length	Hookups	Toilets	Showers	Drinking water	Dump station	Pets	Wheelchair	Recreation	Fee	Season	Can reserve	Stay limit
1 Alder Thicket		•	4	15		V			•	•		H		mid May–mid Nov		7
2 Big Springs			8			V			•	•		H		mid May–mid Nov		7
3 Central Ferry State Park	•	•	69	45	WES	F	•	•	•	•	•	HFSB	$$$	mid Mar–mid Nov	•	10
4 Chief Timothy State Park		•	68	60	WES	F	•	•	•	•	•	HFB	$$–$$$		•	10
5 Fields Spring State Park		•	22	30		F	•	•	•	•		H	$–$$			10
6 Godman		•	8	15		V				•		HR		mid Jun–late Oct		7
7 Lewis and Clark Trail State Park	•	•	34	28		F	•	•		•		HF	$–$$$			10
8 Lyons Ferry State Park		•	52	45		F	•	•	•	•		HFBS	$$	Apr–Sep		10
9 Palouse Falls State Park		•	10	40		P	•			•	•	H	$	Apr–late Sep		10
10 Teal Spring		•	8	15		V				•		H		Jun–mid Nov		7
11 Tucannon		•	13	15		V				•		HF		May–late Nov		7
12 Wickiup		•	5	15		V			•			H		mid June–late Oct		7

Hookups: W = Water   E = Electric   S = Sewer
Toilets: F = Flush   V = Vault   P = Pit
Recreation: C = Bicycling/Mountain Biking   H = Hiking   S = Swimming   F = Fishing   B = Boating
O = Off-highway driving   R = Horseback Riding
Maximum Trailer/RV Length given in feet. **Stay Limit** given in days.
Fee $ = less than $10; $$ = $10-$15; $$$ = $16–20; $$$$ = more than $20.
If no entry under **Season,** campground is open all year. If no entry under **Fee,** camping is free.

1 · Alder Thicket

Location: About 130 miles south of Spokane, near Pomeroy.
Sites: 4 sites for tents or self-contained RVs no longer than 15 feet.
Facilities: Picnic tables, fire grills, vault toilets, dump station; no drinking water.
Fee per night: None.
Elevation: 4,920 feet.
Management: Umatilla National Forest, Pomeroy Ranger District.
Activities: Hiking.
Finding the campground: From Interstate 90 in Spokane, take exit 279 and head south on U.S. Highway 195 for 57 miles. Just before you reach Colfax, turn west onto Washington Highway 26 and drive 17 miles to Dusty. Take WA 127 south for 27 miles to Dodge and then turn east onto US 12 and drive 13 miles to Pomeroy. Turn south onto WA 128, which will become Mountain Road and then Forest Road 40. Drive 17 miles from the turnoff to the campground entrance.

About the campground: Located, naturally, in an alder thicket in the middle of the proverbial nowhere, this campground is quite rustic, bordering on primitive. The choices are to kick back and commune with nature or go hiking and commune with nature. The campground is open from mid-May to mid-November.

2 Big Springs

Location: About 137 miles south of Spokane, near Pomeroy.
Sites: 8 tent sites.
Facilities: Picnic tables, vault toilets, dump station; no drinking water.
Fee per night: None.
Elevation: 4,970 feet.
Management: Umatilla National Forest, Pomeroy Ranger District.
Activities: Hiking.
Finding the campground: From Interstate 90 in Spokane, take exit 279 and head south on U.S. Highway 195 for 57 miles. Just before Colfax, turn west onto Washington Highway 26 and drive 17 miles to Dusty. Take WA 127 south for 27 miles to Dodge and then turn east onto US 12 and drive 13 miles to Pomeroy. Turn south onto WA 128 and drive about 20 miles to the Clearwater Lookout. The road will become Mountain Road and then Forest Road 40 along the way. At the lookout, turn left (east) onto FR 42 (Ruchert Road) and continue for 3 miles to the campground on the left.

About the campground: Nestled below Unfried Ridge, Big Springs is a very basic campground—a good place for roughing it. Hunters use the site in the fall. The campground is open from mid-May to mid-November.

3 Central Ferry State Park

Location: 91 miles south of Spokane on the Snake River, near Pomeroy.
Sites: 8 primitive tent sites, 60 sites with full hookups for RVs no longer than 45 feet, 1 group site.
Facilities: Drinking water, picnic tables, fire grills, flush toilets, showers, dump station, group fire ring, 3 horseshoe pits, 3 boat docks, 2 ski docks, 4 boat ramps, fishing pier, marine dump station.
Fee per night: $$$.
Elevation: 640 feet.
Management: Washington State Parks and Recreation Commission.
Activities: Hiking, fishing, boating, swimming, waterskiing, beachcombing, bird watching.
Finding the campground: From Interstate 90 in Spokane, take exit 279 and head south on U.S. Highway 195 for 57 miles. Just before you reach Colfax, turn west onto Washington Highway 26 and drive 17 miles to Dusty. From there, take WA 127 south for 17 miles to the park.

About the campground: Central Ferry encompasses 185 acres, including 6,500 feet of shoreline on Lake Bryan, backwater of the Little Goose Dam on the Snake River. The water frontage includes 775 feet of unguarded swimming beach. The park is tucked into the wheat fields of southeastern Washington. High bluffs border the park on one side. Resident birds include meadowlarks, bluebirds, Chinese pheasants, killdeer, and swans. The brushy countryside just beyond the park harbors some dangerous wildlife, including rattlesnakes and black widow spiders. The campground is open from mid-March to mid-November. For a fee, you can make reservations by calling Reservations Northwest (see contact information on page 236).

4 Chief Timothy State Park

Location: 111 miles south of Spokane on an island in Lower Granite Lake, near Clarkston.

Sites: 33 tent sites, 33 sites with water and electrical hookups for RVs no longer than 60 feet, 2 primitive tent sites.

Facilities: Drinking water, picnic tables, fire grills, flush toilets, showers, complete disposal facilities, interpretive center, 4 boat ramps and docks, playground, snack bar.

Fee per night: $$ to $$$.

Elevation: 900 feet.

Management: Washington State Parks and Recreation Commission.

Activities: Hiking, fishing, boating, waterskiing, interpretive programs.

Finding the campground: From Interstate 90 in Spokane, take exit 279 and head south on U.S. Highway 195 for 94 miles to the Idaho border. US 195 joins US 95 as the route enters Idaho and continues for 6 miles to Lewiston. At Lewiston, turn west onto US Highway 12 and drive 11 miles back into Washington to the park.

About the campground: This 282-acre park is on an island in a segment of the Snake River that has been dammed to create Lower Granite Lake. The dam is more than 20 miles downstream. The park features 11,500 feet of shoreline, including an unguarded swimming area that is protected from boat traffic. The Alpowai Interpretive Center is built near the original site of a mid-19th century Nez Perce village called Alpowai. The campground is open year-round. For reservations, call the National Recreation Reservation Service (see contact information on page 236).

5 Fields Spring State Park

Location: 29 miles south of Clarkston, near the Grande Ronde River.

Sites: 20 sites for tents or self-contained RVs no longer than 30 feet, 2 primitive tent sites.

Facilities: Drinking water, picnic tables, fire grills, flush toilets, dump station, playground, coin-operated showers, firewood (fee), 7.5 miles of cross-county ski trails, 3 miles of hiking trails, sled run, lighted tubing hill.

Fee per night: $ to $$.

Elevation: 4,500 feet.

Management: Washington State Parks and Recreation Commission.

Activities: Hiking, bird watching, cross-country skiing, sledding, tubing, snowmobiling.

Finding the campground: From Clarkston, on the Idaho border, head south on Washington Highway 129 for 29 miles to the park.

About the campground: This idyllic site in the Blue Mountains encompasses nearly 800 acres on Puffer Butte. It is situated 4,000 feet above the Grande Ronde River on an old Indian route between Oregon and Idaho. The Indians stopped in the area to dig roots. There is a hiking trail to the top of the butte, which offers wondrous views into three states. In 1974, about 70 percent of the Douglas and white fir in this area was damaged by an infestation of tussock moths and subsequently removed. The campground is open year-round, with limited services in winter.

6 Godman

Location: About 150 miles south of Spokane, near Dayton.
Sites: 8 sites for tents or self-contained RVs no longer than 15 feet.
Facilities: Picnic tables, fire grills, vault toilets, dump station, horse facilities; no drinking water.
Fee per night: None.
Elevation: 4,330 feet.
Management: Umatilla National Forest, Pomeroy Ranger District.
Activities: Hiking, horseback riding, snowmobiling.
Finding the campground: From Interstate 90 in Spokane, take exit 279 and head south on U.S. Highway 195 for 57 miles. Just before you reach Colfax, turn west onto Washington Highway 26 and drive 17 miles to Dusty. From there, take WA 127 south for 27 miles, crossing the Snake River, to Dodge. Turn west onto US 12 and drive 24 miles west and south to Dayton. Leave US 12 and turn left (southeast) into town. In a half-mile, turn left (east) onto Mustard Hollow Road, drive almost 4 miles, and turn east onto Eckler Mountain Road. Stay on it (as it becomes Skyline Drive and Forest Road 46) for 24 miles to the campground.

About the campground: This is definitely the end of the road in the Blue Mountains, but it is also where the trails begin. The campground makes a good base for backpacking into the Wenaha Tucannon Wilderness. It is used a lot by horseback riders, too, and by snowmobilers in the winter. The campground is connected by a trail to the Ski Bluewood ski area, 3 miles west. The campground is open from mid-June to late October.

7 Lewis and Clark Trail State Park

Location: 130 miles south of Spokane on the Touchet River, near Walla Walla.
Sites: 30 sites for tents or self-contained RVs no longer than 28 feet, 4 primitive tent sites.
Facilities: Drinking water, picnic tables, fire grills, flush toilets, dump station, amphitheater.
Fee per night: $ to $$$.

Elevation: 1,610 feet.
Management: Washington State Parks and Recreation Commission.
Activities: Bird watching, fishing, hiking, picnicking, sledding, hunting.
Finding the campground: From Interstate 90 in Spokane, take exit 279 and head south on U.S. Highway 195 for 57 miles. Just before you reach Colfax, turn west onto Washington Highway 26 and drive 17 miles to Dusty. From there, take WA 127 south for 27 miles to Dodge. Turn west onto US 12 and drive 29 miles to the campground, which is 5 miles beyond Dayton. From Walla Walla, drive northeast on US 12 for 24 miles to the park.

About the campground: This 37-acre campground is on the Touchet River, which eventually joins the Walla Walla River on its way to the Columbia. The route that Lewis and Clark took on their return journey in 1806 runs right through the park and gives the park its name. Homesteaders used this site to hold post-harvest picnics and games. Today, park rangers host campfire interpretive programs in the summer. There is a 1-mile interpretive trail and a 0.75-mile bird watching trail in the camp, which is open year-round.

8 Lyons Ferry State Park

Location: 126 miles southwest of Spokane on the Snake River, near Pomeroy.
Sites: 50 sites for tents or self-contained RVs no longer than 45 feet, 2 primitive tent sites.
Facilities: Drinking water, picnic tables, fire grills, flush toilets, showers, dump station, 2 boat ramps.
Fee per night: $$.
Elevation: 545 feet.
Management: Washington State Parks and Recreation Commission.
Activities: Hiking, fishing, boating, swimming, waterskiing.
Finding the campground: From Interstate 90 in Spokane, take exit 279 and head south on U.S. Highway 195 for 57 miles. Just before you reach Colfax, turn west onto Washington Highway 26 and drive 17 miles to Dusty. From there, take WA 127 south for 27 miles to Dodge. Head west on US 12 for 9 miles to the junction with WA 261. Turn right (west) onto WA 261 and drive 16 miles to the campground, which is 8 miles past Starbuck.

About the campground: This 1,282-acre park, located at the confluence of the Snake and Palouse Rivers, features 10 miles of Snake riverfront, including 428 feet of unguarded swimming beach. The park also encompasses the Marmes Rock Shelter Heritage Area, site of an ancient burial cave. Archaeologists found human remains dating back 10,000 years in the valley now flooded by Lower Monumental Dam. More recently, the Palouse Indians used the site as a burial grounds. About 400 graves were moved before the flooding. The Lewis and Clark expedition passed through here, and the Lyons Ferry, propelled by the river current, has been crossing the Snake River here for 108 years. Early settlers and the U.S. Army used the ferry to reach the Palouse country. It is currently berthed in the park. The campground is open from April through September.

9 Palouse Falls State Park

Location: 134 miles southwest of Spokane on the Palouse River, near Dayton.
Sites: 10 primitive sites for tents or self-contained RVs no longer than 40 feet.
Facilities: Drinking water, picnic tables, fire grills, pit toilets, observation shelter, barrier-free trail to overlook.
Fee per night: $.
Elevation: 560 feet.
Management: Washington State Parks and Recreation Commission.
Activities: Hiking, picnicking, viewing of falls.
Finding the campground: From Interstate 90 in Spokane, take exit 279 and head south on U.S. Highway 195 for 57 miles. Just before you reach Colfax, turn west onto Washington Highway 26 and drive 17 miles to Dusty. From there, take WA 127 south for 27 miles to Dodge. Head west on US 12 for 9 miles to the junction with WA 261. Turn right onto WA 261 and drive 22 miles west and north to Palouse Falls Road. Turn right (northeast) and drive 2 miles to the campground.

About the campground: Palouse Falls is the only remaining waterfall on the Palouse River that was formed by glacial floods. It is 198 feet high and is most spectacular in the spring and early summer. The park is more popular with day trippers than campers, but the campground is serviceable if you do not expect too much. There is plenty of shade, and the park is located near the confluence of the Snake and Palouse Rivers. The campground is open from April to late September.

10 Teal Spring

Location: 134 miles south of Spokane, near Pomeroy.
Sites: 8 sites for tents or self-contained RVs no longer than 15 feet.
Facilities: Picnic tables, fire grills, vault toilets, snow shelter; no drinking water.
Fee per night: None.
Elevation: 4,330 feet.
Management: Umatilla National Forest, Pomeroy Ranger District.
Activities: Hiking.
Finding the campground: From Interstate 90 in Spokane, take exit 279 and head south on U.S. Highway 195 for 57 miles. Just before you reach Colfax, turn west onto Washington Highway 26 and drive 17 miles to Dusty. From there, take WA 127 south for 27 miles to Dodge. Head southeast on US 12 for 13 miles to Pomeroy, turn south onto WA 128, and drive about 20 miles. The route will become Mountain Road and then Forest Road 40 along the way. The campground turnoff is on the right a half-mile past the Clearwater Lookout.

About the campground: This is a very basic and pleasant campground just off FR 40, the main thoroughfare in these parts. A pack trail leads from camp to and beyond Diamond Peak (elevation 6,415 feet). The campground, which is open from June to mid-November, has a snow shelter used by hunters in the fall.

11 Tucannon

Location: 138 miles south of Spokane, near Dayton.
Sites: 13 sites for tents or self-contained RVs no longer than 15 feet.
Facilities: Picnic tables, fire grills, vault toilets; no drinking water.
Fee per night: None.
Elevation: 2,820 feet.
Management: Umatilla National Forest, Pomeroy Ranger District.
Activities: Hiking, fishing.
Finding the campground: From Interstate 90 in Spokane, take exit 279 and head south on U.S. Highway 195 for 57 miles. Just before you reach Colfax, turn west onto Washington Highway 26 and drive 17 miles to Dusty. From there, take WA 127 south for 27 miles to Dodge. Turn left (west) onto US 12 and drive 9 miles to Tucannon. Bear left on Tucannon Road, which eventually becomes Forest Road 47, and drive 28 miles east and south to the campground.

About the campground: This is certainly the backcountry, way back. Roughing it is your only option here, but the wooded setting is very peaceful. The campground, open from May to late November, is close to the Tucannon River.

12 Wickiup

Location: About 145 miles south of Spokane, near Pomeroy.
Sites: 5 sites for tents or self-contained RVs no longer than 15 feet.
Facilities: Picnic tables, fire grills, vault toilets; no drinking water.
Fee per night: None.
Elevation: 4,000 feet.
Management: Umatilla National Forest, Pomeroy Ranger District.
Activities: Hiking.
Finding the campground: From Interstate 90 in Spokane, take exit 279 and head south on U.S. Highway 195 for 57 miles. Just before you reach Colfax, turn west onto Washington Highway 26 and drive 17 miles to Dusty. From there, take WA 127 south for 27 miles to Dodge. Turn left (east) onto US 12 and drive 13 miles to Pomeroy. Turn right (south) onto WA 128 and drive about 27 miles. WA 128 will become Mountain Road and then Forest Road 40 along the way. When you reach the junction with FR 44, turn left (east) and drive 3 miles to the campground.

About the campground: This campground is way, way down the road, but you are sure to have the place pretty much to yourself when you get there. It is quite primitive, and there is not a lot to do besides relax. Of course, if you get bored, you could always hike up Hogback Ridge, which is a mile or so east of camp. The campground is open from mid-June to late October.

Contact Information

MANAGING AGENCIES:

**Bureau of Land Management,
509-536-1200**
Boundary Dam, 509-536-1200
Wenatchee Resource Area,
509-665-2100

**Bureau of Reclamation,
509-754-0200**

**Naches Ranger Station,
509-653-2205**

**Chelan County Public Utility
District, 509-663-8121**

City of Anacortes, 360-293-1927

**City of Chelan, Parks Department,
509-682-8024, P.O. Box 1669,
Chelan, WA 98816**

City of Entiat, Parks and Recreation Department, 509-784-1500

City of Oak Harbor, 360-679-5551

City of Rockport, 360-853-8808

**Clallam County Parks, Salt Creek
Recreation Area, 360-928-3441**

**Colville National Forest,
509-684-7000**
Colville Ranger District,
509-684-7010
Kettle Falls Ranger District,
509-738-7700
Newport Ranger District,
509-447-7300
Republic Ranger District,
509-775-3305
Sullivan Lake Ranger District,
509-446-7500

**Coulee Dam National Recreation
Area, 509-633-9441**

Entiat City Park, 800-736-8428,
P.O. Box 228, Entiat, WA 98822

**Gifford Pinchot National Forest,
360-891-5000**
Cowlitz Valley Ranger District,
360-497-1100
Mount Adams Ranger District,
509-395-3400
Packwood Ranger District,
360-494-0600
Randle Ranger District,
360-497-1100
Wind River Ranger District,
509-427-3200

**Lake Roosevelt National Recreation
Area, 509-633-9441**

**Mayfield Lake County Park,
360-985-2364**

**Mount Baker-Snoqualmie National
Forest, 425-775-9702**
Darrington Ranger District,
360-436-1155
Mount Baker Ranger District,
360-856-5700
North Bend Ranger District,
425-888-1421
Skykomish Ranger District,
360-677-2414
White River Ranger District,
360-825-6585

**Mount Rainier National Park,
360-569-2211**

**Mount St. Helens National Volcanic
Monument, 360-247-3900**

**North Cascades National Park,
360-856-5700**

Odlin County Park, 360-468-2496

**Okanogan National Forest,
509-826-3275**
Methow Valley Visitors Center,
509-996-4000
Tonasket Ranger District,
509-486-2186

**Olympic National Forest,
360-956-2400**
Hood Canal Ranger District,
360-877-5254
Quilcene Ranger District,
360-765-3368
Quinault Ranger District,
360-288-2525
Soleduck Ranger District,
360-374-6522

**Olympic National Park,
360-452-4501**
Elwha Ranger Station,
360-452-9191
Hoh Ranger Station,
360-374-6925
Kalaloch Ranger Station,
360-962-2283
Lake Ozette Ranger Station,
360-963-2725
Queets Ranger Station,
360-962-2283
Staircase Ranger Station,
360-877-5569

**Pend Oreille County Department
of Public Works, 509-447-4821**

**San Juan County Park,
360-468-2992**

**Snohomish County Parks,
360-339-1208**

**U.S. Army Corps of Engineers,
509-547-7781**

**Umatilla National Forest,
541-276-3811**
Pomeroy Ranger District,
509-843-1891

**Washington Department of Natural
Resources, 360-902-1000**
Central Region, 360-748-2383
Northeast Region, 509-684-7474
Northwest Region, 360-856-3500
Olympic Region, 360-374-6131
South Puget Sound Region,
360-825-1631
Southeast Region, 509-925-8527
Southwest Region, 360-577-2025

**Washington State Parks and
Recreation Commission, Parks
Information, 800-233-0321**

**Wenatchee National Forest,
509-662-4335**
Cle Elum Ranger District,
509-674-4411
Entiat Ranger District,
509-784-1511
Leavenworth Ranger District,
509-548-6977
Lake Wenatchee Ranger District,
509-763-3103
Naches Ranger District,
509-653-2205

**Wenatchee River County Park,
509-662-2525**

**Whatcom County Parks,
360-733-2900**

RESERVATION SERVICES:

National Park Reservation Service, 800-365-2267, reservations.nps.gov/search.com
National Recreation Reservation Service, 877-444-6777, www.reserveusa.com
Reservations Northwest, 800-452-5687, TDD phone 800-858-9659,
    www.parks.wa.gov
USDA National Reservation Line, 800-274-6104

Index

A

Adams Fork 96
Admiralty Inlet 55, 89
Ahtanum Camp 163
Ahtanum Meadows 163
Alder Lake 96
Alder Thicket 228–229
Alpowai Interpretive Center 230
Alta Lake State Park 132
Anacortes, City of 235

B

Ballard 132
Battle Ground State Park 96–97
Bay View State Park 63
Beaches map 34
Beacon Rock State Park 97
Beaver 98
Beckler River 63
Bedal 64
Beebe Bridge Park 184
Belfair State Park 42–43
Bert Cole State Forest 32
Beverly 132–133
Big Creek 16
Big Meadow Lake 204
Big Springs 229
Birch Bay State Park 64–65
Bird Creek 163–164
Blackpine Creek Horse Camp 133
Boardman Creek 65
Bogachiel State Park 16–17
Boulder Creek 66
Boundary Dam 204–205, 235
Bridge Creek 133–134
Bridgeport State Park 184–185
Brooks Memorial State Park 164
Brown Creek 17
Browns Lake 206
Buck Creek 66
Bumping Crossing 164–165
Bumping Lake and Boat Landing 165
Bureau of Land Management 235
Bureau of Reclamation 235

C

Camano Island State Park 87
Camp 4 134
Camp Spillman 43
Campbell Tree Grove 17–18
Canyon Creek 206
Cape Disappointment 35
Cascade Range 58

Cascadia Marine Trail 48
Cat Creek 98–99
Cedar Springs 165–166
Central Ferry State Park 229–230
Charbonneau Park 185
Chatter Creek 134–135
Chelan County Public Utility District 235
Chelan Parks Department, City of 235
Chewuch 135
Chief Timothy State Park 230
Chopaka Lake 135–136
Chuckanut Foot Race 73
Clallam County Parks 235
Cle Elum Ranger District 236
Clear Creek 67
Clear Lake North 166
Clear Lake South 166–167
Clover Flats 167
Clover Leaf 206–207
Coastal Region 8, 13
Coastal Region map 12
Coho 18
Cold Creek 99
Collins 18
Colonel Bob Wilderness 17
Columbia Plateau map 182
Colville National Forest 235
Colville Ranger District 235
Conconully State Park 136
contact information 235–236
Coppermine Bottom 18–19
Corral Pass 99–100
Cottonwood 19, 136–137, 167–168
Cougar Flat 168
Coulee Dam National Recreation Area 235
Council Lake 100
Cowlitz Valley Ranger District 235
Crawfish Lake 185–186
Crow Butte State Park 186
Crow Creek 168–169
Crystal Springs 169
Cultus Creek 100–101
Curlew Lake State Park 186–187

D

Dalles, The 101
Daroga State Park 187
Darrington Ranger District 235
Dash Point State Park 101–102
Deception Pass State Park 88

Dog Lake 169–170
Dosewallips 27
Dosewallips River 44
Dosewallips State Park 43–44
Dougan Creek 102
Douglas Falls Grange Park 207
Douglas Fir 67
Dragoon Creek 207–208
Dungeness Forks 19–20

E

Early Winters 137
East Crossing 20
East Lake Gillette 208–209
East Sullivan 209
Eastern Region 8, 127
Eastern Region map 128
Ebey's Landing National Historical Reserve 89
Edgewater 208
Eightmile 137–138
Elbe Hills ORV Trailhead 102
Elkhorn 20
Elwha 28
Elwha Ranger Station 236
Entiat City Park 187–188, 235
Entiat Park and Recreation Department, City of 235
Entiat Ranger District 236
Evans 210
Evans Creek 103

F

Fairholm 28
Fall Creek 103
Falls Creek 21, 138
Falls Creek-Crest Horse Camp 104
Falls View 21
Fay Bainbridge State Park 68
Ferry Lake 188–189
Fields Spring State Park 230–231
Fish Lake 138–139
Fishhook Park 189
Flat 139
Flodelle Creek 210
Flowing Lake County Park 68–69
Foggy Dew 139
Fort Canby State Park 35–36
Fort Casey State Park 88–89
Fort Ebey State Park 89
Fort Flagler State Park 54–55
Fort Spokane 210, 212
Fort Worden State Park 55

Fox Creek 140

G
Gatton Creek 21–22
Gifford 212
Gifford Pinchor National Forest 235
Gifford-Inchelium Ferry 207
Ginkgo-Wanapum State Park 189–190
Glacier Public Service Center 70
Glacier View 140
Godman 231
Gold Basin 69
Gold Creek 44
Goose Lake 104
Graves Creek 28–29
Grayland Beach State Park 36
Grays Harbor County 13

H
Haag Cove 213
Halfway Flat 170
Hamma Hamma 22
Hannegan 69–70
Hause Creek 170
Hawk Creek 213
Heart o' the Hills 29–30
Hells Crossing 171
Hill, Sam 193–194
Hoh 29–30
Hoh Oxbow 22–23
Hoh Ranger Station 236
Honeymoon 140–141
Hood Canal 13
Hood Canal Ranger District 236
Hood Canal/Kitsap Peninsula map 41
Hood Park 190
Horseshoe Cove 70
Horseshoe Lake 104–105
Horsethief Lake State Park 171
Howard Miller Steelhead 70, 72
Howell Lake 44–45
Hunters 214
Hutchinson Creek 72

I
Ice Harbor Lock and Dam Visitor Center 185
Ida Creek 141
Ike Kinswa State Park 105
Illahee State Park 45
Indian Camp 141–142
Indian Creek 172
Interurban Trail 73–74
Iron Creek 105–106
Island Camp 172

J
J.R. 142
Jackson, John R. 108
Jarrell Cove State Park 45–46
Jarrell, Philora 46
Joemma Beach State Park 46
Johnny Creek 142

K
Kachess 143
Kalaloch 37
Kalaloch Ranger Station 236
Kamloops Island 214
Kanaskat-Palmer State Park 106
Kaner Flat 173
Kayak Point County Park 72–73
Keene's Horse Camp 106–107
Keller Ferry 190–191
Kettle Falls 214–215
Kettle Falls Ranger District 235
Killen Creek 107
Kitsap Memorial State Park 46–47
Klahowya 23
Klipchuck 143
Kopachuck State Park 47
Kwayaylsh, Joe and Sarah 83

L
La Push 37–38
Lake Chelan State Park 144
Lake Creek 144
Lake Creek II 145
Lake Cushman State Park 23
Lake Easton State Park 173
Lake Gillette 215
Lake Leo 215–216
Lake Merrill 107–108
Lake O'Neil 35
Lake Ozette Ranger Station 236
Lake Roosevelt National Recreation Area 235
Lake Sylvia State Park 24–25
Lake Thomas 216
Lake Wenatchee Ranger District 236
Lake Wenatchee State Park 146
Lakeshore RV Park 145
Larrabee State Park 73–74
Leader Lake 146–147
Leavenworth Ranger District 236
Lena Creek 24
Lewis and Clark Interpretive Center 35
Lewis and Clark State Park 108
Lewis and Clark Trail State

Park 231–232
Lilliwaup 24
Lincoln Rock State Park 191–192
Little Naches 174
Little Twin Lakes 216–217
Lodge Pole 174
Lone Fir 147
Long Lake 192
Loup Loup 147
Lyman Lake 192–193
Lyons Ferry State Park 232
Lyre River 55–56

M
Makah Tribal Museum 13
Manchester State Park 47–48
Marble Creek 74
Marcus Island 217
Margaret McKenny 108–109
Maryhill Museum of Art 193–194
Maryhill State Park 193–194
Mayfield Lake County Park 109, 235
Meadows 147, 149
Melbourne 25
Methow Valley Visitors Center 236
Middle Waddell 109
Mill Pond 217–218
Miller, John H. 110
Millersylvania State Park 110
Mima Falls Trailhead 110–111
Mineral Park 74
Mineral Springs 149
Minnie Peterson 25–26
Money Creek 62
Mora 37–38
Moran State Park 89–90
Moran, Robert 90
Morrison Creek 174–175
Moss Creek 111, 175
Mount Adams Ranger District 235
Mount Baker Ranger District 235
Mount Baker-Snoqualmie National Forest 235
Mount Rainier National Park 235
Cougar Rock 111–112
Ohanapecosh 112–113
Sunshine Point 113
White River 113–114
Mount Spokane State Park 218
Mount St. Helens National Volcanic Monument 235
Interpretive Center 120
Lower Falls Recreation Area 114

Mountain Loop Highway 78

N

Naches Ranger District 236
Naches Ranger Station 235
Napeequa Crossing 149–150
Nason Creek 150
National Park Reservation
  Service 236
National Recreation
  Reservation Service 236
Neah Bay 13
Newport Ranger District 235
Nice 150
Noisy Creek 219–220
North Bend Ranger District
  235
North Cascades map 129
North Cascades National Park
  235
Colonial Creek 75
Goodell Creek 75
Hozomeen 76
Newhalem Creek 76
North Creek 114–115
North East Lake Ellen 218–219
North Fork 115, 151
North Gorge 219
North Head Lighthouse 36
North Puget Sound map 60
Northeastern Washington map
  202

O

Oak Harbor City Beach Park
  90
Oak Harbor, City of 235
Ocean City State Park 36–37
Ocean Shores 13
Odlin County Park 91, 235
Okanogan National Forest 236
Oklahoma 115–116
Olallie Lake 116
Old Fort Townsend State Park
  56
Olympic National Forest 236
Olympic National Park 13, 236
Altaire 26
Deer Park 26
Dosewallips 27
Elwha 28
Fairholm 28
Graves Creek 28–29
Heart o'the Hills 29
Hoh 29–30
Kalaloch 37
Mora 37–38
Ozette 38
Queets 30
Sol Duc 30
Staircase 31

Olympic Peninsula 13
Osoyoos Lake State Park 194–
  195
Ozette 38

P

Pacific Beach State Park 38, 40
Pacific Crest National Scenic
  Trail 81
Packwood Ranger District 235
Padilla Bay National Estuarine
  Research Reserve 63
Palouse Falls State Park 233
Panhandle 220
Panorama Point 76–77
Panther Creek 116
Paradise Creek 117
Paradise Point State Park 117
Paradise Visitor Center 111
Park Creek 77
Passayten Wilderness 135
Pearrygin Lake State Park 151
Pend Oreille County
  Department of Public
  Works 236
Pend Oreille County Park 220–
  221
Peninsula 175–176
Penrose Point State Park 48
Peterson Prairie 176
Phelps Creek 152
Pierre Lake 221
Pioneer Park 221–222
Pleasant Valley 176–177
Pomeroy Ranger District 236
Porcupine Bay 222
Port Orchard 48
Port Susan Bay 73
Porter Creek 117–118
Potholes State Park 195
Potlatch State Park 48–49

Q

Queets 30
Queets Ranger Station 236
Quilcene Ranger District 236
Quinault Ranger District 236

R

Rain Forest map 14
Rainbow Falls State Park 118
Randle Ranger District 235
Rasar State Park 77–78
Red Bridge 78–79
Red Mountain 152
Republic Ranger District 235
reservations 236
Reservations Northwest 7, 236
River Bend 153
Riverside State Park 222–223
Roads End 153

Rock Creek 118–119, 153–154
Rock Island 154
Rock Lakes 154–155
Rockport State Park 79
Rockport, City of 235
Rocky Lake 223
Rodin, Auguste 194

S

Saddle 119
Salmon la Sac 155
Salt Creek Recreation Area 56–
  57
Saltwater State Park 119–120
San Juan County Park 91, 236
San Juan Islands and Island
  County map 86
Sawmill Flat 177
Scenic Beach State Park 49
Schafer Brothers Logging
  Company 31
Schafer State Park 31
Seal Rock 50
Seaquest State Park 120
Sequim Bay State Park 57
Sheep Creek 223–224
Sherman Pass Overlook 196
Sherman Valley 120–121
Shifting Sands Nature Trail 40
Silver Falls 155–156
Silver Fir 80
Silver Lake Park 79–80
Silver Springs 121
Skookum Creek 224
Skykomish Ranger District 235
Smith, Joe and Emma 46
Smokey Creek 121–122
Snohomish County Parks 236
Snow Cabin 177–178
Soda Springs 122, 156, 178
Sol Duc 30
Soleduck Ranger District 236
South Cascades map 161
South Creek 156
South Fork 178–179
South Fork Hoh 31–32
South Puget Sound map 93
South Skookum Lake 224–225
South Whidbey State Park 92
Southeastern Washington map
  227
Spencer Spit State Park 92
Spokane and Northeastern
  Washington map 202
Spring Canyon 196
Squire Creek County Park 80–
  81
Staircase 31
Staircase Ranger Station 236
Steamboat Rock State Park
  196–197

Strait of Juan de Fuca map 53
Sugarloaf 157
Suiattle River 66
Sulphur Creek 81
Summit Creek 122–123
Sun Lakes State Park 197–198
Sun Lakes State Park Resort
198
Sunset 123
Swan Lake 198–199
Swauk 157

T
Tahuya River Horse Camp 50
Takhlakh 123–124
Taneum 179
Teal Spring 233
Tenmile 199
Tinkham 124
Tonasket Ranger District 236
Toonerville 51
Torpedo Warehouse, The 48
Tower Rock 124
Tree Phones 179
Troublesome Creek 81–82
Tucannon 234
Tumwater 157–158
Turlo 82
Twanoh State Park 51
Twenty-five Mile Creek State
Park 158
Twin Harbors State Park 40
Twin Lakes 52

U
U.S. Army Corps of Engineers
236
Umatilla National Forest 236
Upper Clearwater 32
USDA National Reservation
Line 236
user's guide 8

V
Van Slyke, Ralph 184
Verlot 82–83
Verlot Public Service Center
64, 78, 82, 83

W
Wallace Falls State Park 83
Walupt Horse Camp 125
Walupt Lake 125
War Creek 158–159
Washington Department of
Natural Resources 236
Washington map 9
Washington Park 83–84
Washington State Parks and
Recreation Commission
236
Wenatchee Confluence State
Park 200
Wenatchee National Forest 236
Wenatchee Resource Area 235
Wenatchee River County Park
159, 236

Wenberg State Park 84
West Sullivan 225–226
Western Lakes 32–33
Western Region 8, 58
Western Region map 59
Westport 13
Whatcom County Parks 236
White Pass Lake 180
White River Falls 159
White River Ranger District 235
Wickiup 234
Wildrose 180
Willaby 33
William C. Dearinger 84–85
Williams Lake 225
Willoughby Creek 33
Willows 180–181
Wind River Ranger District 235
Windust 200
Windy Point 181
Winthrop 151
Wish Poosh 160
Woodland 126
Wynoochee Dam 17

Y
Yacolt Burn State Forest 119
Yakima Sportsman State Park
201

About the author

Steve Giordano began camping at age 5 in an army surplus mummy bag on the beaches of northern California. Since moving to Washington 30 years ago, he has been hitting the highways and byways in search of memorable camping experiences. He has tried motor homes, campers, station wagons, tents, and even bicycle camping, but he still thinks nothing quite matches a sleeping bag under the open sky.

Steve is the author of three previous books, including *Scenic Driving Washington* (Falcon Publishing, 1997). He writes a monthly column for *RV Life* magazine, contributes to skiing guidebooks, and writes for travel magazines and online publications. He is a member of the Society of American Travel Writers and the North American Snowsports Journalists Association.